Sports Guy

Also by Charles P. Pierce

Hard to Forget: An Alzheimer's Story

SPORTS GUY

In Search of Corkball, Warroad Hockey, Hooters Golf, Tiger Woods, and the Big, Big Game

Charles P. Pierce

Foreword by Roy Blount, Jr.

DA CAPO PRESS

The pieces in this book have appeared previously in *GQ*, *Esquire*, *The National*, *The
New York Times Magazine*, and *Boston Magazine*.

A CIP record for this book is available from the Library of Congress.
ISBN 0-306-81005-0

Published by Da Capo Press
A Member of the Perseus Books Group
http://www.dacapopress.com

1 2 3 4 5 6 7 8 9—03 02 01 00

To Abraham, Brendan, and Molly,
something that's not from the airport gift shop.

And in memory of Shelby Strother.

"Truth is an odd number."
—Flann O'Brien
At Swim-Two-Birds

CONTENTS

FOREWORD

Roy Blount, Jr.

"My own personal America," writes Charlie Pierce, "comes with six seconds left and the home team—anybody's home team—with the ball and trailing by a point or a goal. There is barbecue at the concession stand, and there is beer in a paper cup, and a band is playing across the way. I can be happy there." From that perspective, he can look at contemporary stockcar racing, for example, and put his finger on what is wrong not just with big-time sports today, but with American culture-slash-enterprise in general. "Corporate connivance dressed up as populist celebration . . . as raucous authenticity," is leaching the humor out of everything, even Spam. But Pierce still has a fine palate for the salt of the earth. Sportswriting will not lack savor, or humor, as long as Charlie is handsomely sustaining a certain tradition.

A quarter-century or so ago, I was talking to a feature writer who had been assigned by a general magazine to work up yet another story about the dubious hoopla surrounding the Super Bowl. Though her publication was weekly, she struck me as an everyday enough person, not too fastidious or she wouldn't have been talking to me. But at one point she looked around the press room and exclaimed, "Sportswriters!" In a tone of disdain!

I was startled. "I like sportswriters," I said.

She looked startled. "They're such scruffy guys," she said.

"I like scruffy guys," I said. That is not how I should have put it. I should have said, "You can't generalize from their haircuts," or "You must mean 'raffish guys' or 'hungover guys.'" But her remark had thrown me off balance. To me it seemed clear that the least cheesy aspect of the proceedings, aside from the actual blocking and tackling and pass-catching to come, was these guys' persistence in pounding out copy, exchanging pungent anecdotes, and griping about the promotional packaging that was overshadowing the game.

This was back before commercial television had quite permeated the sports atmosphere as it has today, to the point that no sports hero with any sense of how his bread is buttered can be expected to see any value in speaking with the media other than on camera, emptily, to the full satisfaction of Nike, Taco Bell, and the hero's various moneyhandlers. Back then, cities had not yet begun to name their bowls and stadia for amorphous conglomerates instead of agricultural products and mean old sonsofbitches. Back then, a sportswriter still might chew a domestic cigar and sip a medicinal beer while he worked. It was not as though these guys were unacquainted with high style, for they had seen Native Dancer in the paddock in his prime, and he them there in theirs. But they would have snorted at any ascription of positive value to the wearing of Armani. Their sense of couture was best represented by the scribe who wore his new blazer proudly until (and, if the truth be known, even after) an usher came up to him and said, "Hey, buddy, where do we turn these in after the game?"

Today you could call guys like that countercultural. And some of the younger ones could call themselves that back then. They shared the older writers' admiration for tough, salty, rise-to-the-occasion performers whose calluses and glints were in all the right places (Arnold Palmer, Al McGuire, Bill Russell, Darrell Royal, Frank Robinson, Billie Jean King); but their tastes and their politics had been colored by the sixties and Muhammad Ali. They could hang with the crusty old guys and also with long-haired and perhaps herbally stimulated young athletes. They were to sportswriting as Willie Nelson to country music: traditionalist but loose.

I recollect Charlie Pierce as one of those young guys then, and he manages somehow, *mutatis mutandis* (I gather that no employable journalist of any age can stay out as late as we did regularly, lightsomely, back then), to be one of them still. Cognizant of both baseball and rock and roll, he is witness not only to the first lifetime home run of an obscure Tiger named Jim Walewander, but also to the fact that the fans cheering Walewander include Dean Clean, Joe Jack Talcum, Dave Blood, and Rodney Anonymous: The Dead Milkmen.

At this point I would like to quote some of Pierce's best lines, but I would just be stealing them, and you will enjoy them more in context. He has a flair for spontaneous foolery—as you will have learned if you have heard him on *Wait, Wait, Don't Tell Me*, a National Public Radio show on which he and I often fool around together—but he is no snide wisecracker, not one of these snarky junk-ironists who will fill an entire column with obscurely knowing one-liners. Charlie the tough-love romantic can get up for a game, at the high-school or the Olympic level. "I don't understand these sportswriters who don't like sports," he remarked recently. He has the observational chops to examine an icon like Tiger Woods or Magic Johnson both critically and sympathetically, close-up yet with detachment. He has the wit to view with bemused relish the proliferation of superjewelry on today's lavishly compensated players, and also to elicit from one of them the following explanation of why he is not wearing his usual meganecklace: "It's in the shop."

It is not because he is caught up in nostalgia that Pierce evinces such a keen sense of what tends to be missing in sports and other aspects of culture today. It is because he is still resourceful and hearty enough to dig up and appreciate the good stuff. He has been around long enough, and still gets around widely enough, that when he says something is the damnedest thing he has ever seen, he is saying something.

PREFACE

I'm a rummager and a scuffler in my business. Always have been. I love odd bits of business, the strings, old shoe buttons, and battered tin cornets of history. I don't know where it comes from, although my grandmother was an old Irish farm girl who used to tell me the stories that she'd heard from the shanachie, the itinerant storytellers who functioned both as entertainment and as a collective memory in the old Ireland. The shanachie told stories for food and drink. If the story was drab, or if it ran too short, out he went hungry onto the Tralee Road in the rain.

That may be where it comes from—my love for small town libraries, and for tiny museums, where the helpful elderly volunteers always have the skinny on the point guard's grandfather, or memories about the great flood that changed the town's history, and how the celebrity outfielder's neighborhood came to be built on what used to be the town cemetery. The drifting dead, then, become as much a part of the outfielder's story as his glove, or his bat, or his minor-league manager, who (maybe) once was a preacher. And that's the way my stories grow. The best ones, anyway.

There are a number of stories in this collection that can loosely be called "celebrity profiles." This is not an unfamiliar genre; a friend of mine calls them "arugula stories," as in: "(Fill In Your Favorite Greasy-Haired Dyspeptic Young Movie Star Here) looked out over his arugula salad at the trendy Beverly Hills bistro and sighed." We

have them in sportswriting, too. In fact, we have more and more of
them, as athletes increasingly have more and more in common with
other celebrity entertainers. Frankly, they are my least favorite pieces
herein collected.

One of them is about Tiger Woods. It has become somewhat notorious because Tiger said some revolting things, told some lascivi-
ous jokes, and I wrote them down and published them and, the next
thing I knew, Tiger and his father, Earl, were on national television
accusing me of illicit electronic surveillance of a limo driver. What
I'd done was take notes when I was supposed to take notes. Let me
explain.

For the better part of six months, the magazine for which I worked
negotiated with Tiger's people—a fairly new twist, athletes have
"people" with whom you negotiate—to set up a precise slice of time
within which I would hang around with the talented young golfer.
Part of this was the time during which he would have his picture
taken. So I hung around, took my notes, and wrote what I heard,
some of which became controversial because young Tiger heretofore
had been pitched as some odd combination of Ben Hogan and
Gandhi, which meant that when he started talking about black men
and the size of their penises, he was offending against his own image,
which is serious business now that we all accept the bogus axiom that
perception is reality. But, really, how bland is that?

They are throwaways, these celebrity stories, and they teach
lessons as simple and as tedious as flat blacktop. Oh, there is occasionally a burst of neon to them, but they are not the stories I love. I
love the ones that meander, that find themselves turning down into
the shadier places, where blood and bone and history hang over the
road like fingers of Spanish moss, where there is a stirring in the
bushes, a flash of shadows, and then gone again, and you find yourself bursting into a clearing—not where you'd planned to be, certainly, but a better place than where you were.

I love the stories in which you meet guys named Peerless.

There is in this collection a piece about Peyton and Archie Manning, father and son, both quarterbacks, the father the kind of legend

(and the kind of gentleman) in whom the American South seems to specialize. However, as I was visiting Peyton Manning at the University of Tennessee, I noticed that one of his teammates was named Peerless Price. I never had met anyone named Peerless, so I asked to speak to him for no other reason than I wanted to meet someone named Peerless. He became part of the story of Peyton and Archie Manning. There are people who would call this a digression. I say, how can any story be truly complete without somebody named Peerless?

How can a story about Rohan Marley be complete without that of his father, Bob? Bob's mother told me part of Rohan's story, on a sunny morning in Florida, with some of Bob's music playing faintly and vividly under our conversation, and she gave a blessing to me for the upcoming birth of my daughter, who can flat dance now, seven years later. Rohan was a linebacker, but his story was much more than that, if you followed it where it led, into the music and the sunshine.

"The blessing of Jah upon your little girl," the old woman told me, even before my daughter was born.

There is no point in talking about Danny Nee if you're not going to talk about Vietnam, in which he fought, and about the Gulf War, through which he coached, and about the distance over which the country had traveled between them. The stories Abe Lemons tells, and the impossibly funny way he tells them, are unthinkable without the Dust Bowl and the Depression, and a huge black cloud looming above a small town, the picture of which Abe still carries in his wallet. (OK, so Steinbeck's fingerprints are still on the story, too, but he never met Abe, who'd've had the Joads in stitches on the day they loaded up the wagon.) Jeff Hartwig and his pole-vaulting, and his snakes in Jonesboro are forever shadowed by gunfire erupting over a playground. I walked the woods there, past the sniper's perch, and the ground seemed to quiver still.

I love the stories about places as much as I love the stories about people. I love the way the wind stirs the grass on the grave of James Naismith in Lawrence, Kansas, where I learned that the old gentleman once played a hot version of "Little Brown Jug" on the fiddle.

That led me to the Driscolls of Russell, Kansas, the traditional Democratic hometown opponents of Bob Dole. I love the way there is
snow in the air all through wintertime in Warroad, Minnesota, so
you can hunker down by the fireplace in the town library, and read
the local lore about the Ojibwe—one of whom, Henry Boucha, became a local legend because of the way he played ice hockey, to
which Warroad has given its heart. I'm better for having sat there in
the barn, one thundery and flashing afternoon, with Junior Johnson,
as big in his time and place as Tiger Woods is in his, and Junior with
the tang of the outlaw still fresh upon his legend.

I drove up to his house that day—no phone call, no "people" with
whom to negotiate. I drove up through the backroads of North Carolina, along which Junior and his friends used to run moonshine,
past the hollows and the glens once thick with the law, now becoming flat and open places, ready for Authentic Country Living (starting at $80,000) and office parks. I drove up the long driveway toward
the mansion that Junior built on his farm, after auto racing made
him rich and Tom Wolfe made him famous. He's out in the barn, the
lady told me.

Well, Junior said, y'all might as well come in and talk.

We sat and talked. Lightning lit up the sky beyond the huge barn
doors. You could smell the ozone burning through the rain and over
the aroma of the sweetgrass in the fields. The story was about
NASCAR, so it was about Junior, of course, but it was about the
country, too, about how even the outlaws have agents nowadays. It
also—crucially, deeply—was about the hills lying tamed out there in
the rain, and the smell of summer lightning.

There are people to thank, of course. My family, which has tolerated
my regular absence over the past 16 years, especially my wife Margaret, who now knows more about the infield-fly rule than she ever
thought she would, and for that I apologize as well. She is the best
editor I have, and that leads me to all the others.

Once, if you asked my toddler son who the worst people in the
world are, he would've answered, sweetly, "Editors." It was an editor from whom I first learned that trick, and his name was Bob

Sales, and he was the first great editor I ever had. Subsequently, I have worked with estimable people on the stories in this collection—chief among them, David Granger, with whom I have traveled nearly a decade over three different national publications, two of which even are still extant. There are others, of course: T. A. Frail, Rob Fleder, Andrew Ward, Frank Deford, Neil Cohen, David Rosenbaum, Mike Roberts, John Strahinich, Craig Unger, and Robert Vare. All of them were willing to follow the stories wherever the stories went.

I learned about fact-checkers late in life, and I have come to appreciate them as pitchers do great shortstops—they can make your blunders disappear in the next day's boxscores. I am enormously grateful to Susan O'Donnell, Andrew (The Dark Prince) Chaikivsky, and to the redoubtable one, Ms. Sallie Motsch Brady, and to the rest of the people whose fingerprints are all over these stories for which I get to take all the public credit. Thanks also to Glenn Stout and Dick Johnson—friends, archivists, and lifelong Red Sox victims—for digging out a couple of the stories of which I'd long ago lost my own copies.

David Black and everyone in the sprawling Black Inc. empire knows that I love them madly.

For the past six years, on almost every Friday afternoon, I have been blessed with the opportunity to talk sports with Bill Littlefield on National Public Radio's *Only A Game*, which doesn't necessarily mean that we talk about sports. Occasionally, we talk about soccer. (That got him!) We also talk about shoes for industry *and* shoes for the dead. My thanks to Bill, and to the whole OAG sports team, past and present: Gary Waleik, David Greene, Katy Clark, Karen Givens, Doug Haslam, (Only A) Gabe O'Connor, and Jon Marston. Apologies for that crack about the dulcimer music.

Kevin Hanover from DaCapo called me up one day and asked if I would like to be anthologized. I said, certainly, it sounded like fun, and not at all like being trapped in a glass sarcophagus, and it has been fun. I am flattered and grateful to have been asked—this is also Albert Murray's publishing house, which is cool—and I would like to thank Kevin, John Radziewicz, and Carmen Mitchell for the opportunity and the privilege of putting this book together. Thanks also to

Roy Blount, Jr., for the kind words, and just for being the thorough-going, American-icon, national resource that he is—and not just because he knows more than should any living Christian soul on the subject of Songs About Food.

And, last of all, there are the people—famous and not so famous, and everything in between—who allowed me to rummage around in their lives for a spell in order to tell these stories, which is the only job I ever wanted. As we rounded out of the last century, there was a lot of dreary, dismal talk—some of it extremely well-founded—about athletes and the sports that they play. There are people who believe we are going to hell here in America. And, then, there are those of us who believe, with everlasting gratitude to the One Great Scorer, that we're all still pretty safe—until some shoe company lands the contract to make the handbasket.

Charles P. Pierce
Summer 2000

A Big Game

Upon arriving in a new town, some people visit museums. Other people find the theater, or they go off in search of whatever the local newspaper says is the best restaurant in town. I have one friend who haunts courthouses, collecting exotic criminal proceedings the way some folks collect roadside reptile farms. As for me, I seek out the arena or the ballpark. Even after years of traveling to games, I still listen for distant cheering and look for the glow of lights above the near horizon.

I am a sucker for a Big Game. Which is not necessarily the same as a Championship Game. It is not necessarily the same as an Important Game, as defined by television hucksters. A Big Game is more than that. It is a piece of living history, a theater of the generations with an outcome more compelling than theater of any other kind. Thousands of actors have played Hamlet, but Hamlet always dies. Thousands of players have played in the Harvard–Yale football game, and very few of them have the same story to tell. If all the elements are right, and if history has aligned correctly with the emotion of the moment, I would rather be at a Big Game than almost anywhere else in the world.

In this capacity, I have rooted for small-college basketball teams in Wyoming and for small-college football teams in Mississippi, for minor league baseball teams in North Carolina and for high school hockey teams in Minnesota and for a thousand athletes whose names I have long since forgotten. I have been an Alcorn State Brave and a Mishawaka High School Caveman. (Our women's teams, it should be noted, are gallantly called the Lady Cavemen.) I have been a Reno Silver Sock and an Asheville Tourist. (The centerfield scoreboard read VISITORS and TOURISTS, which I thought was right friendly.) It has been said that we all carry our own America with us. My own personal America comes with six seconds left and the home team—*anybody's* home team—with the ball and trailing by a point or a goal. There is barbecue at the concession stand, and there is beer in a paper cup, and a band is playing across the way. I can be happy there.

In Lawrence, Kansas, where stands the University of Kansas, they long ago set up a memorial to the old man on a bare and windy hill just inside the cemetery gates. But they buried him a few degrees south, in a shady plot, with his family and his fellow Masons, beneath a tall marble tower with a great marble ball set on top of it. His marker is flat, set right there in the ground, the stone so darkened and weathered that it looks like a small vein of iron in the earth. NAISMITH, the stone reads, and beneath it, in smaller letters, JAMES and MAUDE.

Basketball had a single inventor. That we can say this with authority makes the game unique among sports. The Scottish shepherd who first hit a rock with a curved stick, thereby inventing both golf and recreational prevarication, is lost to antiquity. It has never been clear whether the inventor of American football was the first man to run with the ball, the first man to throw a forward pass or the first man to devise a point spread. Baseball has at least four creation stories (at least one of which is an absolute lie), all of which obscure the fact that America's putative pastime is really a British mongrel. Basketball, however, began irrefutably in this country with James Naismith, who is buried in this shady plot in Lawrence, Kansas, where he came to coach at the university and in which function he remains the only men's basketball coach at the University of Kansas with a losing lifetime record.

I mention all of this because it is within basketball that the growth of sports—for good and ill—can be most vividly seen. After all, in certain places, even high school sports have become afflicted with a giantism similar to that which has afflicted the professional games. I can be fairly sure that old Jamie Naismith would not approve of much of it. He was said to be rather stiff-necked in the area of personal deportment. Still, there is evidence that he was not entirely an old fud: we know, for instance, that he played the fiddle, and that "Little Brown Jug" was his party piece.

Across town, on this breezy morning fresh with the onrushing springtime, Kansas is preparing to play Kansas State in basketball for the 237th time. I think that if he could, Naismith—1–1 lifetime against the Wildcats—would be there on Saturday. I think he would cheer. I think he would shake a pompom. I do not think he would chant "Bullshit!" at a referee—even though nobody ever had better credentials to do so. (Naismith was death on profanity.) But I think he would enjoy a Big Game. I think he'd have—and I'm sure he will one day forgive me for saying so—a hell of a time for himself.

More than anything else, a Big Game needs to have a sense of place. It radiates outward from the arena. It spreads itself beyond the stadium. Children slide down an icy sidewalk toward the warmth of the field-house doors. Halfway up the block, they can smell the popcorn. Time stops at midafternoon. The old men come out in their blazers. The women all wear camellias. The air itself seems to quiver and shake. The first time Florida and Florida State played football last season was a Big Game. It was in Tallahassee, all raucous with accumulated tradition, cheers echoing back through time and the generations. The second time they played football was in the Sugar Bowl. This was not a Big Game. It was merely for the national championship.

Alas, more and more, the Big Game is being overshadowed by the Championship Game, which increasingly is becoming just another television show. For example, there is no more entertaining sporting event in the country than a football game between Mississippi and Louisiana State, particularly if the game is played in Baton Rouge.

First of all, the game is played in Louisiana, which, as we all know, is not part of the United States of America in any sense that really matters. Second, the game is played at night, fog swirling through the paludal air and Spanish moss hanging like ghostly fingers from every tree. Third, surrounding the game, there is a sprawling celebration that is pretty much what the Druids would have thrown if they'd had sororities. The game will probably never be a Championship Game, because neither LSU nor Ole Miss has competed for any kind of championship since God was a boy. The people in charge of such things will probably never designate it as an Important Game, either. But it is a Big Game, every year. Big Games are not about trophies and banners. They are not about ratings and rights fees. Instead, memories are at stake, entire lifetimes of them. Bright as midnight torches, they are as warm and genuine as primal fire.

In or near the town of Monona, Iowa, there once was a highway patrolman named Howard Bell. It seems that Bell once nabbed Kansas coach Roy Williams for speeding along Highway 52. Williams was in town recruiting a local high school star named Raef LaFrentz. The following evening, lurking still, Bell ticketed LaFrentz. Three years later, LaFrentz is preparing to play Kansas State, and he has just told the story on a conference call that included representatives of the *Sporting News*, *Sports Illusstrated* and the Associated Press. Howard Bell is now famous, and he doesn't even know it. That is the way things happen today. Radar at the ready, Trooper Bell now cruises the information superhighway.

LaFrentz is preparing to play in a Big Game, though it has ceased to be much of a competitive rivalry. Kansas has won the game nine times in a row going back to 1994, and Kansas State is winding up a thoroughly miserable season. Nevertheless, on the running track that circles the basketball floor in Allen Fieldhouse, students have been camped out for tickets for nearly three days. In one corner, engineering students work out a design assignment using what appear to be Popsicle sticks. Two students have set up a small video arcade near one of the darkened popcorn stands, and a number of others are asleep under blankets. This will be the last home game for six Kansas seniors. The fans are urged to bring flowers and to shower the court with them before the game.

Allen is a genuine field house, one of the very few left. The stands rise steeply away from the court. At either end of the building, the walls come to a peak, with windows set into them. Kansas has been playing in this place since 1955, when it was dedicated to Dr. F. C. "Phog" Allen, Naismith's successor and the man to whom Naismith confided his theory that basketball cannot be coached, that it can only be played. Allen cannot have taken the old man too seriously; Phog coached at Kansas for thirty-nine years.

They have tucked and trimmed and embroidered the place down through the years. In 1990, as part of the unending renovation, they bought a new scoreboard. This presented them with the problem of what to do with the old one. They planned to sell off the electrical components piecemeal and the metalwork for scrap. Then someone in the athletic department called Kelly Driscoll and told him that if he hustled he could have the old scoreboard for his saloon. Driscoll fired up his truck and took off up Naismith Drive.

On the night before the Kansas State game, the Yacht Club is loud and merry. The fans of one school are indistinguishable from the fans of the other. Up front, near the door, Kelly Driscoll sits at his personal table and watches a Big Game come through the doors of his saloon.

Driscoll is a native Kansan. His hometown is Russell, where his family has been involved for years in Democratic politics and has been something of a burr in the side of Russell's most famous son, Bob Dole. (Around the Driscoll hearth, Dole is remembered fondly as "the only county attorney we ever had who never won a case.") Recently, when Russell County went Democratic in the state's gubernatorial election, Dole was heard to comment that the Driscolls must have been working overtime. One of Kelly's brothers lives on a farm next door to Russell's other claim to fame: a purported landing area for extraterrestrial spacecraft. What with space aliens coming down from the sky one day and the Washington press corps arriving the next, Russell has had a rough, if redundant, couple of years.

When his friend called him about the scoreboard in 1990, Kelly Driscoll was trying to make a success out of an old singles bar that he'd bought. He ripped the leatherette off the walls and renamed the place the Yacht Club, decking it out in a nautical motif that was approximately as appropriate to Kansas as a rodeo ambience would be to Hawaii. Right from the start, Driscoll's friendship with then coach Larry Brown and with Brown's star player, Danny Manning, made the Yacht Club a sort of unofficial headquarters for the 1988 champions.

The scoreboard dominates the Yacht Club the way a great landscape dominates a Tudor banquet hall. "There was no way we could get the thing through the doors," Driscoll recalls. "So we knocked out one of the back walls and fit the scoreboard right into the hole. That scoreboard is part of the wall. I don't know what will happen if we ever sell the place." The scoreboard is permanently set at Kansas 83, Oklahoma 79, the final score of the 1988 championship game. The score is brighter on a Friday night than anything else in the place. You can see its glow through the windows from the sidewalk.

It began in 1886 as a cheer for a victorious science club. At odd points during a game, Kansas fans intone, "Rock. Chalk. Jayhawk. Kayyy-*yewww!*" The melody of it had whispered at me for years. As I lounge in my seat in the field house just before the game, it finally occurs to me that it is a snatch of Gregorian chant, the same haunting strains that I first heard at a Trappist monastery near where I grew up in Massachusetts. It is a serious, signifying chant, and it brings back a flood of memories, and not merely of basketball games but also of something bigger than myself, which is what the people who wrote the chants had in mind. For a long moment, I am home again.

The crowd has brought their flowers. Every time a senior is introduced, the air fills with blossoms. Dressed in tuxedos for the occasion, the band plays hard and loud, albeit with an unfortunate tendency towards '70s Toyota-commercial standards. The chant is much more impressive in its gravitas. Not many people even in

Kansas would argue that this is an Important Game, but it is a Big Game because it has begun to feel like one. Time stops for a moment. The air in the field house begins to quiver and shake.

Kansas plays a terrible first half, but its team is so patently superior that it takes the game away easily in the second. As the minutes wind down, the forgotten seniors at the end of the bench are in the game, and everybody pleads with them to score, and they all do, and everybody is very happy and pleased. After the game, nearly everyone stays in his seat, and all six Kansas seniors get to give a little speech in order to say good-bye.

I do not stay for all these valedictories. The Savior is mentioned early on, and I have a strict rule regarding the theological speculations of athletes. I discreetly make my way to the door, walking out into a softening evening.

This was not a Championship Game. It was not even an Important Game. However, it was a Big Game. It was a Big Game because of the band in its tuxedos, and because of all the flowers cascading onto the floor, and because of all the little speeches and because of all the people who packed in to watch it at the Yacht Club across town. There is a sense of community here, not only among the people attending the game but also with all the people who attended the previous 236 games Kansas and Kansas State played against each other, all the way back to January 25, 1907, when James Naismith himself masterminded a 54–39 Kansas victory. It is for all of them—all the players and all the coaches, but also for all the people whom the game has ever touched. It is for Raef LaFrentz and for Trooper Howard Bell. It is for the people at the Yacht Club and for the people in Russell—for the Driscolls and the Doles, and maybe for the odd space alien, too. It is for James and Maude, and it is also for me.

Because everyone has stayed for the speeches, the lawn outside the field house is empty and silent. As I walk toward my car, I can still hear the cheering inside the building. Basketball began here. It is a constant and unbroken line from James Naismith—an athletic theologian himself, truth be told—to the seniors giving the speeches in a field house named for one of Naismith's protégés. I believe the old man would have had a time for himself. I believe he would have en-joyed the band in their tuxedos. ("Maude, do you think they know 'Little Brown Jug'?") He would have Rock-Chalked himself hoarse. I think the old man would know a Big Game when he felt it. And maybe, at a loose moment, when Maude wasn't watching, James Naismith would have thrown a few flowers into the air.

GQ

Bottom of the Ninth

People will come, Ray.

No, really, they will. They'll come for reasons they can't even fathom. They'll turn up your driveway . . . well, not really *your* driveway. It's Ilitch the Pizza Guy's driveway. Anyway, they'll turn up *somebody's* driveway, not knowing for sure why they're doing it, although some possible reasons—like Genuine Authentic Replica Gear!—will be suggested at top volume by the kids howling in the backseat.

They'll walk through what used to be called a neighborhood before we had new "urban villages" with "shops, restaurants, offices, and other attractions." They'll enter through one of three gates: the one with the eighty-foot bats, the one with the two immense sculpted tigers, or the one that has big bats *and* a big tiger and that faces the new "restaurant/retail" complex at the other end of the avenue. People will come, Ray.

There'll be one cash register for every 125 fans. (Did you know, Ray, the typical ballpark has one cash register for every 200 fans?) They'll wander through the food court. They'll ride the carousel. Later, perhaps exhausted, they'll sit in the large, open-air beer garden. They won't even have to come inside, Ray. They'll sit on the roof decks along Witherell Street, which will be "easily accessible" from the food court and the carousel and all levels of the ballpark.

The one constant through all the years, Ray, has been baseball. America has rolled by like an army of steamrollers, but this field, this game, is a part of our past. It reminds us of all that was good and could be again if we can just line up the bondholders. And now, Ray, look out there. Now it's baseball that's rolling by like an army of steamrollers. Not clumsy metaphorical ones but real ones, the kind that build new and modern things, like urban villages and genuine authentic replica ballparks.

Oh, people will come, Ray. People will most definitely come. They'll arrive at your door, innocent as children, longing for the past.

And, by God, Ray, we'll be there to sell it to them.

(Is this heaven?)

No, Ray. It's Detroit.

The ball has a cushioned cork center and the signature of someone named Gene Budig. It also has a black splotch where it came off the bat, and, tight against one seam, there's a very suspicious-looking scuff mark approximately the width of two fingertips, which may account for the fact that a promising young Detroit Tiger infielder named Frank Catalanotto was able only to loft the ball foul, along the third-base line, through the velvet evening rain and up into the outdoor auxiliary press section at the very top of Tiger Stadium.

I found the ball there, sitting in a small pool of rainwater. I was alone. There's little call for an outdoor auxiliary press section during a game between the Detroit Tigers and the Anaheim Angels on a softly flowing night at the beginning of May, not even at the beginning of the last May in which baseball will be played at Tiger Stadium. There was nobody to fight me for the ball.

I am not sentimental about old stadiums. Which is odd, because I have spent most of my life around Boston, where ballparks and arenas generally find themselves afflicted with talismanic characteristics as though they were concrete Kennedys. The relentless palaver about Fenway Park leaves me cold because, far too often, especially during night games in April, so does the ballpark. (David Halberstam claims to love even Fenway's smells. I don't know. Maybe the smells remind him of the good old days in the Mekong Delta.) In the first game I ever saw at Fenway—and, yes, I saw it with my father— the Red Sox lost by a fat pile of runs on their way to a 62–100 season. There were about ninety-five hundred of us there, and nobody was talking about history, tradition, quaint patriarchy, or lyric little band-boxes.

Because I am not sentimental about old stadiums, I am equally un-moved by the new ones, the plasticine nostalgia palaces that have sprung up in places like Denver and Cleveland and, most famously, Baltimore, a place of the kind of ersatz instant tradition perfect for a time in which television anchormen fancy themselves historians. The new ballparks are comfortable tributes to the modern service economy, and they are not as ugly as old Crock-Pots, and that is all that can be said for them.

Now, on this soft and liquid evening, Tiger Stadium was about as empty as Fenway was the first time I saw it. The two parks are rather married to each other; both opened on April 20, 1912, al-though neither event received the attention it might have, since the *Titanic* went down that same week. However, whereas Fenway has become an icon, Tiger Stadium is looked at now as an anachro-nism: old, a bit leaky, and possessed of far too much inherent archi-tectural democracy to meet the oligarchic demands of modern baseball economics—to wit, luxury boxes, club seating, and a babe-licious young hostess to bring you refreshments. Even to those people whose memories of the place are the longest and the fond-est, Tiger Stadium is ending its days as something of a public in-convenience.

"It's time," says Ernie Harwell, who broadcast his first game for the Tigers in 1960. "I mean, I'm ready. I'm not one of those Good Old Days guys. History and tradition are great, but it's time for them to go forward in a new ballpark."

I looked down from the outdoor auxiliary press section. The field was bright and wet and impossibly green. Tiger Stadium always has been an odd mix of impressions. From the outside, it dominates the corner of Trumbull Street and Michigan Avenue with a blank and cheerless facade. (Harwell and Al Kaline both had the same initial reaction to the park; they thought it looked like a battleship.) Inside, however, it is a warm, self-contained universe.

Tiger Stadium is the only major league ballpark that is double-decked all the way around, from home plate to the thin wedge of bleachers in dead center field. It is done up in deep blue and bright orange, like a child's happy castle, and running along its top level is a series of wooden enclosures that look for all the world like the running chutes in a stockyard. Unlike Fenway, which forces baseball to adapt to its weird, procrustean angles and corners, Tiger Stadium encompasses the game within itself.

Next season, the Tigers will move into Comerica Park, a $290 million nostalgia factory along lower Woodward Avenue for which the public will pay nearly half the tab. I will miss Tiger Stadium, which is remarkable, because I've been here only six or seven times in my life, and even more remarkable because baseball has very little to do with why I'll miss it.

I rolled my last souvenir of the place around my hand, and my fingertips once again stuck in the peculiar abrasion along one of its seams. I don't trust immaculate history, impeccably straight-line, survey-course, and sound-bite ready. Give me history that's suspiciously scuffed, a touch of rough mischief that you can put your fingertips on so that you can make it sail and dive, a kite in gypsy breezes. It can break all the rules, this history. You can make it dance.

Shortly before the turn of the century, Samuel Brooks built his lumberyard on the corner of Cherry Street near Michigan Avenue. It was a time of frenzied woodcutting, with thousands of newly arrived Swedes and Germans and Lithuanians plunging into raffish settlements deep within the wide forests around the Great Lakes, and Samuel Brooks prospered. In 1896, he saw a baseball field rise on what was once an old hay market at the corner of Michigan and Trumbull. Over the next twenty years, after Samuel handed the business down to his son, Arthur, the Brooks family and their employees watched as what was once Bennett Field became Navin Field.

Then when the great teams were in town—the Athletics with Al Simmons and that burly gobblehog Jimmie Foxx, or the Yankees with Ruth and Gehrig—the men working in the lumberyard would hear the crack of the bat and look up through the spreading twilight for the ball. The men would chase after the ball. You could get a half dozen in one afternoon if you were quick enough.

Arthur Brooks handed the company down to *his* son, Arthur, who is retired now and living in Florida. His first memory of what would become Tiger Stadium is of sprinting from Jefferson Intermediate School in order to make the 3:00 P.M. starting time. In the days before night baseball, the games started at three so the men coming home from work might be able to catch the last few innings. Arthur Brooks would run to Trumbull Avenue and hop a streetcar to the ballpark. He'd pay his fifty cents and sit in the bleachers, and he'd watch the home runs soar into his father's lumberyard.

"They wouldn't always find them all," Brooks says. "Used to be, especially if those Yankees were in town, I could still find half a dozen balls all over the lumberyard."

The home runs stopped coming regularly in 1938, when Walter Briggs finished the job of enclosing the stadium that had been started by Frank Navin, Arthur Brooks's godfather. It was a whole new ballpark, considered to be state-of-the-art. There would be no more rickety temporary bleachers, the fans atop the last row standing and craning their necks until it seemed the whole structure would capsize onto Cherry Street. Baseball was contained within itself. The cheers reached the streets in softened roars. To hit one into the lumberyard now required a luckless conjunction of Homeric power and a truly terrible curveball. "Ted Williams did it a couple of times, though," Brooks recalls. "He put a couple into the yard for us." Reggie Jackson almost did it in the 1971 All-Star Game, but his rising line drive banged off a transformer that sits stop the right-field roof in what is still one of the defining home runs of the age.

The baseballs don't come as frequently these days, but Brooks Lumber is still where it always was. It's baseball itself that's moving now. The home runs will soon go sailing by the Hard Rock Cafe and into a whole neighborhood that is part of the ballpark as surely as the whole ballpark was once part of a neighborhood, baseballs falling into the new urban village like so much captive rain.

One day in 1987, a Tiger scrub named Jim Walewander knocked a ball into the right-field seats to win a game. It was Walewander's first career home run. It was also his last. There was a nice crowd that day, and everybody cheered, especially four sallow youths sitting in the boxes near the Detroit dugout. Their names were Dean Clean, Joe Jack Talcum, Dave Blood, and Rodney Anonymous. They were the Dead Milkmen.

No matter how hidebound its bureaucracy, baseball was the sport of choice among the countercultural Left. Back in the days when only FBI informants had any money, baseball's bleachers were always cheap and, therefore, suffused with the spirit of "participatory democracy," that charmingly impossible philosophical template so central to, among other things, the Port Huron Statement, composed by Michigan native and Tiger fan Tom Hayden.

This has not always been easy for the game's purists to accept. George Will, who has replaced the late Bart Giamatti as baseball's preeminent dilettante nuisance, once even blamed the rise of those awful multipurpose stadiums in places like Cincinnati and Pittsburgh on the "wretched excesses" of the sixties, on which Will also blames the popularity of professional football. It should be noted that those same purists—a coalition of corporate and political elites—are behind most of what have been called, with no apparent irony, the "new vintage ballparks."

Rather, the people most directly involved in that "wretched excess" of the sixties hated football—*too militaristic, man*—and loved baseball, which is why the center-field bleachers in Tiger Stadium were once regularly bathed in the aroma of certain American Indian religious compounds. In fact, that same season in which Walewander brought joy to the Dead Milkmen with his one and only home run, Tiger Stadium also played host to something called the Eugene V. Debs Memorial Kazoo Marching Band.

So, as the tie-dye faded and the Grateful Dead turned into a cabaret act, it was no real surprise that the young ballplayers of the eighties developed a jones for ham-fisted drumming and atonal guitar strangling. And the ham-fisted drummers and atonal guitar stranglers came to love baseball. Thus did the Paycheck Lounge in Hamtramck meet Tiger Stadium. Walewander hit his dinger, and the Dead Milk-men cheered, and everybody got together afterward in the Tiger clubhouse, where Walewander talked about his homer and the Milk-men talked about their breakthrough album, *Big Lizard in My Back-yard*. After a while, Detroit manager Sparky Anderson came out of his office and sized up the Milkmen.

"Jeez," Anderson said. "Them boys don't see much sunlight, do they?"

There are people who come to Tiger Stadium and can still hear Ty Cobb cursing the pitcher from second base, or they can still hear one of Hank Greenberg's home runs hitting the second deck in right field, echoing deep and solid like a ripe melon dropped into a barrel. Me? I look down at the boxes along the first-base line and hear my favorite Milkmen single, "Methodist Coloring Book": "But don't color outside the lines / Or God will send you to Hell."

Alas, the Dead Milkmen broke up in 1994, and Jim Walewander was out of baseball not long after that. People say he's in California now, working as an investment banker, which isn't bad for a guy who once used Hefty bags for curtains.

On the last weekend I was there, Jon Beavers and his friend Louis Koroyanis had come to Tiger Stadium as part of their annual spring ballpark tour. They found themselves trapped in the no-alcohol fam-ily section deep in the left-field seats and were returning from a thirsty eastward pilgrimage through the grandstand as the rain fell, steady and percussive, on the empty seats. Far away, Tiger center fielder Gabe Kapler caught the better part of a fastball. The ball stayed on a line, nearly flat, dipping just slightly as it approached the low fence in left field. Jon Beavers, beer in hand, turned back toward the plate just in time for Kapler's home run to hit him right in the stomach.

Louis Koroyanis, of course, in the tradition of all those who once ran through the Brooks lumberyard, immediately dove past his wounded friend and grabbed the ball.

"Do you believe this shit?" Beavers said, laughing. "I get hit in the gut, *on television*, and he winds up with the ball."

My personal history of Tiger Stadium took its last little mystifying break when Gabe Kapler went long to Jon Beavers's midsection. It sailed with the Eugene V. Debs Memorial Kazoo Marching Band, and it dipped once each for Jim Walewander and Dean Clean and Rodney Anonymous. My history here had some stuff on it. It never moved the way things will move in the true urban village, which will be a safe and convenient place, where the line will run straight and true, from Ty Cobb to Gehringer and Greenberg, to Cochrane and Kaline and Alan Trammell, who played shortstop for twenty years and who played it only in Detroit.

Before the game, Trammell talked about the old ballpark and the new one and about the difference between history and sentiment, a subtle distinction often lost on the people who build new stadiums or write about baseball. In fact, it's a distinction that eludes quite a few historians who look for life to color between the lines because they're afraid we'll all go to hell if it doesn't.

"Look, I'm not saying that I'm not going to miss this place," Trammell said. "This was home, and I'll cherish that. But you don't erase twenty years. I'll have that right here." And he puts his hand over his heart.

"But," Trammell went on, "the history will travel. It will come with us, I hope, and there will be some new history in the new ballpark."

I have a little piece of that history to carry with me, an inauspicious foul ball that fell into a small pool of rainwater during an extraneous game on a rainy night in May. The ball is nowhere near as significant as the one that hit Jon Beavers amidships, or the one Reggie Jackson pounded off the transformer, or the one with which Jim Walewander delighted the Dead Milkmen, or even most of the ones that went rattling through Brooks Lumber. There is a black mark on my ball, and there is a suspicious scuff on it, and that's why it will bring forward for me Tiger Stadium, where history always dove and sailed and fooled you, because it was a place where history always had its very best stuff.

The Tigers moved into their new Comerica Park before the 2000 season. They hiked ticket prices an average of 103 percent. The team continued to bungle. Crowds dropped precipitously. Somewhere, Eugene V. Debs is warming up, smiling.

Esquire **August 1999**

Soul on Ice

The Sioux would come up the river toward the big lake, and they would steal the ponies of the Ojibwe people who lived along the banks of the river. The Ojibwe would follow, ten or twenty or a hundred, down the shores of the river, down a narrow trail that fell breathlessly toward the water. There would be a great battle, and many Ojibwe and many Sioux would fall, and there would be blood staining the snow along the narrow path, and blood running red down the river, too. There were many battles along this trail, and there was so much blood that the Ojibwe people called the little path Ka-beck-a-nung, "the Trail of War."

The French came first, heading north to the islands in the big lake. An explorer named Pierre de LaVerendrye arrived in 1736, on his way to settle in Fort St. Charles, on the north shore of the big lake. He camped along Ka-beck-a-nung, which he translated as "Chemin de Guerre." Once, LaVerendrye sent his son and a priest north from Fort St. Charles for supplies. He got them back without their heads. Then the English came, and there were wars, and then there was the United States of America, drawing a complex and bizarre boundary between Canada and what came to be known as Minnesota. The Ojibwe—whom the English called Ojibway or, more often, Chippewa—were sent south and away from the big lake and the river, but their spirit lives in the name of the place: a town that the Americans came to call Warroad.

19

At the turn of this century, the U.S. government opened the old Ojibwe land for homesteading, and in 1901, a Saint Paul man named William P. Christian became bored working for the telephone company. Homesteading looked like both a good deal and a great adventure. The government gave him eighty acres to farm near what was by then being called the Warroad River. In winter, as the river and the lake became clotted with thick, black ice, it seemed that the world ended right there on those banks. Great swirls of snow rose straight up off the ice as the winds that began in Manitoba swept across the lake like a hail of razors; they didn't blow themselves gentle until they hit the Ozarks. But the farming was good, there was a booming local economy in the timber and lumber business, and William Christian still thought it was a good deal.

Three years later, George Marvin got off a Canadian National train at the Warroad depot. He had come to begin the rest of his life. He'd left school in southern Minnesota after the ninth grade, gone off to Canada to work for the Canadian Elevator Co. Now, a rising star in the firm, he'd come to Warroad, barely over the border, to take charge of the company's grain elevator, and also to manage its lumber and fuel interests. As George Marvin stepped off the train and into the snow-edged January gale, a young man offered to help with his bags.

"By the way," the young man asked George Marvin. "You don't play hockey by any chance, do you?"

Sports rarely flourish in tiny places anymore, particularly professional sports, which have far more in common with Twentieth Century Fox these days than they do with, say, the Rochester Royals or the Canton Bulldogs or some of those other Mesozoic aggregations beloved by America's smaller cities at a time when America believed in things like smaller cities. Back then, the identity of a team was inextricably entwined with a specific sense of place. A team was rooted in a community, which involves more than simple geographic boundaries. The team was a manifestation of the shared values that cause people to come and live together.

Community is virtually lost to sports today. A team does not arise within a city. It is laid upon it, often by forces beyond the community's control. Even the last real vestige of the way it was—minor-league baseball—has in the past decade become a national merchandising bonanza; there is nothing more preposterous than seeing some yuppie dweeb wandering Boston's Back Bay wearing a glen-plaid suit and a Durham Bulls cap. It's like naming your Afghan hound "Spike."

College sports is a hopeless cause as well. What was once perceived to be the exclusive property of men in raccoon coats and women festooned with camellia blossoms is now merely another vehicle of mass entertainment. In turn, this has brought the attention absurdly down to the high-school level. Grown men who work for television networks—which is not yet entirely oxymoronic—get paid for speculating on the career paths of 14-year-old basketball players. It is not cupidity that has drained whatever innocence sports may once have had. It is a kind of informational greed, the abiding public hunger of an age that demands to know the sexual predilections of the duchess of York. For, as she discovered to her toe-sucking dismay, it is no longer possible to excel privately at any level of any sport. There are very few tiny places anymore.

For almost a century now, the town of Warroad has obsessed about ice hockey. It is a city of 1,600 people, and it has two indoor hockey rinks and is about to open a third. Children begin playing organized hockey at the age of 4, and the best of them are still playing somewhere when they are 40. Drive along Route 11 from International Falls, the country spreading wide and white and flat in every direction, and a water tower, "WARROAD" written across it, slowly rises on the horizon. There is what appears to be a great X on either side of the town's name. Closer now, just over the little bridge that crosses the clotted river, and the X's become plainer. They are hockey sticks, crossed above the blades.

Once the locals played on the river, and they played on the lake, and they even played in their boots on the slippery, unpaved streets. Occasionally, a horse would come down the street, leaving behind it a trail of fresh hockey pucks, needing only to be frozen: It took an even braver man to be a goalie in those days. In a very real sense, Warroad's historic soul is on ice, skating its lane.

William Christian's grandsons—Gordie, Roger and Bill—all throve within the sport; Bill and Roger won gold medals as part of the 1960 U.S. Olympic team at Squaw Valley. William's great-grandson Dave won another one, as part of the 1980 team that improbably won in Lake Placid, thereby touching off the first public signal of the imminent Reagan Era. As it happens, no U.S. hockey team has ever won any kind of Olympic medal without at least one player from Warroad on its roster. Dave now plays for the Chicago Blackhawks, and the rest of the Christian family operates Warroad's third-largest industry. They make hockey sticks: "Hockey sticks by hockey players" is the slogan.

The Christian brothers—yes, they occasionally get mail intended for the winery—have built their factory directly across Route 11 from the Marvin Windows plant. Covering forty acres and employing more than 3,000 people, that company is the legacy of the life that George Marvin came to Warroad to build. It's one of those small-town companies thought long since lost to junk bonds and automation. Even at the height of the Great Depression, the plant refused to lay off any of its employees. The outgrowth of George Marvin's success in the lumber business, it now makes fancy window frames that are shipped all across the country: "Built for northern windows with southern charm" is the slogan.

George had five sons, and they played hockey in the streets with the other children of the town. It hooked young Cal Marvin deepest of all. He played all the time, cardboard stuffed in his socks as makeshift shin pads. In 1943, Cal joined the Marines. He fought in the Pacific, landing in the first wave on Guam. The best hockey player he knew was killed on Okinawa. Cal Marvin returned from the war wanting more than anything else to play. "I came back with the idea that we needed an arena in town," he says. "It was very difficult then. I mean, the town needed a library. The town needed sidewalks. The town needed streets. So here I am, trying to talk business leaders into building an indoor rink." Even as the scion of the town's leading employer, Cal had a hard sell.

But eventually, with a set of blueprints borrowed from the University of North Dakota, Cal began to build his rink. He found a perfect place for it, at the corner of Main and McKenzie streets, right in front of the depot where his father had stepped off the train and just down the street from the Northland Tap, a popular watering hole for Marvin Windows employees. Cal and his friends poured the concrete by hand. Ed Christian (son of William) handled a lot of the carpentry work. They opened the rink in 1948 and they called it the Memorial Arena, but, being hockey folk to the bone, they began to refer to it as the Gardens. "You know," Cal says today, "Maple Leaf Gardens. Boston Gardens. Warroad Gardens. It fits."

The Gardens is the town's communal heart, even though Cal later managed to get the second arena, the Olympic, built, and he has been instrumental in the construction of the state-of-the-art facility that will open this fall, just off Route 11 behind the Christian Brothers factory. The Gardens is a smallish place, with high and arching wooden rafters, and to sit shivering in the unheated bleachers on a winter's night is to feel as though one has stumbled into the world's only rolltop glacier. They've all played the Gardens. All the Christians, and Dan McKinnon, and Alan Hangsleben, and Blaine Comstock. The Mites play at the Gardens. So do the Squirts, the Peewees and the Bantams. So do the Warroad Warriors, the high-school team. So do the Lakers. At the Gardens, if you wait long enough and there is a great one coming, you can see him for years off, the way that you can see the water tower with its hockey sticks from a mile up the road. It is a place where little legends are born, no less precious than any others you can name.

His mother is of the Ojibwe people, the handful who stayed on the Buffalo Point reservation, in Canada, on the old lands near the big lake. Henry Boucha's father was a Canadian fisherman whose own father had long ago truncated the family name of Boucher for reasons that remain unclear. Henry is his mother's son. In 1969, in one magical hockey season, it was his mother's people whom everyone summoned when they talked about Henry Boucha, the greatest high-school player Minnesota ever saw.

"You look back," he says today, "and you think about how naïve you were—last year, let alone twenty years ago. You're just out there having fun, not a care in the world." He smiles at this, dark eyes crinkling under darker eyebrows. His right eye, embroidered lightly in scar tissue, does not move at all, souvenir of a martyred career.

They saw him coming at the Gardens. They saw him coming all over town. Henry Boucha was the best anyone had ever seen. He was a good enough placekicker that Notre Dame had offered him a scholarship. "I saw him come to where we had a baseball game and a track meet going on," recalls Frank Krahn, a teammate of Boucha's at Warroad High School. "He'd play in the baseball game and then come over and win the 440 or something." Because he was dark and handsome and unmistakably Ojibwe, the inevitable comparisons were drawn: Henry Boucha was Warroad's Jim Thorpe. He touched some chord in the town's common history.

Ironically, he had not been raised in the Native tradition at all. There was a strong assimilationist pull to his upbringing. "My mother spoke Indian," he recalls, "but there isn't a reservation here. There's reservation land here, but it's just woods. There were only four or five Indian families here. So I didn't have a lot of traditional Indian culture. She tried to teach us on occasion, but we weren't really that receptive because nobody else was doing it. It was not a fashionable thing at the time."

He was drawn to hockey because he was an athlete and because he lived in Warroad. "It was just what you did," he says. "We went to the rink to play all the time. Because Warroad didn't have a Zamboni back then, we scraped the ice between periods. Really, it was all we did all winter."

He was a defenseman, but he played the entire ice. By the time he was in eighth grade, he was playing on the Warroad Warriors' varsity team. By the time he was a senior, in 1969, the Warriors were ranked number one in the state, and they were preparing to enter the Minnesota high-school tournament, over which the state annually loses a good bit of its mind, in much the same way Indiana yearly goes off its trolley about high-school basketball. Like Indiana, Minnesota in those days organized its hockey tournament so that every high-school team in the state was eligible regardless of the size of its enrollment. This made Warroad, which then had fewer than 200 students enrolled, an irresistible story from the start. Henry Boucha made Warroad a sensation.

Early in the tournament, he took a stick to the head but returned to the ice and, bloody bandage and all, took a pass from Frank Krahn and scored a goal with one second left to beat Eveleth 3–2. Today, that goal is variously described as coming from fifty, seventy-five or a hundred feet. "Hey, it was in the slot, right at the top of the circle," Boucha demurs. The legend grew as the tournament went on, until Warroad made it to Minneapolis for the finals, and everyone wanted a piece of the little high school, with its Indian star. Warroad was quaint, and Boucha was impossibly exotic.

Even without knowing about Cal Marvin and his Gardens, most of the state informally adopted the Warriors as a kind of plucky out-of-nowhere underdog. "It was strange," recalls Krahn. "We'd be walking downtown in our Warroad jackets, and people'd come up and shake our hands."

The Warriors won their way into the state-championship game, in which they played Edina High School. Edina is a wealthy Minneapolis suburb—one of its players that year was the son of the president of Northwest Orient Airlines—and what had been a fairly conventional David-and-Goliath plot line suddenly veered full tilt into Frank Capra territory. In the second period, Edina held a 2–1 lead, when Boucha made a rush up the right side. The crowd rose as he shot and the goalie deflected the puck into a corner of the rink. Boucha went after it, and he threw it back out in front of the net. At that point, an Edina defenseman named Jim Knutson ran Boucha into the boards, catching him in the head with an elbow. Boucha went down flat and stayed on the ice. Horrified, the crowd in the Metropolitan Center fell silent.

"He slapped my head up against the glass, and I broke my eardrum," Boucha says. "I lost my equilibrium, so when I did get up, it looked like the ice was lopsided." Boucha left the ice, lost for the rest of the game—in fact, he spent the next three days in the hospital. Warroad now owned the crowd, and the Warriors managed to tie the game, 4–4, and then to take it into the first of two overtimes, during which at least one Warroad shot hit the goalpost. Finally, Edina scored, winning the game and the championship. The Edina players were booed as they accepted the trophy. Because the Bouchas were unable to afford Henry's medical costs, the people in Warroad collected $1,300 to pay his hospital bill.

(In Warroad, where the presumption remains inviolate that the Warriors would have won had Boucha not been injured, Knutson's check is described as everything from tough hockey to involuntary manslaughter. "I don't know," says Krahn. "It looked okay to me.")

Boucha recovered and, almost immediately, got married and signed with the Winnipeg Jets of the Western Canada Hockey Association. At 18, he was ready for neither one. The marriage soon fell apart under the stress of his constant travel.

After winning a silver medal on the 1972 U.S. Olympic team, Boucha joined the Detroit Red Wings when it was still remarkable for an American to play in the NHL. Even beyond that, he was a personality. In order to keep the sweat from falling in his eyes, Boucha took to wearing a headband—almost no one wore a helmet—and it brought out the Ojibwe in him, to the point where Native American activists were publicly critical of Boucha for allegedly exploiting his background. The American Indian Movement referred to him as "Uncle Tomahawk." Nevertheless, Boucha marketed the headbands for $15 apiece, and they soon became his trademark.

In 1974, Boucha was traded to the Minnesota North Stars. His popularity in the state was still immense; he got ovations in the Met Center that rang loudly with memories. It was widely rumored that he would be the North Stars' captain the following season. On January 4, 1975, in a game against the Boston Bruins, Boucha got into a fight with Dave Forbes, a young and marginal player trying to make his bones with the notoriously roughhouse Bruins. Both men were sent to the penalty box. When they came back onto the ice, Forbes skated up and rammed the butt end of his stick into Boucha's right eye. Again, Henry Boucha fell to the ice. Again, the Met Center fell silent. Again, Henry Boucha didn't get up. The socket around the eye was shattered, and some of the muscles that control the eye's movement were destroyed. He would have double vision for the rest of his life.

The attack was so vicious that the district attorney for Hennepin County charged Forbes with aggravated assault. Boucha wound up suing Forbes, the Bruins and the NHL, a case that was settled in 1980. His career was essentially finished. He bounced around some, signing with the Minnesota Fighting Saints of the World Hockey Association and then jumping back to the NHL's Kansas City Scouts, who later became the Colorado Rockies. It was a maddening time for him. He could still skate, and his hands were as deft and quick as they ever were. But every time he looked down, he saw two pucks at his feet. "Then, you start kicking around down there and you get leveled," he says. "You wind up looking at those GEs on the ceiling." He retired in 1977. He was 26 years old.

"I was bitter," says Boucha, who still keeps a videotape of the Forbes incident near his television set. "It lasted a long time. I had a hard time adjusting. I mean, your life is cut off right there, and I was unprepared as to what I was going to do afterward."

He moved to Seattle, then Spokane, where he tried to start a meat company while he pursued his protracted lawsuit. The meat company failed, as did his second marriage. He briefly took a job selling advertising in Detroit, then moved to Idaho, where his sister lived. He hunted and he fished, and he helped grow a huge garden. Gradually, he decided that he wanted to come back to Warroad. "This has always been home," he says. Now he sells real estate, and he helps coach the Warriors, one of whom is a dark and handsome young forward named Henry Boucha, Jr., who moved north to be with his father and to be part of the program that had nurtured his father long ago. "It's fun," says the young player. "He's kind of a legend around here. People come up to me and they tell me that they saw my dad do this and that."

"I'm really a student of the game now," says Henry senior. "I grew up a little. I'm 41 now. I probably didn't grow up until I was 32 or 33." And people still point at him and whisper, watching him through younger eyes.

Cal Marvin is in the Gardens this night. So is Henry Boucha, standing behind the bench as the Warroad Warriors take out Bemidji, 5–0. It is 31 degrees in the place, and it feels colder, as though they eventually are going to have to pry the trumpets off the lips of the kids in the pep band. Warroad's best player is a sophomore forward named Wyatt Smith, whose family moved to town because Wyatt's father got a job at Marvin Windows. Other towns in the region are failing; Thief River Falls is losing its retail business to a mall that opened up outside of Grand Forks, North Dakota. Because of the Marvin Windows plant, and because of the Polaris Co., which makes snowmobiles, and because of the Christian Brothers Co., Warroad's economy has proved relatively well bulwarked against the recession. This has provided the town with at least one ancillary benefit: Wyatt Smith, who right now is lighting out on a scoring rush that makes the chilly fans stamp their feet and think of Henry Boucha.

"He's going to be a good one," says Cal Marvin. "He's got the tools."

Down the street, warmly lit against the night, is Frank's Place, which used to be the Northland Tap until it was bought by Frank Krahn, who gave Henry Boucha the assist on the big goal against Eveleth. It is a beer joint and, given the state ordinances, a 3.2-beer joint at that. It does have a rather staggering variety of bar snacks, however. These include turkey gizzards, as well as beef jerky, moose jerky, elk jerky and venison jerky.

"I guess you have to say the hockey tradition really started with Cal," muses Krahn. "It became a tradition with him, anyway. Now, though, we've got some people who don't love hockey, who are coming here just for the jobs."

By custom, and by common consent, Warroad has defined itself by its ice hockey, and its ice hockey is indivisible from the history of the town itself. It has not been imposed as some kind of favor from distant and wealthy people who understand little and care less. So the new people will play hockey if they stay, and they always stay, the way that George Marvin stayed, climbing off the train at the depot across the street. He happened to play hockey, you know. The way that William Christian stayed, here on the old lands where, in winter, the snow blows in a flash upward off the big lake and, angel-white, it spreads everywhere like dreams and wishes.

GQ March 1993

The Snake-Handling
Pole-Vaulter

This is about three places in a very small place. It is about a house
and a barn and a schoolyard.

The house sits back from a fork in the road that leads into a neighborhood that someone carved out of a bean field on the south side of
the town. In the house live six dogs, two monitor lizards, forty con-
strictors of various breeds, an iguana named George, and Jeff
Hartwig, the best pole-vaulter in the world. That makes this house
different from any other house in Jonesboro, Arkansas.

The barn rises from a bean field not far away, and it looks like
every other barn in every other bean field, all triangles of corrugated
tin, the property edged with low-slung barbed wire in which are tangled the rusting innards of a dozen old machines. Inside the barn,
there are people pole-vaulting, and that makes this barn different
from all the other barns in Jonesboro, Arkansas.

The schoolyard is north of the house and the barn, away from the
snakes and the lizards and the pole-vaulters, up out of the bean
fields, and toward the edge of a ridge. It is an open place facing a
stand of woods, the trees bare and gnarled in the pale winter sunlight. From the woods, you can see right down into the schoolyard,
and there is a sign at one end of it. ALL NEWS MEDIA MUST REPORT

TO THE SUPERINTENDENT'S OFFICE, it says, and that is why this schoolyard is not like any other schoolyard in Jonesboro, Arkansas.

Life, it seems, can be a parabola. You rise and rise, up toward something precious—a goal, a great love, a perfect family—and you get there and get over, or you get close and then fall away because life has somehow raised the bar on you. You get close, and then you fall away, out of the sky, steady as rain, swift as a gunshot.

That is the story of these three places in a very small town: the schoolyard with the sign, the barn with the athletes, and the house with the pole-vaulter and the lizards and all the snakes in the front bedroom. Jonesboro is an open place, tucked into the northeast corner of the state, its watersheds and tiny streams mere vestigial children of the great mother river to the east, a place where you can see flags against the distant horizon and where stories travel, boundless as hawks over the spreading bean fields.

The House

If, for any reason, you decide to enter the house through a front window, it is best not to pick the north window. Step through the south window and the worst that can happen is that a small spaniel will fasten himself onto your pant leg. Step through the north, however, and your right leg will go through the glass and onto a fourteen-foot Burmese python, which will not appreciate the attention. Your left leg will encounter a twelve-foot albino python curled nestlike around her eggs. Presuming that neither of the pythons takes particular offense, you might then find yourself eye to eye with an Asian monitor lizard—cousin to the Komodo dragon so beloved of cheesy special-effects wizards and viewers of *Wild Kingdom*. (Ah, Marlin Perkins. "The Komodo dragon can chase a man down and eat his leg. If disaster is chasing you down and eating your leg, call Mutual of Omaha.") Even assuming that the big lizard is open to negotiation, it is unlikely that you will be in any condition to explain your presence to its keeper, who happens to be the best pole-vaulter in the world.

"A lot of people," explains Jeff Hartwig, "I can't talk to them about the technicalities of the pole vault, but they've got all kinds of questions about the snakes. All they know is that I'm the Olympic pole-vaulter who keeps big reptiles."

Like most vaulters, Hartwig is long and lean; it is a sport meant for sleekly powerful, split-rail types. His eyes are bright and intelligent, with just enough eccentric gleam in them to mark him as a vaulter. Sprinters have snipers' eyes—narrowed, focused, and unfriendly. There is the strained glow of a stolid fanatic behind the eyes of weight heavers. A vaulter's eyes, though, are encompassing, as befits anyone who hurls himself toward the sky.

"We're all eccentric to some degree," Hartwig admits. "Most people think we're crazy. It's not like skydiving. I mean, in skydiving, you take that step and then it's over. You've done what you came to do. In pole-vaulting, you've got to stay focused mentally while you run down there and do something that most people would consider extremely scary. You're not really out of control until you let go of the pole. Hopefully, you're headed in the right direction.

"One thing we all understand is that it is an event based on failure. Unless you break a world record, you always try higher, which means that even when you win, you miss your last jump. Your event always ends in failure."

The United States—country of the Wright brothers, John Glenn, and Evel Knievel—was once a pole-vault nation. We had the first man over fifteen feet (Cornelius Warmerdam), the first over sixteen feet (John Uelses), and the first over seventeen feet (John Pennel). We had Bob Richards, who later came to sell us Wheaties, a breakfast cereal that tastes only marginally better than the sawdust in which the Vaulting Vicar used to land. Up until 1972, when some dubious Teutonic bureaucracy disqualified all of Bob Seagren's poles, the United States had won every Olympic pole-vaulting gold medal. Since then, and coincident with a steep national decline in interest in track and field generally, the pole vault has belonged increasingly to Frenchmen, Poles, and the towering Ukrainian figure of Sergei Bubka, still the only man to clear twenty feet.

"The U.S. was lucky to dominate for as long as we did," Hartwig explains. "We won a lot of competitions in jump-offs and on fewer misses. Part of it is that track and field is now a forgotten sport here in non-Olympic years."

Since making the 1996 Olympic team, Hartwig has been the most consistent vaulter in the world. That year, he not only cleared nineteen feet for the first time, he did so after losing the heart of the season to a broken hand. By March of this year, Hartwig had not only become the first American to clear six meters (19 feet 8.25 inches), he also had broken both the American indoor (19 feet 6.25 inches) and outdoor (19 feet 8.5 inches) records. In 1998, he cleared nineteen feet in twenty-two of the thirty-one meets in which he competed, and, though he was ranked only second in the world, most vaulters believe that his consistency made Hartwig the best in the world at the event.

"Every year," says Earl Bell, a former Olympian who coaches Hartwig out at the barn that sits in the bean field, "Jeff got a little bit better. I think if you'd come to me six or seven years ago, I'd have said he'd already overachieved."

Hartwig found devotion to the vault and his reptiles in Jonesboro. Raised outside of St. Louis, he began vaulting in high school. After graduating, Hartwig heard of the little vaulting empire that Bell had been building in Jonesboro at Arkansas State, where he had gone to college. Hartwig enrolled at ASU, graduating in 1990. Then, in 1991, a vaulter named Lane Lohr came down to Bell's new barn from Illinois to train. Lohr had a ten-foot Burmese python named John. Hartwig was fascinated with the animal, and when Lohr took a coaching job back in Illinois, he left the snake with Hartwig. Alas, shortly thereafter, John the python passed to his snakish reward.

"After that snake died," Hartwig says, "I spent two months reading anything I could about snakes." He compiled an extensive library, and he also bought himself as many as forty snakes at a time, some of which he bred for pet stores. As his vaulting improved, Hartwig found his snakes as popular a topic as his athletic success. He did programs at the schools around town, watching as entire classes of fifth graders strained to lift Niki, the fourteen-foot Burmese python who was as calm and gentle as milk around them.

Hartwig got married, and he settled into the house at the fork in the road. The snakes moved into the north guest room. He liked Jonesboro. "I grew to really enjoy living here," he says. "You can leave your doors unlocked, and you can sleep with the windows open at night." He helped Bell build the training center out in the bean fields. One day, Hartwig heard Bell talking to the construction foreman. The crew was pouring concrete in a hurry, and Bell asked why.

Because tomorrow's the opening of hunting season, and all these guys won't be here, the foreman replied.

Well, they wouldn't work for my company, Bell said.

We tried firing folks, said the foreman. Didn't matter a damn.

The Barn

Inside the barn, there is a radio pounding classic hits—except when Hartwig shows up and changes it to a local hiphop station, which usually drives Bell out into the bean field amid the barbed wire and tractor gizzards. "He's a vaulter, so you figure he's a little eccentric, and you can understand the snakes," says Earl Bell. "But I haven't figured out the rap music yet."

At one end of the barn, down past the video corner and the walls full of poles hanging like harpoons in their racks, there is a vaulting pit: Two uprights rise toward the ceiling above a large, inflatable bag, the same bag in which Hartwig landed in Atlanta when he finished eleventh at the 1996 Olympics. On the wall behind the pit, exactly 19 feet 8.5 inches off the floor, there is a line drawn to celebrate Hartwig's American record. It's nearly the height of a two-story building. It's twice the height of a basketball rim. From the floor of the barn, it's a staggering height to consider rising toward, let alone falling from. But it does not reach the top of the wall. There is still ample clearance inside the barn.

"It takes a great deal of courage to do what Jeff is going to do," Bell explains.

Earl Bell's father was a military doctor assigned to the Canal Zone. His mother was Panamanian. The family moved to Jonesboro when Earl was five. As a family project, his father set up a sawdust pit in the backyard, and the whole family vaulted. (Dr. William Bell is now seventy-seven, and he still regularly clears ten feet.) Like Hartwig, Earl Bell grew long and lean. He stayed home to go to ASU and became a regular on the United States national teams throughout the 1980s, as the rest of the world was catching up with this nation of vaulting fools. He studied the people who vaulted as much as he studied the vault itself.

"Guys that love the pole vault, they're like surfers," Bell muses. "Like how surfers will got out there and wait and wait for that one wave? That's what compels people to pole-vault. It's the challenge to go higher, but it's also the ride."

In 1991, Bell bought the bean field southwest of town and began collecting pole-vaulters from all over the country. He works with high school kids as well as with Jeff Hartwig. Unlike, say, solitary sprinters, vaulters need training partners as much as they need their poles. "Maybe you're not having your best day," Hartwig says. "Then somebody goes down there and jumps real high, and you start thinking, Maybe I'd better concentrate on this workout."

Bell had worked to develop Hartwig's most conspicuous gift: his ability to jump consistently high. They do not push the envelope in training. They don't make a try at twenty feet just for laughs. Instead, they make sure that Hartwig's technique is so sound that he can clear nineteen feet on almost every attempt. Do that, Bell and Hartwig believe, and twenty feet will take care of itself. After all, if Hartwig can reliably clear nineteen six by seven inches, he is vaulting twenty feet whether the bar is set there or not. "I know I can jump the world record," Hartwig says. "I can see where I can jump twenty feet. It's a matter of how everything lines up. That's where consistency comes in. In 1996–97, the Americans were so strong over eighteen feet. They made eighteen eight every single meet. Then the bar would go to nineteen feet, and guys that were jumping eighteen eight and clearing nineteen feet every time would miss. To me, that's a mental barrier."

On the morning of March 24, 1998, Jeff Hartwig got up, drove over to the barn in the bean field, and threw himself into a workout. Afterward, he drove to Memphis to buy some snakes. On his car radio, he heard someone mention Jonesboro. He turned it up. Back in the barn, a vaulter named Kim Becker saw her neighborhood on the small television set. There was her house, and there was Westside Middle School. There were dozens of police there, and ambulances, and children lying on the ground. A teacher was dead. Four children were dead. Ten children were wounded.

Two other children were arrested.

Kim Becker ran to her car. It took her a long time to get home. Earl Bell walked out of his barn and thought about his hometown, the kind of place where this kind of thing didn't happen, looking out at the road that twisted toward the west side, where the bean fields fall off down the ridge toward the rice country.

The Schoolyard

It is nearly a year later, and the children are on vacation. The schoolyard is quiet. The woodland nearby, where two boys named Andrew Golden and Mitchell Johnson—good, God-fearing Christian children, the kind that are taught by their daddies and granddaddies to kill the ducks that feed on the sweet lowland rice—parked a van loaded with guns and ammunition, where they took their combat stances in ambush, where they sighted down the barrels of their weapons and opened up on their classmates as though their classmates were ducks themselves, these woods are silent except for the calls of angry crows and the wind that rattles the bare branches as though they were unsettled bones.

That day, just as Kim Becker was leaving the barn and trying to get home, Suzann Wilson wandered dazedly over the killing ground at Westside Middle School. She was looking for Britthney Varner, her eleven-year-old daughter, a smiling child with bangs and wide, happy eyes. Suzann found Britthney on the ground, one of the four children whom Andrew Golden and Mitchell Johnson—good, God-fearing Christian children dressed like Happy Meal Rambos—had shot dead in the schoolyard.

"Going and searching for your child and seeing your child's face on the ground in the middle of a crowd huddling together, that's a feeling I will never forget," Suzann Wilson says. "The terror that you see in other people when they look you in the eye, and you *know*."

Jonesboro has worked hard at healing. A year later, civic leaders will tell you that life has moved on, mentioning that Westside was the last place on earth that you'd expect something like this to happen. Except that everybody here has a gun and knows how to use one, and the children pose with rifles the way some kids pose with rattles and toy trains, and everybody takes the day off for the opening of duck season. Construction workers pouring concrete for a barnful of pole-vaulters quit for the day. Children skip school.

Suzann Wilson has stayed in town, a great and good place, and she's intrigued to hear that Jonesboro has become a haven for the country's pole-vaulters, that people come here from all over America to work with Earl Bell, to leap and jump and rise toward the ceiling of a barn in a bean field, and that a town where children once murdered other children may one day be at least partly redeemed by a snake-handling pole-vaulter who is the best in the world.

"I think I've seen that place," says Suzann Wilson. "It's out there off the bypass near 226."

Jeff Hartwig has been trying to schedule one of his snake presentations at the Westside Middle School so the fifth graders there can yelp and giggle and throw their heads back as they try to lift a snake that's almost as long as the entire class is tall. He also goes out to the barn, working on his technique, looking up, then running, rising up above the bean fields and the rusting machine innards, up above the schoolyard and the ambush woods, up above all the snakes in his house and all the snakes in the history of a small place, up in the almighty parabola, and then over the top and falling, down and away. In the mind's dark sky, a white flag flutters on the battlements of paradise.

Jeff Hartwig still owns a houseful of reptiles and the American record in the pole vault. Shortly after this piece appeared, Eric Harris and Dylan Klebold went off to Columbine High School for the last time.

Esquire June **1999**

Heavy Metal

The midsummer heat shimmered across 125th Street in New York City and settled upon the Minnesota Twins like a great, musty shawl. It was 1987, and the Twins were headed on their bus to Yankee Stadium. They also were on their way, eventually, to a world championship, but at this moment the bus had taken on the air of a caged and sullen van on its way to Rikers Island. Their opponents this day were the Yankees, whose season had left in it only the persistent threat that the Principal Owner might once again start channeling Vlad the Impaler. It was an airless, dead time in a long and ordinary season.

Various Twins slouched in varying degrees of indolence, lounging in the thickly sweet hydrocarbons. The bus stopped at the light on 125th Street, and a white Mercedes-Benz with Texas plates pulled up alongside. The car glistened like an uncut diamond, and it caught the attention of the Twins, particularly of Kirby Puckett, the bright and talented outfielder whose personality enlivened even that sodden summer's morning. Puckett looked out the window at the white Mercedes with the Texas plates, and he saw that the driver was Walter Berry, a former basketball All-America at St. John's University who was then in the employ of the San Antonio Spurs and who would continue in their employ until the rest of the NBA caught on that Berry's right hand was of less use on a basketball court than a socket wrench would be. On this day, however, Berry was living fat.

He had his contract and his white Mercedes, and he had his gold chain around his neck.

It was not specifically a chain in that it was not made of individual links. It was a rolled tube of solid gold about the thickness of a man's thumb. And not your thumb or mine, either. Walter Berry's thumb, say. Or Kirby Puckett's. In fact, it looked like nothing more than a length of golden garden hose. Its glint caught Puckett's eye, which was not surprising. Its glint likely could have caught the eye of a pilot on a DC-10 westbound to Denver out of LaGuardia. Lord Carnarvon dug holes in the desert for years to come up with that much gold. Puckett leaned out of the window of the bus. His teammates snapped to attention.

"Hey, Walter!" Puckett yelled. Very coolly, Berry looked up and gave a small wave. Puckett pointed at Berry's neck.

"Yo, Walter," Puckett asked. "What cost more, your car or your jewelry?"

The bus, alive at last, rocked with laughter. The light changed, and the Twins rolled along toward the happy end of their baseball season, while Walter Berry sat there for a long time in his car. Kirby Puckett leaned back in his seat and laughed the best laugh in all of professional sports—one that came from deep in the satisfaction that he, Kirby Puckett, late of the Robert Taylor Homes in Chicago, had succeeded to the point where he could laugh at other rich people over their conspicuous ostentation without worrying that the laughter came fouled by envy. It was his due, this laughter, and he could laugh it, full and loud, until it shook his own golden medallions and they sang across his chest.

Historians agree that throughout medieval times, it was the men who wore most of the jewelry. They adorned themselves with garish hereditary trinkets and opulent religious gewgaws. The latter came into vogue as just-converted Christian rulers sought to express their newfound faith without abandoning their comfortable pagan vulgarity. Charlemagne wore a talisman that consisted of two huge sapphires set in gold, between which was lodged an alleged piece of the True Cross. It was buried with Charlemagne, but it was considered such a hot little token that Emperor Otto III dug it up in 1000, and Napoléon wound up giving it to Joséphine as a wedding present.

It was those spoilsports behind the French Revolution who changed everything. In *The Story of Jewelry*, Marcus Baerwald and Tom Mahoney explain that jewelry became a feminine thing after the revolution, when European fashion began to pattern itself after English dress. Moreover, because most of the men's jewelry up until that time had to do with one's respective rank within the aristocracy, possessing a particularly stylish medallion in the time of the Terror was a way to ensure that one likely would not long have a neck from which to hang it.

Of course, we Americans were a bit more delicate about how we chucked the landed aristocracy out of our country. Since then, however, we have been engaged in a fairly constant search for an indigenous gentry within the limits of our democratic pretensions. By and large, in the twentieth century, we have settled upon those people who excel in our media of mass entertainment. This is an aristocracy open to anyone who can sweat on-camera, play four chords on a guitar, sneer at Gene Shalit or dunk on the Dallas Mavericks.

For a time, sports performers considered themselves to be apart from actors and singers and other show-business professionals. Somehow, sports was different—less contrived, more uncertain, less lucrative and more manly. Today, money has broken down whatever barrier once kept sports removed from the other vehicles of public performance. Today, there is little left in their public lives that separates Shaquille O'Neal from Jack Nicholson, Eddie Vedder or Ice-T.

Thirty years ago, no athlete would have dreamed of taking the field with a cross dangling from one ear. Today, Barry Bonds is never without one. Thirty years ago, no athlete would have considered being photographed for the cover of a national magazine festooned in gold. Today, Deion Sanders stares off of *Sports Illustrated* looking like Queen Nefertiti's pool man. Any qualms an athlete might have about appearing effeminate have been obliterated by that athlete's desire to tell the world that he belongs to the only viable American aristocracy.

"People want other people to know they've made it," says Michael Craig, a New York jeweler who designs pieces for several hundred professional athletes. "It's important to them to make people know that."

Sports jewelry was an isolated phenomenon for many years. ESPN baseball analyst Jim Kaat remembers a little wizened man in San Francisco who would haunt the clubhouses in Candlestick Park with his sample case. "He didn't have much, but he had the same players coming back to him every year," Kaat recalls. In the late 1970s, when large medallions came into vogue, the National Basketball Association banned on-court jewelry, a prohibition that is still in force today. "You had guys getting their fingers snagged in them," says Jerry Sichting, a former NBA player who now broadcasts for the Boston Celtics. "You'd come around a pick, and one of those things would fly up, and you'd have guys losing teeth out there."

Competing while wearing jewelry can indeed by a complicated business. One day, Yankees manager Billy Martin completely unglued fractious Boston pitcher Dennis "Oil Can" Boyd by making the umpire remove the Can's chains on the entirely specious grounds that the gleam off the gold was distracting Martin's hitters.

Much of the original sports jewelry involved religious medals. This was particularly true in baseball, where the influx of Latin ballplayers brought to the game the ostentatious Catholicism of the Caribbean basin. But as the barrier between sports and the rest of the entertainment world broke down, athletes began to respond to fashion imperatives from outside the tight little confines of their own occupation. By the mid-1980s, for instance, hip-hop fashion had come into sports because so many athletes were listening to Afrika Bambaataa and Grandmaster Flash. I can vividly remember a St. John's basketball player named Willie Glass, who used to wear a necklace with his nickname, "Hollywood," that was the size of a license plate. One day, Glass showed up for practice without it. I asked him where it had gone.

"Sorry, man," he said. "It's in the shop."

Quite naturally, this all did not go down well in the more hidebound precincts of the sporty world, especially when the drug scandals of the late 1970s broke. Functionally incapable of dealing with any cultural phenomenon more radical than Rosemary Clooney, the sports Establishment wasted no time in deciding that since dealers wore gold chains, any ballplayer who wore them must somehow be connected with drugs. There was more than a little unsubtle racism to all of this. "This was part of it," says Red Sox outfielder Otis Nixon, who battled drug problems himself. "People thought you came from 'that kind of environment.'"

The 1980s were what finally brought sports jewelry into the mainstream. Suddenly, it ceased being gauche to parade one's vast wealth down America's main streets. Nancy Reagan was running through Parisian design houses as though they were the back racks at Kmart, and Donald Trump was deciding that the thing a luxurious midtown apartment building needed was its very own waterfall. In the climate of the times, Charlemagne could have worn his talisman to a White House dinner and ended up looking like one of the Poor Clares. Conspicuous consumption belabored good taste, and good taste went down like Walter Mondale.

Which is about where we stand today. One of the more remarkable baubles I saw during my brief time hanging around baseball players was worn around the neck of a veteran catcher. He was a stolid, no-nonsense type who had attended the same grammar school I had. One day, while interviewing this fellow, I noticed that he was wearing a pendant of the suffering Christ, crowned with thorns. The Lord's head was gold, and at every point where a thorn had punctured the divine brow, there was a tiny ruby depicting a drop of blood. I couldn't keep my eyes off the crucifix. It was the single most tasteless item I had ever seen. Who makes these things? I wondered. In this secular and godless world, where do you go if you just must have a Jesus bleeding rubies?

"I know that piece," says Michael Craig with a sigh. He does not make a Jesus bleeding rubies. Not yet, at least: "I can't imagine anything I wouldn't make for somebody," he says.

Several times a year, Michael Craig dresses up like a bum and tours the hotels in mid-town Manhattan, the posh ones where the ballplayers stay. With him are two of his associates, both of whom are armed. "I'm probably carrying $200,000 worth of stock," Craig explains, sitting in a warehouse that he shares with a designer of hip-hop clothing. This September, he will open his own showroom on 47th Street, a place where a visiting athlete can come and shoot pool, lounge on the huge leather wraparound couch and allow Craig to help him demonstrate how truly wealthy the athlete is.

"The feeling is that they are part of an exclusive club, so why hide it?" Craig explains. "A lot of sports personalities . . . they came from nothing and instantaneously they've got $8 million and, basically, the thought is, Why practice denial? The first stop usually is either me or the Mercedes dealership."

Craig fell into his current business, which he says nets him an income that "you can say is multimillion dollars." Eleven years ago, he was hustling around New Jersey, selling cheap gold chains to a clientele of hairdressers: "I was going around to hair shops selling the crappiest stuff you can imagine and getting a lot of aggravation and an ulcer." He abandoned that and began designing custom jewelry for karate champions and bodybuilding stars. "I was making jewelry for people with the egos to wear it but not the incomes to match," he says. In 1988, he made a tiny gold dragster for champion driver Joe Amato. That piece caught the eye of baseball player Jack Clark, an automobile aficionado so devoted that when he finally ran himself into bankruptcy, he owned forty cars. Still flush at this point, Clark bought one of Craig's little dragsters, and he introduced Craig to Amos Otis, a former star with the Kansas City Royals, who was the jeweler's entrée to the big leagues.

Craig and Otis worked both clubhouses in San Diego, where Otis was living at the time. "When I walked into the Montreal Expos locker room in San Diego and saw their reaction," Craig says, "I knew I was onto something. I cut my first big deal within about five minutes of Otis walking in there." Since then, his business has expanded into all major sports. Craig works largely through his catalogue, which is mailed to every player in care of the ball clubs. There are rings, bracelets, watches, pendants, gold baseball gloves, gold footballs and tiny gold hockey skates in Craig's catalogue. The most outré items are the Amato dragster and a sprawling school of diamond-encrusted marlins that Craig made for Marsha Bierman, a champion angler.

"I would say that the most conservative jewelry-purchasing group would be hockey players," Craig says. "Next would be football. Baseball is definitely getting to be a little more flamboyant, and basketball is absolutely the most flamboyant, in terms of what the jewelry is and the amount of diamonds that we use." He is only now branching out into the entertainment world. Mark Jackson of the Los Angeles Clippers brought Craig around the L.A. music scene. Now he's outfitting rockers and rappers, and he went to the Grammys with his newfound clientele. "There's not that much difference," he says, "between a singer making $20 million a year and a player that makes $20 million a year. If they want something badly enough, they'll buy it."

It is the shank end of the NBA season, and the Orlando Magic are in Boston to play the suddenly woebegone Celtics in a game that means absolutely nothing to either team. Before the game, Shaquille O'Neal comes out to practice his free-throw shooting, which needs improvement. Children stand gawking along the baseline. Some of them dare to dart forward and snap a picture, often without aiming the camera at all. Shaq takes his shots, coolly and smoothly, a huge gold hoop dangling from his left earlobe. In the days when the NBA played in places like Fort Wayne and Syracuse, nobody came out to shoot around looking like Captain Hook.

"I remember when I was 13, I got an earring, and my father told me to take it off," O'Neal says later. "He told me I could get one if I straightened up and did well in school. Later, I talked to my mother, and she said, 'Okay, go get one. You're a man now.' So when I was a sophomore in high school, we lost a big game, so I went and got one. I've had one ever since."

Not surprisingly, a backlash is growing. The Philadelphia Phillies forbid the wearing of earrings on or off the field, perhaps the only nod given by that rambunctious crew to baseball convention. "Ask me with the notebook open and I'll tell you that I don't think they have any place in the game," says Phillies general manager Lee Thomas. "Close the notebook and I'll tell you what I really think of those guys." Of course, in May, Marge Schott, the swastika-hoarding owner of the Cincinnati Reds, told a group of Cincinnati public officials what *she* really thinks of those guys: "Only fruits wear earrings."

Thomas and Schott are fighting a lost war. O'Neal is on the winning side. He comes by his jewelry through the sport he plays, the way he plays it and the different streams of culture that now form the culture of his game. For instance, in one of his rap videos, he wears a Superman ring that is the approximate radius of the average waffle iron. ("I never weighed it," he says with a smile. "But I know it's big.") He is a basketball player, certainly. But he also is an entertainer, with roots and influences from dozens of different arenas. He wears the gold hoop not because Bill Russell did but because that is what rich and successful entertainers do in 1994. His endorsement is on page 22 of Michael Craig's catalogue, along with a gold money clip, a chain with a gold basketball, two gold rings and a pendant of a ball going through a hoop. The basket's net is made of fine silver. The ball is gold, and there are diamonds on it.

For the foreseeable future, there will be athletes bejeweled and studded, draped in gold and their own headlong affluence. The gold and the jewels are not like the fantastic salary figures that appear in the newspapers, the ones that set off the torrents of greed and envious loathing without which sports-talk radio would wither and die. The gold and the jewels are not abstract columns of numbing figures. The gold and the jewels are right out front for everyone to see, especially those people who are less and less able to afford tickets to the performances and whose cars always cost more than their jewelry. The jewels are the signposts to a different world, to an aristocracy grown as distant as the one that so exercised the spoilsports who brought about the French Revolution. A different world entirely, where bright gold game fish leap toward the sky, while the Savior bleeds rubies in the sunshine below.

GQ July 1994

The Sport That Time Forgot

Once, before everything was a commodity, the rules for every sport were drawn up like this—drawn up by the people who actually played the game, drawn up in the basement of an actual tavern in an actual neighborhood, like the Haven in South St. Louis, where the Sportsman's Corkball League is meeting on a misty night as spring comes slowly down the Mississippi. This is how sports used to change—behind history's back, when the world wasn't looking.

For nearly fifty years, the league has played its games in Tower Grove Park, a lovely, sylvan spot with little bright gingerbread gazebos peeking out from between the trees. This season, though, the club is moving to the fields at Jefferson Barracks, because a lot of the players have become "uncomfortable with the neighborhood" around Tower Grove, says one club member, corkball being a predominantly white and predominantly male exercise in a nation that's becoming predominantly neither one. For good and ill, corkball's history is now full of the history of the city in which it was born.

"It wasn't like we wanted to leave," says Lee Renfrow, Jr., a second-generation corkballer. "There's a little bit of a problem with some element, but nothing had ever affected us. But then, if guys are telling you in your ear, 'Well, we're not going to bring our kids down here because we're scared to,' that makes you start thinking."

The move to Jefferson Barracks has prompted the club to discuss an adjustment of the rules no less profound than that which baseball had to make when people began building ballparks with fences in the outfield rather than strands of rope. The Sportsman's Club is deciding whether to begin the millennium by allowing players to hit something besides singles. It is the second month of the new century, and extra-base hits may be coming to the league.

"All right," says Renfrow, the club's president, fighting to be heard over the chiming beer bottles. "You've got three choices: singles only, singles and home runs, or singles, doubles, triples, and home runs."

Corkball did not begin as an outdoor exercise. It began in St. Louis bars, where the Germans and the Italians and all the other people who worked at the city's numerous breweries came to consume their own product. One night around 1900, some brewery worker or another popped the cork—or "bung," which is the last time it will be referred to as such here, by the way—out of a barrel of beer, wrapped it in tape, and threw it toward one of his colleagues, who tried to hit it with a broomstick. Soon, corkball cages had sprung up inside dozens of saloons, or in the alleys outside of them. St. Louisans who joined the Navy during World War II rather famously played corkball on the flight decks of aircraft carriers, and returning veterans helped spread the game throughout the South. "Basically," says one old corkballer and Navy vet, "the Pacific was a home run."

It is a simple game. It involves a pitcher, a batter, and a catcher. There are no bases, and therefore, no base runners and, therefore, a great number of men who play corkball into their fifties and beyond. There are three outs, and every swinging strike is an out, provided the catcher hangs on to the corkball, which looks like a baseball shrunk to the size of a Titleist 4. Five balls is a walk. Foul balls and caught fly balls are outs, and any hit that travels fifteen feet, on the ground or in the air, is a single. Four singles equal a run, making corkball as much a station-to-station game as the D train. Runs are scarce, however, because the ball is small and the bat is thin and because the pitchers are encouraged to bring it with speed and movement only a touch below that seen downtown in Busch Stadium.

"No kidding," Renfrow explains. "We've got some guys that can part your hair with that thing. They have to be able to, because everybody in this league can hit a fastball." Nevertheless, a .250 batting average is a good season; in 1950, though, Dutch Weissflug hit .576, a mark that is still spoken of with reverence and awe.

At Tower Grove, the Sportsman's Club played singles only, not least because nobody ever quite figured out how to parcel out the extra bases when somebody hit one up into the branches of a tree. However, at the Jefferson Barracks fields, there are no trees to complicate play, and the distances for doubles, triples, and home runs actually are set out in lines burned into the ground. (A home run has to carry 250 feet.) The game can change there.

Moreover, Jefferson Barracks for years has been the home field of the South St. Louis Corkball League, the city's most famous loop, long the domain of the late Don Young, whom the papers always called "Mr. Corkball." Moving the Sportsman's Club to Jefferson Barracks is very much like moving the Mets into Yankee Stadium, and there is an undercurrent of mildly outraged traditionalism about the balloting.

"We had thought about just going down there and playing with the simple rules," Renfrow explains. "But with such a big move, we decided to bring it to our membership and let them decide."

The game changes by a vote of 13 to 10 to 3. They will play with the full panoply of extra-base hits. There is some moaning from the assembled pitchers, because pitchers will get blamed. Pitchers always get blamed. You can imagine Alex Cartwright in a place like this basement, puzzling out on a napkin the notion that the bases themselves should be ninety feet apart, perhaps struck suddenly by the rationale that, with four bases, a runner would score after having traveled the exact number of feet as there are degrees in a circle.

"Circling the bases," Cartwright would muse with a smile as baseball is born so that, a few decades later, some brewery workers in St. Louis can develop a recombinant form called corkball. There is cold beer in a tin tub and trophies on shelves along the wall. Two darts have been stuck in the dartboard for so long that nobody remembers who tossed them there, and Abner Doubleday, that useless old fraud, is nowhere to be found.

Before you understand corkball, you must understand its birthplace. There is no element in the history of American sports more underrated than the influence of the city of St. Louis. It is here that the very name of the sport is distinctly pronounced: The *o* becomes a harsh, almost corvine *a* sound that stops just short of a full Gaelic brogue. "Caharkball" is close. It is southern, but it's filtered through all the German and Italian and Irish accents that came down the river to work.

Moreover, the city of St. Louis has been giddily creative in constructing games around the concept of hitting a thrown object with a bat. In addition to corkball, the people of St. Louis have also devoted themselves to other, even more esoteric variations on baseball. There is fuzzball, in which the batter tries to hit a tennis ball with its bristling cover burned away. There is also the strange competition in which the batter attempts to make contact with a bottle cap, which can be made to dip and spin and confound the player with its gnat-like aerodynamics.

Fuzzball often is considered a minor league system through which young players pass on their way to their corkball careers. (Old-timers regularly bemoan the future of corkball on the grounds that not enough young people play fuzzball anymore, and they sound like old baseball writers wailing about the diamonds that lie empty throughout the suburban summer.) The game of bottle caps, on the other hand, is simply nuts. "You can really get carved," explains Renfrow.

So St. Louis has a love for mutant baseball that is richer and more diverse than even that of New York, which has produced stickball, which hardly anyone plays anymore. New York has had it easier, however, simply because so many of its former stickball players grew up to be gifted writers. Hence, the literature of stickball is far more vast than that of corkball, despite the facts that: a) because of its speed, corkball is more interesting; b) because it is played in peaceful parks and not on busy streets, corkball is safer; and c) corkball is still vibrantly alive, having spread at least in a small way from St. Louis southward.

In fact, down in Macon, Georgia, in the house where they all lived before they got famous, the members of the Allman Brothers Band engaged in notoriously rowdy corkball games; the late Duane Allman, it is said, was a helluva catcher. In sum, through its professional teams and provincial pastimes, St. Louis may have touched more people in places far more widespread than even New York did through the Yankees.

The mighty signal of KMOX Radio made Cardinals fans out of Tennessee moonshiners and Iowa wheat farmers, New Orleans rounders and Alabama Baptists. It made a lifelong Cardinals fan out of a poor boy in Indiana named Larry Bird. The New York ball clubs may have owned the urban salons of the Northeast, and, in their avaricious migration, those same teams may have conquered the West Coast, but for most of the century just concluded, between baseball and corkball, St. Louis owned almost everything in between.

There is very much a there there, the present hooked to the past and not dislodged and floating the way it is in so many places. Consider, for example, not the Cardinals but the old St. Louis Browns, now d/b/a the Baltimore Orioles. In the early 1900s, the Browns were owned by one Chris Von der Ahe, a manic German publican who went so spectacularly broke that one of his creditors had him hauled off to jail in Pennsylvania. He was an owner, and he lost all his money. His team now plays in Baltimore. In his saloon, the employees played corkball. Their great-grandchildren play it today. Something, at least, abides.

In the old days, Herb Markwort used to be a hot tennis player in the parks on the city's south side. He couldn't afford to have his racket restrung, however, so he learned to do it himself. Gradually, word got around to the other players, and Herb began to make a living for himself stringing tennis rackets on his back porch. From this came the Markwort Sporting Goods Company, tucked into an old factory-warehouse district just off the interstate. Today, it is the country's—nay, the *world's*—leading supplier of corkball equipment.

"The cork from the barrels is what they started using in the taverns, and outside the taverns later on," explains Herb Markwort, Jr., the founder's son. "Then they started putting tape around it to get it more spherical, and then some of the guys decided, Well, let's just start making little baseballs, then. So some of them were actually made in homes here in St. Louis." A man named Bill Pleitner is credited with making the first corkball with a proper cover on it, in 1936, and he kept on making them until he retired in 1995. Some leagues—most notably the South St. Louis League—refused to play with anything except a Pleitner ball.

For a while, the Rawlings Sporting Goods Company sold corkballs, most of which were made by hand in St. Louis. The Markwort company would buy its corkballs from Rawlings. In the 1960s, however, Rawlings moved out of the corkball market and the Markworts began having their own corkballs manufactured—first in Haiti and, later, in China. Today, the company markets corkballs and bats with an eye toward the nostalgic haze that surrounds everything remotely connected to baseball. Each corkball comes in a box with Smithsonian lettering that seems taken directly out of Chris Von der Ahe's saloon.

"This style, with the pinstripes, is supposed to convey the history of baseball," Markwort says, admiring one of the boxes. "This is trying to portray its longevity in the history of American baseball. Our sales were up 40 percent last year. And this year, we expect another jump like that."

To hold a corkball is an odd sensation, especially to anyone accustomed to the feel of a regular baseball. The stitches are too close together and in the wrong places. The whole thing can disappear into the palm of your hand. "Stan Musial came to our banquet once," recalls Joan Young, the widow of Don Young, who was Mr. Corkball for nearly forty years. "It just amazed him, that little cork ball." And when she says it, it sounds like the ancient chorus from a forgotten folk song, "That Little Cork Ball."

Lord, lord.

Don't she roll.

Another basement, then, this one in a neat little home in a neat little neighborhood tucked down into the gentle slopes of a hill now crowned by four-lane blacktop and every franchise known to God, man, and the onion ring. The history of St. Louis corkball is here, tucked into boxes and hanging on the wall. "When my husband died last year," explains Joan Young, "at the funeral, one of my daughters said that you couldn't die or have a baby, or do anything important, on Wednesday, because Wednesday night was for corkball.

"They always put things in for the wives, because they were kind of neglected in the summertime. But we used to have a picnic every year. We always teased that we were going to put in an application to join the league, but we never did."

They met at the Casa Loma, an old ballroom down on Cherokee Street. Don Young was a second-generation corkballer. His father, Bill, helped found the Grupp League in 1936, and Don began playing in 1945. (His son still plays, making the Youngs a third-generation corkball family, which is not unusual.) After he retired from active play in 1976, Young set about documenting a systematic history of corkball in St. Louis. He compiled reams of scorecards. He chased down ancient team rosters.

He even pursued and recorded the game's creation mythology back beyond the brewers and their barrels, all the way back to 1763, when Pierre Laclède landed his men on the banks of the river, and the Indians threw dirt clods at them, and Laclède's men hit them back with spears. Of course, this would make Pierre Laclède the father of baseball, corkball, fuzzball, and bottle caps, which would make, say Father Jacques Marquette look like something of a piker, discovery-wise. Don Young didn't necessarily believe this story, mind you, but he told it anyway, which was the important part.

He told all the stories, wrote them all down, and told them again: about the time he played in the lowest-scoring game in corkball history because the ball broke in half and he was awarded only half a run. About long balls and shutouts. About a hundred other games and a thousand other players. About how he got both the 1964 and 1967 world champion Cardinals team to sign a corkball for him.

About how when one of the players died, he would send a wreath, and at its heart would be a corkball bat. When Don Young died, the funeral procession detoured on its way to the cemetery and brought him back for a lap around the grounds at Jefferson Barracks, one more time.

"He became disabled when he was seventy-six, and he couldn't play anymore," his widow recalls. "So he began to put all the records together." It was the social aspect of the game that kept him coming back on all those summer evenings, which was all right with his wife, who had become accustomed to a life grown tight as a vine around a little local game.

Come back in August, they said. Come back when all the teams get together at Jefferson Barracks—Sportsman's, the South St. Louis guys, the people who play in Georgia and Florida—and come back for the picnic and the barbecue, and the spinning, running, laughing children, and come back for the corkball, too. For the World Series of corkball, at the Barracks, where the Sportsman's Club now has decided to play.

"My first memories of corkball are the picnics," says Lee Renfrow. "I can remember going out with my father and brothers and sisters, and we'd watch the guys playing bottle caps. We still do that at our annual picnic here. We get out a big bucket of bottle caps and old broomsticks and go to it."

There is no snobbery here. Corkballers are proud to play bottle caps, and vice versa, but it is corkball that has flourished beyond the other games. "I mean, corkball's in my blood, and I've been in the club since '91," Renfrow says. "There were times when I thought about leaving, but I don't know what I'd do with my summers. I'm thirty-four, and my arm's gone. I can remember going home every Wednesday night, icing it up, laying there with it, just agonizing, just trying to get it ready to go again the next week."

The meeting has adjourned. The membership has gathered upstairs at the Haven, where a light Thursday-night crowd is talking over the NCAA basketball tournament on the big-screen television and somebody keeps playing Fleetwood Mac songs over and over on the jukebox, drowning out the commentators on the television, but not the conversation, which flows and eddies in the past and the present. There are legends to corkball, most of them apocryphal, as though that ever matters for the best of them.

There is the remarkable tale people tell about Hammering Hank Stoverink, who fills a spot in the history of corkball roughly akin to that held by John Henry in the history of the American railroad. Seems that one day Hammering Hank got hold of one and drove it out of the Barracks grounds entirely. The ball rolled down a steep slope and into the Mississippi, which carried it, rolling and tumbling, down in the Gulf of Mexico and off to Cuba, to Venezuela, to memory and the misty isles, to Avalon.

Is the story very likely an aged and mellow crock of beans? Of course it is, and I don't believe a word of it, just as I don't believe in John Henry, except when Mississippi John Hurt sings about him, and then I so believe in him that I expect him to come up my walkway and ring my doorbell, and I'm disappointed when he doesn't. I don't believe for a second that Hammering Hank Stoverink once hit a corkball out of Jefferson Barracks and off toward eternity, until somebody tells me the story, and there's a thrill in his voice, and then I believe in Hammering Hank. In my bag, there's a corkball now, and I roll it in my fingers, and it seems to disappear in my palm, and it's as though baseball itself is shrinking, as though the game has become manageable again—as though, somehow, in this strange, beloved mutation of itself, you can get a grip on it again.

Esquire June 2000

Hooters Golf

Ah, Brandy, Misty, and Amanda, come out and sit on the veranda.

Come down near Tunica, Mississippi, to celebrate the final round of the Harrah's Casino Classic, a piece of the professional golf tour sponsored by Hooters, the internationally renowned restaurant chain that employs them in its Memphis franchise. Decked out in the chain's internationally renowned corporate uniform of barely epidermal tank tops and orange hot pants, they caused quite a stir out on the veranda, did Brandy, Misty, and Amanda.

They'd missed the previous week when a soaking tropical rain drowned the River Bend Links, which winds through the cotton fields and alongside the levees, an adjunct of the casinos that light up the heart of the Mississippi Delta with fungal neon, like some sort of Area 51 for the mud-flap gambling set. The tournament schedule foundered almost immediately, and the golfers played only fifty-four of the scheduled seventy-two holes, mainly in front of themselves, tournament officials, and the odd Harley-Davidson T-shirt gone missing from the craps tables. The only sign throughout most of the tournament of the sponsoring corporation was the bug-eyed owl that festooned every flagstick, the bug-eyed owl being the second most familiar trademark of Hooters of America, Inc.

Like the sun, the sponsor's three field representatives came out only on Sunday, for championship day, when golfers in the Hooters Tour contested one another for the right to have a $15,000 check handed to them on the veranda by Brandy, Misty, and Amanda. A quintet of players had finished tied at the end of the truncated competition, and now here they came down the first playoff hole—all five together, all five, uh, abreast.

They played the eighteenth hole twice, and two of the players fell away. Which left three: Jason Caron from Massachusetts; Chad Wellhausen from Mississippi; and David Howser, who'd driven down from Memphis in his 1980 Blue Bird Wanderlodge, the wood-grained rolling condominium that he and his wife and their boxer dog had taken almost sixty thousand miles around the country since buying it two years ago. It ran very well, except when it didn't.

Now the Wanderlodge was parked in the lot along the tenth fairway, and all around it were the trailers, trucks, and recreational vehicles of other people who had come here to gamble on other games. Gypsy dreamers, all of them, even the Howsers—perhaps especially them.

David Howser knocked his tee shot straight down the middle of the eighteenth fairway for the fourth time that day. He and his wife, Ashleigh—on the Hooters Tour, almost every caddie is a wife or a girlfriend—walked up along the rolling landscape. Night was beginning to fall over the cotton fields and over the levees, but not over the casinos, where night simply settles for a draw against the garish neon. David addressed his ball and smacked it up toward the green, up toward the clubhouse, up toward the big $15,000 cardboard check, and way up toward where sat the sponsor's representatives, sirens of the misty isles where cold beer and hot pants do make a man a king. Way up toward the veranda, where sat Brandy, Misty, and Amanda.

Walk out through the casinos and remember there once was real blood-stakes gambling here, in the jukes and the roadhouses, where people waved knives instead of platinum cards. The casinos technically are not in Tunica. They are in Robinsonville, where the great bluesman Robert Johnson once lived, and a couple hours' drive from where he died in a dispute that did not involve the $9.95 all-you-can-eat breakfast buffet. Down on the floor, a band is murdering the old local music, and remember as you walk by that if these grayboys had played those songs that way fifty years ago, nobody ever would've found the bodies.

Walk out into the hot Mississippi morning and remember that there was once illicit sex here, the genuine furtive kind, under the Jim Crow radar, not at all as safe and removed as the kind of sex that sells crab legs and blackened fish at chain restaurants all across America.

Walk over to the golf course, a tight, neat place carved out of the cotton fields, and remember that professional golf was born in places as small as this, but not as neat. It came from sweaty men in shirts without logos, betting money they did not have on shots they could not hit, as raffish a passel of cutthroats as the old blues guys ever were. There was Jimmy Demaret, who won three Masters despite the fact that all indications point to him not sleeping at all in the 1950s. There was Sam Snead, who titled the first chapter of his autobiography "Peckerwood Kid," meeting legendary hustler Titanic Thompson back in the 1930s, on a day when Thompson had so many side bets going on that Snead's head spun, and learning so well that he formulated a life's rule out of the experience: "Never bet with strangers until they become friends."

The battered old courses were their roadhouses. The old clubhouses were their jukes, smelling of moldy towels, with linoleum floors scarred by hundreds of cigarette burns and fluorescent lights buzzing above the card game in the corner. They came out of places like that, and they shook golf free of the country clubs.

But the people in the country clubs fought back. They always do. They put the names of their companies on the hats that the sweaty guys came to wear. They opened their country clubs to the sweaty old guys, and pretty soon the sweaty old guys gave way to a generation as far removed from the scarred linoleum and fluorescent lights as the House of Blues is from Junior Kimbrough's old joint.

The people in the country clubs bought up every last scrap of the old, weird America, to borrow Greil Marcus's vast and useful phrase. And now golf, even at its roots, even at its most primitive, starveling level, has a corporation to sponsor it, and that corporation uses sex to sell its seafood, a sailor's whispers transformed into a salesman's beery boasts. And the corporation drops a tournament into a place where gambling sings soprano now, where it has buffet breakfasts, forgotten lounge comedians, and valet parking.

Walk all the way out, however, and look at the people who play in the tournament, and you can catch just a glimpse of what used to be, like the lights of a juke amid the distant trees, where the glare of the neon doesn't reach. Maybe we'll all be saved from manufactured jackpot redemption. Maybe there's enough left of the old unshaven dreams. And maybe, just maybe, the presiding image of America as the millennium crashes down doesn't have to be a three-hundred-pound woman with oxygen tubes up her nose stuffing coins into the nickel slots at 2:00 A.M., wearing a T-shirt that reads, JESUS SOLVES MY PROBLEMS.

Slight, with a bit of a slouch to his walk, David Howser has over-achieved at his sport ever since his father moved the family into the home along the course at Colonial, near Memphis. "When David was ten years old," recalls his father, John, a prominent Memphis neurosurgeon, "he'd go out on the practice tee and hit balls for two hours." One day, after a bad round, David laid his clubs down on the ground and cried.

"That was the proudest day of my life," John Howser explains. "He was crying because he couldn't hit shots that *nobody* could hit. I knew I had a winner then."

David moved on to the University of Arizona, where he played his way into a scholarship. He also met and married Ashleigh, a bright and funny art-history major from the University of Memphis. After they were married, in January 1997, David and Ashleigh decided to go out on the Hooters Tour together.

They put the Wanderlodge on the road, bouncing from Puppy Creek to Boonville, from the Delta Pontiac Performers Classic to the Jackaroo Steakhouse and Sauce Classic, from Missouri to Indiana by way of Florida and South Carolina. The Hooters Tour began in 1988 as the United States Golf Tournament. Three year later, a real estate magnate named Rick Jordan financed it, but Jordan lasted only two years. Hooters took over the sponsorship in 1993. One of the first things the company did was bump the total purse for each tournament up to $100,000, which is a considerable temptation for those players unable to land a spot on the Nike Tour, the official gateway to the Big Tour itself.

Hooters is a strange, suspended existence. Its tournaments in fact are a more accurate miniature of the PGA Tour than the Nike tournaments are. Hooters golfers play seventy-two-hole tournaments. There are leader boards. Yet they know that to win on the Hooters Tour means to have a chance to have a chance at the Nike Tour, which is a chance to have a chance at the biggest payoff of all. Hope's equations can be the most inexorable. That's why casinos and professional golf survive.

"How long have I been out here?" says Hooters Tour member Zoran Zorkic, who, for four straight years, has missed the final stage of the PGA's qualifying school by a single shot. "Too long."

David's father agreed to sponsor him on the tour. (Most of the Hooters players have individual sponsors.) "My dad was adamant about that," explains David. "That way, I could bypass a lot of the frustration you get by asking people to pay your way. Anybody I'd have asked would've been friends of my family, and that would've gotten complicated, too."

David and Ashleigh looked for a way to cut their expenses. Most of the golfers drove between tournaments, and the Howsers decided they'd save on motels and food. They set about looking for a motor home and found one at an estate sale in Union, Mississippi. (As is his wont, David methodically researched motor homes and found that the Blue Bird is known as the Cadillac of the form.) They bought it immediately, and the three of them—David, Ashleigh, and their boxer, Samson—took off for the open highway.

And then they broke down. A lot.

"It was in great shape to look at. We haven't done anything to the cosmetics of it," David explains. "But we've replaced the transmission, and the refrigerator, the air conditioner, the water pump, the engine-block heater, and it goes on and on." Their honeymoon was enlivened when the pumps froze and, when they got to a campground outside Oklahoma City and hooked up the water, the pipes exploded.

"I'm keeping a scrapbook," explains Ashleigh.

In the middle of the 1997 tour, they set out for a tournament in Sikeston, Missouri. Riding along with them was Casey Martin, who would become famous the following year for riding a golf cart in the U.S. Open because of a rare circulatory disease that affected his legs. Martin is one of the Hooters Tour's most successful alumni. But after his ride in the Wanderlodge, Martin is lucky he lived long enough to become controversial.

"First thing that happened," David recalls, "is that we had an infestation of mice or rats that dropped a lot of feces and urine down under the driver's chair. So it gets to smelling terrible, and I open a vent, and it lets this odor back, and Casey almost falls off the couch."

Later, Martin was nearly asphyxiated by fumes from the Wanderlodge's toilet tank and nearly drowned when a clamp came off a water-pump hose. When they finally got to Sikeston, Martin fairly leaped from the Wanderlodge.

"Ashleigh," he said, presumably over one shoulder as he fled, "you're my hero."

By Sikeston in June of that year, David's game had gone sour, and he told Ashleigh that he was going to quit playing competitively if he didn't improve. The way he was playing didn't justify the expenses of keeping the Wanderlodge running. Just then, however, he had a chance to work with David Leadbetter, the famous swing doctor, near Orlando. David and Ashleigh dropped the Wanderlodge off near Blue Bird world headquarters, in Fort Valley, Georgia, and went down to see him. They picked it up six weeks later, en route to Dallas and David's first tournament in six weeks. Brimming with confidence, the Howsers took the Wanderlodge back out on the road. It broke down along Highway 80, outside of Selma, Alabama.

"We were stuck there for fifteen hours," says Ashleigh. Three weeks earlier, the police had run a sweep of the local crack dealers, so tensions were still running high. Two mechanics came out to help, and when a car slowed approaching the Wanderlodge, the mechanics stepped into the Howsers' headlight beams so that the driver of the car could see their guns.

"They told us that if anybody came knocking, not to wait, just to shoot through the door," David recalls. They didn't get to Dallas until four in the morning the day before the tournament started. Exhausted, David went out and shot 21-under, and then lost in a three-way playoff. Since then, he has been one of the fifteen or twenty players who can actually make a living on the Hooters Tour. This year, through the midseason break, David Howser has won $26,779.50.

"I'll never stop as long as I keep improving," he says. "I believe that I have what it takes to be a player on the PGA Tour. I mean, the good thing about golf is I don't have to worry about what somebody thinks of me. It's just my scores. I mean, you can win your way through."

However, the Howsers are taking the Wanderlodge off the road. Someday, when they have children, they are going to tell them all the stories, and even that long night on Highway 80 is going to shine in the telling. "I'm going to miss it," says Ashleigh. "Of course I am. We have stories that we can tell for the rest of our lives. It's the freedom you have with it that I liked. That is, when things were going well."

The final straw came last winter, when they were driving back from a session with Jim Flick, David's regular coach, in Arizona, and they were planning to spend Christmas with David's brother in Fort Worth. The Wanderlodge developed a vacuum leak and died outside of Odessa, and the Howsers ate Christmas Eve dinner—pinto beans and grilled cheese sandwiches—at the Warfield Truck Terminal.

Christmas at the truck stop. Can you hear the old song ringing in the story, drifting out of time, old as sin and whiskey, light as the night breezes that dance along the levee?

Far out on the fairway, you can see their heads fall. David Howser has struck his approach shot fat, and it drops into a bunker short of the eighteenth green. Ashleigh's head drops first. You can see the bob of her ponytail. Then David's head drops out of his follow-through, and the two of them walk through the spreading twilight up toward the clubhouse. John Howser is sitting inside. He doesn't want to watch.

But David recovers. He nestles a lovely pitch about eleven feet past the hole. Chad Wellhausen also has played the hole to par. Jason Caron, however, bumps in a birdie putt from the fringe and wins the tournament. A bit dazed by it all, Caron comes up to the veranda to get his big cardboard check, and he poses, blushing, with Brandy, Misty, and Amanda.

David Howser misses the scene. He walks back through the descending evening and into the parking lot where the Wanderlodge is parked. All around him, people are flying out of their campers and recreational vehicles, marching in determined procession toward the casinos, every bit as inexorable as the children in *Village of the Damned*. David opens the door to the Wanderlodge, and Samson jumps out, begging to be walked.

It has been a frustrating day for David—pure, torturous golf. Four times, putts that would have won him the tournament either lipped out of the cup or stopped a half turn short of it, those slivers of an inch all the difference between the $15,000 winner's check and the $5,205 second-place money that David brought back to the Wanderlodge. "It would've been easier if I'd been putting badly," he says as Ashleigh and Samson go off through the lot. "But I wasn't."

All around him, the people march off to take carefully calibrated chances, to walk gingerly through a country of manicured risk, and David Howser has his life riding on a ball that stops one roll short of the money that is, in fact, two stops short of the big money. It is a life of scrap and danger, a life of guns in the night in a very strange place, and pinto beans for Christmas Eve dinner. The Wanderlodge seems then as if it's rolled out of a lost dimension, out of an older America, ringing with the old levee moans and the cries of the gamblers playing for blood stakes in places where they didn't have valet parking. A time machine, almost, bringing the old unshaven dreams forward across a modern landscape of unoriginal sin.

The Howsers have taken the mobile home off the road. Meanwhile, the Hooters Tour makes sure that it faxes me the final results of every tournament that it holds. I'm telling you, the IRS doesn't keep up as well as these guys do.

***Esquire* October 1999**

Thieves of Time

The press conference was over, and two men from New Castle, Pa., named Robert Retort and Ed Grybowski had been charged with interstate transportation of stolen property, which is a federal felony. In the conference room of the FBI field office in Pittsburgh, an agent named Bob Reutter was looking over the stolen property, examining it, not with a G-man's eyes, but with those of a fan. There were baseball uniforms—thick, heavy flannel things with the names of the great, lost teams on them. The Memphis Red Sox. The Kansas City Monarchs. There were autographed baseballs, and old, sepia-shrouded pictures of young men wearing the heavy flannel uniforms of the great, lost teams. Looking at them, you could see back through time, all the way to the outskirts of town. Bob Reutter spent a long time looking.

It all belonged to an 86-year-old former security guard at the St. Louis City Hall named James Bell. In 1922, when he and the world were young, James Bell was pitching one hot day for the St. Louis Stars in the Negro League. It was late in the game, and there were men on base, and at the plate was a signifying hitter named Oscar Charleston. If the Negro League had a Babe Ruth, it was Oscar Charleston. The 19-year-old pitcher stared down the alley, and struck Oscar Charleston out of there, saving the game.

Lord, the other Stars thought, that young man is cool. So that's what they called him. Cool Bell. But Manager Bill Gatewood thought the nickname lacked sufficient dignity for the grave young man with the thoughtful eyes. He's older than that, thought Gatewood. Cool Papa, that's who he is.

Cool Papa Bell.

The man had style. Anyone could see that. In the Negro League, the wardrobes always cut like knives. A player named Country Jake Stevens told Donn Rogosin, the author of *Invisible Men*, that he knew he'd made the big club when the owner took him out and bought him three new suits and two new Stetson hats. Even in this company, Cool Papa was sharp. When he walked through Compton Hill in St. Louis, children danced in his wake.

He played for 29 years and for seven different teams. He was the fastest man anywhere in baseball, so swift and deft on the basepaths that, when it looked like Jackie Robinson was going to be chosen to shatter the segregation of the major leagues, Cool Papa once ran wild just to show the young shortstop what kind of play he could expect when and if Robinson were called up. Jimmy Crutchfield once told a baseball historian named Robert Peterson that, when Cool Papa hit one back to the pitcher, everybody else in the field yelled, "Hurry!" Satchel Paige claimed that Cool Papa could hit the light switch in the hotel room, and that he'd be in bed before the room got dark. That was the story they always told about Cool Papa Bell. They even told it when he was inducted into the Baseball Hall of Fame in 1974.

He is old now, and half-blind. For years, he held court in his house on what is now Cool Papa Bell Avenue in St. Louis. He would tell stories, and sign autographs, and he would show the curious everything he had saved from his playing days. The uniforms. The programs. The pictures. He always was an obliging man, was Cool Papa Bell. Even when his health began to fail, he always was that.

"He always had all of this memorabilia," says Norman Seay, Bell's nephew and an administrator at the University of Missouri at St. Louis. "People came from everywhere, from Timbuktu, to get autographs from Uncle Bell. It was a normal occurrence around that house."

Then, on March 22, all that changed. Bell was visited by Grybowski and Retort, who had driven 17 hours to St. Louis from New

Castle, where Retort owns a company called R.D. Retort Enterprises. It operates within the bull market in what are called baseball collectibles. By all accounts, Retort is an aggressive collector. "He called here a lot, and you couldn't get him off the phone," says a source at the Baseball Hall of Fame in Cooperstown. "He never quite made it clear what the purpose of his research was, but he made a lot of requests for uniform numbers, and for what teams certain players played for. He didn't seem to have much of a working knowledge of baseball history, but he kept us on the phone a half-hour at a time."

Retort has declined comment on the specifics of the case against him, but does say that "when it all comes out, you'll see there's one huge world of difference between what I've been charged with, and what really happened. It's a situation where, basically, I was there to get autographs from a Hall of Famer, and I was in the wrong place at the wrong time."

It is possible that Retort and Grybowski were invited to come to St. Louis by Bell, who rarely turned down such a request. The two spent several days there. Bell signed a lot of autographs, but it was a slow process. The FBI says that Retort paid Bell $100 for the various autographed items. That is all that Retort says he did there. The FBI does not agree.

According to investigators, Retort and Grybowski returned on March 25, and began to remove from the Bells' house several cardboard boxes filled with the paraphernalia Cool Papa had collected over the course of his career. Bell and his wife, Clarabelle, told both the local police and the FBI that they had felt "trapped" by the two men, and that they were too intimidated to try and stop them. In fact, the Bells said, they were so intimidated that they didn't even report the incident until their daughter, Connie Brooks, discovered what had happened a week later.

Retort, 38, and Grybowski, 65, were arrested on April 9. Both are free now, Retort on $25,000 bond and Grybowski on $10,000. They will stand trial this summer in St. Louis. Most of the memorabilia was recovered. Connie Brooks has flown in from New York, and she has spent a month helping investigators identify some of the articles.

It is a federal offense to take more the $5,000 worth of stolen mer-
chandise across state lines. The estimated value of everything that
was taken from Cool Papa Bell's house is $300,000, which has flatly
flabbergasted some people who are close to him.

"I couldn't believe it when they said that," says Norman Seay. "I
mean, a half-a-million dollars? To me, he was just my Uncle Bell,
and all that stuff he had, I thought its real value was an internal kind
of thing, that its value was intrinsic to him."

But that is not the way the world is today. There are people who
would call $300,000 a modest price for what was taken from Cool
Papa Bell. These are people who understand a new and unsettlingly
volatile marketplace in which the past is raw currency, and what en-
ergizes that marketplace is that same feeling that came over Bob
Reutter, when he looked into the FBI's conference room and saw an
exposed vein of pure history stretched across its walls.

"I have to admit that I'm a fan, and I looked the stuff over," admits
the agent with a chuckle. "I saw those uniforms and I thought, 'How
did they ever play in those heavy things?' It was all really interesting
to me."

Perhaps the Fourth Lateran Council had the right idea after all. In
the 13th century, the Roman Catholic Church was awash in very
pricey relics, including not only the purported heads of various
saints, but also enough alleged pieces of the True Cross to build du-
plex homes for half the yeomanry in Western Europe. Embarrassed
by this unbridled profiteering in the sacred, the church called the
Council, which forbade the practice in 1215, whereupon the price of
a saint's head crashed all over Christendom.

That sort of naked interference in the free marketplace would not
be tolerated today. We live in an acquisitive age, a trend encouraged
from the very top of the political and cultural elite for more than a
decade now. It manifests itself in everything from the leveraged
buyout to the current desire of every cherubic four-year old to sur-
round himself with replicas of pizza-chomping, Hey-Dude amphib-
ians who are built like Ben Johnson. Indeed, today we have
collectibles the instantly accrued value of which almost totally rests

with the immediate demand for them. How much more, then, must genuine relics be worth?

It hit the art world first. In his book, *Circus of Ambition*, journalist John Taylor describes the rise of what he calls "the collecting class." Taylor writes that, in the 1980s, "Collectors were returning in droves. One reason was the huge surge in income enjoyed by the individuals in the higher income brackets." In one telling anecdote, Taylor overhears a rich young couple at an art auction. The husband complains that, "We're unhappy with the Cezanne." His wife responds, cheerily, "That's OK because we're going to *trade up!*"

Substitute "Pete Rose" for Cezanne in that conversation, and you've pretty much got what happened when this dynamic hit sports, the only difference being, of course, that, unlike Rose, Cezanne wasn't around to pitch his own paintings on the Home Shopping Network. It is estimated that the trade in sports collectibles has become a $200 million industry in this country. It is manifested best by all those things that give the willies to the baseball purists. These include card shows—and the almost universally condemned notion of the $15 autograph—as well as the public auction of old baseball equipment.

When Taylor writes that, "Many of these collectors were frankly more interested in art as an investment than as a means of cultural certification," it's hard not to hear the complaint that echoes across the land every time another one of yesterday's heroes starts peddling his memories. It's hard not to hear the guy at Cooperstown saying that Robert Retort's "working knowledge of baseball" was lacking.

As is the case with any good capitalist enterprise, if you push it far enough you find yourself passing through greed and moving all the way into the criminal. The case of Pete Rose is instructive here. First came the reports that there were several bats in circulation that were purported to be the one that Rose used to break Ty Cobb's record on Sept. 11, 1985. Now, accounts of that historic at-bat indicate that Rose used only one bat. Where the other three (or four, or eight, or 12) came from remains a mystery, especially to the gullible people who bought them. In this, Pete Rose was lucky he only had to face the late Bart Giamatti. The Fourth Lateran Council would've had him in thumbscrews.

Now, however, it's been revealed that Rose failed to declare to the Internal Revenue Service the cash income that he made at card shows, and in the sale of various memorabilia. There is some symmetry, at least, in the fact that, in the same week, Pete Rose and Michael Milken, symbols of their age, both faced a federal judge.

Nor is Rose the only criminal case in which baseball collectibles figure prominently. We have the odd affair involving National League umpire Bob Engel, who is alleged to have attempted to steal 4,180 baseball cards from a store in Bakersfield, CA. And, believing that his bats were being lifted by enterprisingly larcenous clubhouse personnel, at least one American League superstar has taken the radical step of having the bats sent directly to his home rather than to the ball park.

But the case of Cool Papa Bell is far more serious than either of these other two. After all, it involves the alleged intimidation of an 87-year old, half-blind, sickly man, and it also involves a federal felony even more serious than the one committed by Pete Rose. There would have to be a huge payoff involved for Retort to have risked such a crime. Experts say that there was, and that it has everything to do with the nature of the memorabilia itself.

In the first place, there is a finite number of Negro League collectibles available. When Jackie Robinson signed with the Dodgers, the Negro League essentially collapsed. Therefore, there's no futures market in Negro League memorabilia.

In addition, the people who played in the Negro League are mainly quite old now—Bell is about the average age for a Negro League veteran—and there are not many left who even played back then. That means there are only limited prospects for the lucrative trade in replicas, in which a retired player will authorize (and autograph) things like duplicate bats and uniforms. The FBI charges that Retort and Grybowski forced Bell to sign a letter authorizing such replicas. Retort denies the charge.

Because Negro League memorabilia is so passing rare, there is no established price scale for any of it. Thus, traders are free to ask whatever price they want because there are no benchmarks by which that price can be measured. "If I saw a ball signed by the 1919 Black Sox, I'd know what that was worth," says Alan Rosen, a New Jersey entrepreneur who's known among memorabilia collectors as Mr. Mint. "But if I saw a ball signed by the original winners of the Black World Series, I wouldn't know how to authenticate the signatures. I wouldn't know how to price the thing."

This is not an insignificant admission. Mr. Mint has been known to show up in the living rooms of baseball-card collectors with a briefcase full of cash. Indeed, if you were to skulk around Colin Cliveishly and dig up Christy Mathewson, Mr. Mint probably could price the bones for you. Nevertheless, Negro League memorabilia has brought top dollar at a number of auctions. An authentic poster advertising a Fourth of July doubleheader featuring Satchel Paige once sold for $2,400. A program from an exhibition game between a Negro League All-Star team and Dizzy Dean's barnstorming club went for $700. Intact tickets from the Negro World Series, or from the annual East-West All-Star game have fetched up to $500 apiece, and an autographed ball from the 1940 East-West game was sold to a collector for $850. A man named George Lyons even got $1,500 for an authenticated contract between a Cuban League team and one James Bell of St. Louis.

"Nobody really has any independent judgment regarding what to pay for something," explains Herman Kaufman, a collector and auctioneer who specializes in Negro League memorabilia. "I'd say that 99 percent of collecting is pure enjoyment, but that the other one percent is knowing that you have something that nobody else has."

Which brings up the question of how far a collector is willing to go to get what nobody else has. Investigators probing the recent massive art theft at Boston's Isabella Stewart Gardner Museum say privately that, while they're confident that they will apprehend the thieves, most of the actual paintings are probably gone forever, quietly sold to collectors and now hanging in someone's library.

Kaufman dismisses the idea of a memorabilia underground— "Why buy something if you can never show it?" he asks—but others in the field are not as sanguine about the possibility. They think Cool Papa's lucky that the FBI got most of his things back.

"If you're asking if sometimes guys'll come to me and say, 'Look, I got this stuff here, and keep it between me and you where you got it,' and that's the deal, I'd have to say, yes, that happens," says Joe Esposito of B&E Collectibles in New York. "You have to remember that you're dealing with collectors. They'll do anything."

Cool Papa was hospitalized shortly after the incident with Retort and Grybowski. "He's at the point of death," says his wife. He's at home now, but other family members wonder whether or not it's time for him to leave the house on Cool Papa Bell Avenue and live out his days in a retirement home. They doubt whether Clarabelle can adequately care for him anymore.

"He's very fragile and he's very weak," says Norman Seay. "I don't know what we're going to do. You know, it's funny, all those years growing up next door to him, I didn't realize that he was a celebrity. He was just Uncle Bell. I never realized how great he really was. You know, as an African-American athlete, he never got the respect he should have. It was kind of a second-class identity for him."

That, perhaps, is the real crime here. It's more than a simple threat. It's a kind of crime against history. Because of the entrenched racism of major league baseball, Cool Papa Bell never was able to profit fully from his enormous skills. At the very least, then, he ought to be able to profit fully from the accoutrements of that talent, or he ought to be able to leave it alone, snug in boxes in the basement. If what the FBI says is true, then that is the real crime here, not the mere pilfering of things to meet the demands of a marketplace gone dotty, or to satisfy an acquisitive age. It is the further robbing of a man who's already had too much of himself stolen.

There's a man named Tweed Webb who knows what the crime is. He is the unofficial historian for the Negro League in St. Louis, and he is a friend of Cool Papa Bell's. "I go back to about 1910," he says. "I kept all my records because if you don't have records, you can't prove nothing happened. It's like nothing ever did happen, if you don't have records.

"Cool Papa, he's been sick for 18 or 19 years, but we talk, you know? He told me about what happened right when it happened.

The FBI come out here to talk to me because, you know, I got valuable stuff myself. I got all my records, all my scorecards. Certain people'd love to get their hands on the stuff I got. But I don't sell none of it. I pass along learning to people, but the records are priceless. At least, they're priceless to me."

Oddly enough, both the investigators and the defendant express concern for Bell's health. "I did a lot of work on this out of loyalty to Cool Papa," says Bob Reutter, G-man and baseball fan. "I heard that he wasn't doing too well, and I wanted to get that stuff back for him. I don't imagine the publicity's going to help much, either. I mean, it probably isn't good for him that people know he's got a quarter-million dollars worth of stuff in his basement."

"I'm worried about what all this will do to his health," says Robert Retort. "It's got to take a toll on the poor man."

It will come to trial sometime this summer. For now, Connie Brooks stays in St. Louis, identifying pieces of her father's past for the investigators. And Cool Papa Bell stays at home. He doesn't get up much any more. In the twilight, Cool Papa Bell is already in bed. Someone else turns out the light.

Nobody was ever convicted of any crime in connection with Cool Papa Bell's memorabilia. Cool Papa died on March 7, 1991 and he's buried in Hilldale Cemetery near St. Louis. His fame lives on in the name of a popular Detroit funk band.

The National May 10, 1990

Basketball Nation

The holy man is a custodian at the high school. Or, conversely and with infinitely more reverence, at Wyoming Indian High School, the custodian is a holy man.

He is as familiar with the old rituals as he is with his own blood. He carries in his bones liturgies, prayers and supplications that are older than anything on this wide, wavery Wyoming plain except the wide, wavery grasses. The holy man wears a baseball hat and a belt with a wide blue buckle, and he comes to work every morning to a cluttered storeroom in the back of the high school. His friend Dick Thunder is waiting for him. He is going to kid around some with the holy man.

"Morning, stud-hoss," says Dick Thunder to the holy man.

"Not me," replies the holy man. "You're the stud-hoss around here. Really, this guy right here is the stud-hoss. Believe that." And then someone comes in and asks the holy man for some napkins.

It is midday at Wyoming Indian High School, and they have run out of napkins in the cafeteria. So the holy man rises from his old tin chair. He walks back, into the shelves full of carpet cleaner and floor wax, and returns with a box of napkins, because that is the holy man's job these days. Then he and Dick Thunder sit back in their chairs, and they talk the rest of the morning away, two men secure in their time and in their place. Outside the doors, the calling of a crow rises and falls on the long winds from the north. "What I know," the holy man says, "goes back as long as we do."

The Wind River Indian Reservation, in central Wyoming, is a land grown thick with tall grass and holy men. The Shoshone holy men came first. Then came the Arapaho, chasing the buffalo west from Minnesota, bringing their sun dance to a land where the crow is the messenger of good things from the Father and black is the color of joy and promise. Then the white holy men arrived: The Jesuits came and founded their mission, and the Episcopalians founded theirs. Once, an Arapaho named Runs Mysteriously on Ice fell in with the white holy men and came back to his people calling himself the Reverend Sherman Coolidge, confusing the Arapaho to no end.

"I pity all Christians," says Francis Brown, a holy man because his father and grandfather were, and a custodian because that pays the bills. "They don't know who God is."

The school looks like every other high school in every other part of America. Brick and squarish, it seems huge, squatting deep in a swale on an otherwise empty prairie. There is a broad lobby, and there is that odd institutional smell that sets off a nearly uncontrollable craving for macaroni and cheese. There is also a gymnasium. Outside the gymnasium, there is a trophy case. On many of the trophies dangle nylon nets, brought back to Wyoming Indian High School over the twenty-four seasons that Alfred Redman has taught its boys basketball. "We wanted our kids to graduate from high school," says Alfred Redman. "They had no place to go. They needed someplace to go."

In 1972 Redman helped found the Wyoming Indian High School on the grounds of the old Episcopal mission in Ethete. Back then very few children of the reservation entered high school. Those that did went to public high schools in the nearby towns, or they were shipped to boarding schools in other states, ostensibly to learn a trade. Most of them came home lonely and confused. They told of being taunted. Many of them spent most of their time fighting. The dropout rate neared 88 percent, and the ones who finished high school returned to a reservation on which the unemployment rate hovered around 65 percent and still does. "The kids—our kids—

were being pushed out to Lander, to Riverton," says Redman. "They weren't being accepted as students; they weren't being accepted as people. So they'd leave and come back home, and they'd have no place to go."

The same year the high school was born, Alfred Redman started a basketball program. Since then the Chiefs have won five Wyoming state high school championships. Since 1990 they have finished the season as no worse than regional champions, and they once won fifty games in a row. They run and they press and they shoot, and they leave bigger teams exhausted, bent double and gasping raggedly. "It's fun to play as a team," Redman explains. "We'll run all night and press you. That appeals to the kids here."

It is a truism fading toward cliché that basketball's most redoubtable characteristic is its ability to flourish in dire circumstances. There is intense devotion to basketball among native people from the Dakotas to the Aleutians. Among the Dine people in Arizona, there is a fervent following for women's basketball. The game has taken root as securely on America's reservations as it has in America's cities, and that is probably not an accident at all. A ghetto is a ghetto, and here, as in the other ghettos where it is played, basketball's basic appeal is that it offers fellowship, a sense of belonging, a means of drawing strength from something larger than oneself. The difference is that there already existed a tradition into which the game's appeal folded itself quite naturally, a feeling of being part of something as vast and inclusive as the tall grass and as stubborn and durable as the wind that stirs it. Something older than basketball is operating when Alfred Redman's teams come out and play.

His family has lived on the Wind River Reservation for as long as Francis Brown's has. There are huge extended families throughout the reservation: the Goggles, and the WallowingBulls, the Browns, the Weeds, and the Redmans—all the sprawling clans that trace their histories back to the Arapaho and Shoshone hunters who first chased the buffalo into Wyoming. The Goggles children have played for Alfred Redman; so have the Weed children, the Brown children, the WallowingBull children and even the Redman children, the sons of Alfred's late brother. Vincent Redman was a holy man. He blessed the school, and there is a mural of him on the wall outside the gymnasium, and it is that mural that marks the place as very different from the suburban high school it appears to be from out on the prairie road.

In 1835 the Arapaho nation split into northern and southern factions, with the greater portion of the people moving south. What became known as the Northern Arapaho remained in what later became Wyoming and Montana. They lost some of their lands in 1851 in the Treaty of Little Arkansas. Later the Arapaho fought bravely under Red Cloud and under Crazy Horse, who used them as shock troops in the campaign that ultimately led to Little Big Horn, in 1876.

Come 1877, however, circumstances had changed to the point that the Northern Arapaho were given a choice: They could move to "Indian Territory" in Oklahoma, or they could settle on the Wind River Reservation that had been established for the Shoshones in 1868. This was a difficult decision. Neither tribe had much use for the other; in 1874, for example, the Shoshones had joined the U.S. Cavalry against the Northern Arapaho at the Battle of Bates Creek. Nevertheless, the Northern Arapaho grudgingly agreed to split the Wind River Reservation with their old adversaries.

"The main thing that makes this place unique is that you've got two traditional enemies living side by side," explains Don Chavez, a history teacher at the high school.

(Once, for reasons lost to history, a man named Tim McCoy moved to a ranch adjacent to the reservation. McCoy later became a silent-movie cowboy and was so popular around the reservation that Shoshones and Arapaho would ride in the same railroad car just to talk with him. "We are not riding with each other," one Arapaho man explained. "We are riding with him.")

Alfred Redman's parents were ranchers in Wyoming. They sent him to Lander to go to high school, and he played a solid guard on the basketball team. At 19 he joined the air force for four years. Upon his discharge, Redman went to a business college in Billings, Montana. While working in an office to put himself through school, he met his wife, Mary Alice. She was an Assiniboine Sioux, which made things rather complicated.

By 1967 Redman was back home. He received a Robert F. Kennedy Fellowship, and he raised money to help start the Wind River Educational Association, a nonprofit foundation that allowed him to look around for further grants to establish a high school on the reservation. He led a delegation to Washington, D.C., where the Bureau of Indian Affairs (BIA) and the Department of Health, Education and Welfare both became intrigued by the project. The BIA provided a $25,000 planning grant and another $100,000 to begin operation of the high school. "Yeah," he says today, rather wistfully, "we had a lot of friends in Congress back then."

In January 1972, despite some resistance owing to the old tribal rivalry between the Arapaho and the Shoshones, the school opened under BIA auspices on the grounds of St. Michael's, the old Episcopal mission that had been founded in Ethete in 1913. There were thirty-six students being taught by nine teachers on the first day of school. The mission's Parish Hall was used as both a classroom and a cafeteria.

But the Episcopalians had done Redman an incalculable favor in 1928. That year they built themselves a gymnasium, which they called Faith Hall. Redman began coaching basketball there every day after school. The student body voted overwhelmingly to call its teams the Chiefs. "We're not as vocal as other people about nicknames," Redman says. "Although I have to say that I kind of don't like that [Cleveland] Indians mascot very much."

Ultimately, the school merged with the Mill Creek public school system, removed itself from the control of the BIA and became a regular member of the Fremont County public schools. In 1989 a new building was opened on a hillside that overlooks the old mission grounds. There are 190 students now.

By the time the new building opened, Redman's basketball team had already won the state championship in 1984 and 1985; the Chiefs had finished as the runner-up in 1986 and as the third-place team in 1987. They won again in 1989, 1991 and 1993. In the past two years, they lost in the state finals and in the state semifinals. The big schools nearby—Lander and Riverton—won't play the Chiefs, a refusal that prompts more than a little local chortling. So the team cadges a schedule where it can, traveling all over Wyoming to play, sometimes embarking on one- and two-day road trips over the Rockies in the middle of February. In basketball, it seems, they have found a place where the old traditions can survive despite what time and circumstance have done to them.

"It must be a cultural thing about being together," says Don Chavez. "It allows for the competitive thing within a common effort, and that's part of our values here. One of the strengths I've always looked to on the reservation is the idea of the extended family."

Few of the Chiefs go on to play college basketball. In the first place, no hotshot college recruiter is going to drag his sweatsuit and his bag of shoes into the Pow Wow Lounge of the Riverton Holiday Inn and eat pan-fried trout so that he can recruit from a team where only a few people ever reach six feet. More to the point, however, is the fact that the mission of the high school—preparing its students to leave—is still a new one. It's been only twenty-four years since Alfred Redman and the rest of them moved into St. Michael's at the bottom of the hill. The habits of centuries die hard. It is a place of long memories, from the gymnasium to the custodian's storeroom.

"It has been the way for a long time," muses Francis Brown, the holy man. "Our students didn't want to go to school in the white communities. They got into fights. There were problems. We had a need for a high school here so that our children could learn that they could learn."

"When I went to high school," says Dick Thunder, "a lot of the schools wanted the Indian kids to come out for sports. I went and played ball at Lander. One thing about Arapaho—we're natural-born basketball players. Ain't worth a damn at football, though." Sitting on his tin chair, the holy man thinks this is very funny, and they both laugh a long time.

Practice is roaring around him, and Alfred Redman is very happy, not least because it means he is finished doing calisthenics with his team. He is 59, and a year removed from a near fatal encounter with meningitis, and he is not as spry as he once was. "These guys," he says, walking a bit like Groucho Marx, "are going to kill me here." There are nearly forty players on the floor. All of them will play, somewhere, for the Chiefs this season. They will be on the varsity or the junior varsity or the freshman team. It is a freewheeling collection, all the more striking for the long braids that swirl around the action under the backboards. They come from all over to play for him now, the children of the Arapaho diaspora, the distant families.

Ken WallowingBull grew up in Montana. Before last year, he'd been to Wind River only once. "I came down for a funeral," he explains. "My whole family was there, and I mean my whole family. Most of the people there lived on the rez here. It was pretty packed." Last year, dissatisfied with how little his son was playing, Ken's father sent him to Ethete to live with relatives and play for the Chiefs. Thus is another concept added to Arapaho tradition.

Playing time.

"I came here because of the way Coach's teams play," Ken says. "Everybody plays because everybody runs. Hey, that's Indian basketball. Plus, the fact that you can tell Coach really loves what he's doing."

He is asked if he ever feels like a foreigner, whether it ever feels as though he's leaving one country and going to another when the Chiefs drive over the mountains to play. "You mean, like, racism?" he asks, the same way he might ask, "You mean, like, snow?"

"Yeah, it's hard sometimes," he says. "You feel like the guys you're playing with are the only thing you belong to, like there's home and there's everyplace else. All you can do is blank it out and go play."

The dropout rate at WIHS is down to 22 percent now, and there even are two players from last year's team—Craig Ferris and Dennis Shoulderblade—playing at Casper College. Ultimately, it is a hopeful place. There are two worlds here then. There is the world that's largely lost and that lives only in the traditions handed down, the world of the old families, the world of the first holy men. And there is that other world that has never been comfortable with the first one, the world of the Jesuits and the Episcopal preachers. Pity the Christians, the holy man said, who don't understand who God is.

And it was those Episcopal preachers who once built a mission so that Alfred Redman and the old families could one day build a school, and who built a gymnasium so that Alfred Redman could one day build himself a basketball team in which all the traditions and both worlds could converge and rise.

At the very top of the hill, above the high school and the mission grounds, is the old Episcopal cemetery. You can see the entire history of the place in that cemetery. You can trace the sorrow of the great families. There are several dozen homemade crosses in the little cemetery. There are seven children buried there who did not live a year, four of them from the Goggles family alone. Three members of the Goggles family now work at the high school. Two of them played ball for Alfred Redman. The tall grass waves between the crosses, and a huge crow flies into the graveyard. A messenger of the Father. The crow sits in a bare tree, looking past the headstones and down toward the school and the old mission grounds, leaning out, stark and bold, against the long winds.

Now 63, Alfred Redman still coaches at the Wyoming Indian High School. The team placed second in the 2000 Wyoming state class 2A tournament.

GQ February 1996

Friday Night Fever

The steam rises in two great pillars, one from each of the towers of the nuclear plant. On the clear days, they dominate the wide sky over the valley of the Susquehanna. Driving east along Route 11 in eastern Pennsylvania, you can see the two columns from miles off. You can watch them rise to where, finally, the upper-level wind currents catch them, spreading them out at the top until the steam from the nuclear plant looks every bit as white and flossy and natural as all the other clouds that sweep across the mountains and are gone.

Route 11 runs straight through the town of Berwick, and the two great columns of steam rise above the trees and above the old factories and above the visitors' end zone at Crispin Field, and that is where they look most natural of all. They are there in the summer when various Berwick High School Bulldogs come down to the field house, and the heavy air is full of the clang of weights and triumphant groaning. They are there in the fall when the Berwick High School Bulldogs play their football, beating almost everybody almost all the time, while 10,000 people rock the valley with their cheering and Mr. Garrison sounds his siren and the people line up for the halftime happy hour at Terry Bower's Bulldog Lounge, across the street from the stadium. Coming up Route 11, you can find your way to Berwick simply by following the two great columns in the sky. They rise above the town, constant and parallel, a pair of Asgardian goalposts created by man's industry and the whims of God's own breezes.

One can argue convincingly that, in this country, high-school football truly represents that lien on the national soul that baseball so relentlessly claims for itself. Despite the rhetoric of its earnest propagandists, baseball remains slightly aloof from the culture, particularly as compared to high-school football. Minor-league baseball is imposed upon the small towns in which it is played. Little League divides the town into subgroups of children representing various restaurants and dry-cleaning shops. However, where football is popular, the high-school team has an ongoing, organic connection to the place in which it is played. Fathers and sons wear the same colors twenty years apart. One brother follows another into the backfield, and a third waits his turn and cheers.

Over the past decade, no high-school football program in the country has been more successful than the one at Berwick, including the teams that make up the vast industry of high-school football in Texas, the renegade conferences in Florida and the sprawling urban-suburban jumble in California. In the past eleven years, Berwick has twice won the national championship as defined by *USA Today*—which, after all, exists only to define such things. And while Berwick has always been a football town (the 1941 Bulldogs were undefeated, and an ad in one of the programs reminds the reader that the 1929 team was 10–0–1), it has only been since Coach George Curry took over the program, in 1971, that it has taken flight nationally. Curry's career record at Berwick prior to this season was 232–51–3. Since 1981, it is a staggering 152–17–1. "You pinch yourself," he says. "If you had told me we were going to win 232 games in twenty-three years, I wouldn't have believed it."

USA Today has come to town twice. Almost every major newspaper on the East Coast and at least two from Texas have come here to follow the giant goalposts in the sky. Two years ago, when the Bulldogs again went undefeated, they were led by Ron Powlus, a powerful senior who was reckoned to be the best college prospect in the country. One of the schools pursuing Powlus was Notre Dame, which meant that Berwick found itself dealing with the vast and fervent Notre Dame alumni network. "I made up a highlight tape," says Cam Melchiorre, one of Berwick's prominent boosters. "I wound up having to send 250 of them just to Chicago [alumni]." A booster named Dan McGann—alas, a Domer himself—was fielding three calls a week from a Notre Dame fanatic in Montana. "He found me," McGann says, "because he had the alumni book and I was the only guy in there from Berwick."

(A note here to America's college-football recruiters: If you want to blend in, remember that the town's name is pronounced so that the *w* disappears. Repeat after us: "Bur'ik." This will not get you a free beer at the Bulldog Lounge, but it may buy you a little time before someone with either a long-standing allegiance to your program or a deeply held grudge against it descends upon you.)

Berwick is a stubborn, willful place. Indeed, one of its more famous citizens was a certain Colonel Clarence Gearhart Jackson, who was certainly one of the stubbornest members of the Army of the Potomac. He was also one of the unluckiest. The good colonel signed up with the 84th Pennsylvania Volunteers just in time to get rolled up, wounded and captured by Stonewall Jackson at Chancellorsville. He was sent to the infamous Libby Prison, from which he escaped, only to be recaptured. He then was exchanged for a Confederate prisoner, and he rejoined his outfit just in time to get rolled up, wounded and captured by James Longstreet in the battle of the Wilderness. This time, he was sent to Andersonville, thereby completing an extraordinarily unpleasant penal parlay. While imprisoned, Jackson busied himself designing the house he would build when the war was over. Upon his release, he came home to Berwick and built his dream house. He lived in it for three years and then died. That house is now Berwick's town hall. It is a stubborn, willful place.

For nearly seventy years, the town's central industry was the American Car and Foundry Company. AC&F made railroad cars. During World War II, it was one of the country's biggest producers of tanks and armored vehicles. At that time, 10,000 people worked there. The plant closed in 1961. Some local businessmen quickly reopened it as the Berwick Forge, and it exists now as a skeleton of itself, just behind the home team's end zone at Crispin Field. All summer long, that end of Vine Street resounds with ringing steel from the Berwick Forge and from the Bulldog weight room. One is not very much louder than the other.

The town's primary extant employer is the Wise potato chip factory, Earl Wise having founded the family business in his mother's kitchen here in 1921. Nevertheless, the local economy is not unlike that of many smaller industrial cities throughout the Rust Belt. The unemployment rate is slightly above the statewide average, and the median income is slightly below that of the rest of the state. It is an older population. The young people are moving away. That 10,000 people regularly attend Bulldog games is all the more remarkable when you consider that only 11,000 people live in and around Berwick. "On Friday nights," Terry Bower says, "the town shuts down."

This is what brought *Nightline* to Berwick last year. The Berwick Bulldogs became an ongoing *Nightline* miniseries, rather like the ayatollah used to be. We saw the Bulldogs win, and we saw them lose. Poor Dan Pecorelli, last year's starting quarterback, had Ted Koppel addressing the issue of his broken collarbone on national television. However, it is clear that *Nightline* came to Berwick with a story that it wanted to tell—the Beat-up Small Town and Its Plucky Little Football Team—and that it was going to cram Berwick into that story line whether the town fit it or not. But while the area around the old AC&F plant *has* seen better days, that factory, in fact, closed thirty-three years ago. And while there is more than a little plywood mottling the downtown storefronts, there also are wide suburban developments along the east side of Berwick. The surrounding countryside is mountainous and lovely.

After watching *Nightline*, one arrives in Berwick half expecting to find an open-pit coal mine in Colonel Jackson's old backyard. This is why, should Ted Koppel ever return to the Bulldog Lounge, he can count on a slightly chillier greeting than he would receive in, say, the Kissinger home.

"I threw the camera crew out of here once last year," Terry Bower recalls. "I mean, jeez, that's all I need. What if someone's in here with somebody else's wife?" Well, there's that, too.

Berwick is a small town, and it does invest a great deal of its soul in this football team full of its children. The team does not command the town the way high-school teams sometimes do. It rises from the place, full and whole, every first week in September, a combination of one man's industry and God's own good fortune.

"This is the damnedest place," says George Curry, driving back to his office after breakfast. "Nobody works. Everybody hangs around in restaurants."

He is a town character now. The old men in the restaurants and coffee shops slap him on the rump as he walks out. He is squat and unmistakable, rather like a chunkier, muscular Joe Pesci. For the past twenty-three seasons, Curry has worked on building Berwick football. In the process, he has built himself an empire. Some of his hardest work involves not letting the whole thing get completely out of hand.

"It all has to do with the head coach," he explains. "I honestly believe that part of my job is to prevent that. I mean it. My players and I talk about it. I am on their ass all the time. If the head coach allows his kids to get consumed by it, then he is not doing his job."

Curry grew up in Larksville, north of Berwick, deep in the anthracite belt that the Pennsylvania people call hard-coal country. When George Curry was young, there were five collieries in Larksville alone. "Tough kids grew up in that area," he says. He won a football ride to Temple University, where he helped coach the freshman team after graduation. Anxious to run his own shop, he took a job coaching at Lake Lehman High School, not far from Berwick. In 1971, Curry was still teaching and coaching there when a Berwick native on the Lake Lehman faculty told him that the position at Berwick had come open. "They'd had some tough years in the 1960s," Curry says. "Between 1961 and 1970, they had three winning seasons, and those were all 6-and-5's."

Curry set about developing Berwick football into a townwide phenomenon. Today, most of the youth-league coaches are former Berwick players. Talented athletes are spotted as early as the sixth grade; in fact, Curry has been known to drop in on touch-football games played by even younger children. "I have an idea of who our quarterback is going to be for the next I don't know how many years," he says. "I got the top three athletes in the sixth grade. I know their grades. I've looked at their parents so I know how big they're going to be." He has also worked at connecting Bulldog football with almost every other aspect of life in town. Curry's players do benefit telethons. They sign autographs for charity. "If you tell George 'Hey, I need some kids to help clean out my basement,'" says Terry Bower, "they'll be there. And they're bulls, too. Hard workers."

The town quickly embraced the team as the manifestation of its own identity. By 1975, the games were selling out every Friday night. Reserved-seat tickets came so dearly that some people included them in their will. Bower bought the Villa Capri restaurant in 1982, and he quickly remodeled the bar into the Bulldog Lounge, with bulldog lamps and tiny paw prints painted on the floor. Some people in the area became unnerved by the whole business. Curry was accused of recruiting players (which he denies). There also was some indiscreet grumbling about the fact that Curry makes in excess of $50,000 per year, an admittedly large sum for a high-school football coach in rural Pennsylvania.

Having built his empire, Curry needed to control it. He instituted a strict code of discipline. Players have a ten o'clock curfew every night except game nights. (Ron Powlus once was bagged driving home at 10:05, and he ran laps the next day.) There are rules involving hair length (nothing long or unruly) and rules involving academic progress. "I've suspended kids," Curry says. "Football will not run you. I want them to use this as a means to an end." He has had players go on to gain admission to every Ivy League school and all of the country's military academies. He also must be the only high-school coach in America with one graduate currently playing at Notre Dame and another one starting at MIT. "Starting?" Curry says. "He made all-league, whatever league they're in."

Berwick first broke nationally in 1982, when the Bulldogs beat Gonzaga Prep, from Washington, D.C. A year later, they were anointed national champions by *USA Today*. Recruiters began streaming up Route 11. First they came for Bo Orlando, who plays today with the Houston Oilers. Then they came for Jake Kelchner, a quarterback who got bounced from Notre Dame and wound up starring at West Virginia University. (When Kelchner was at West Virginia, he appeared on national television one Saturday only to have Curry call him on Monday to complain about the length of his hair.) In 1992, however, Curry and Berwick broke the bank. They won another national championship, and Ron Powlus was named the best high-school player in the country. The Bulldog Lounge became a happening place.

When her son was in eighth grade, Sue Powlus took a phone call from George Curry. Ronnie was off playing basketball with his friends. Everybody thought he was going to make the Bulldogs a terrific fullback someday. George Curry asked Sue Powlus to go and get her son, who Curry thought might make a quarterback. "Ronnie was very calm about it," she says. "But, oh, my heart was pounding. When your son plays football, you're pretty impressed when Coach Curry calls." Four years later, at a packed press conference, Ron Powlus announced that he would be attending Notre Dame, and some guy from Montana was bouncing joyously around the Rockies. Before he was 18, Powlus had already spent four years having adults depend on him for their happiness.

"It's strange," he says. "It didn't really bother me or our team, which is hard to explain, because you'd think it would. But I think everybody just wanted to win so badly, wanted to win so badly for themselves. The pressure from the outside wasn't so bad because we were putting so much pressure on ourselves. I had kids tell me, kids who didn't play, 'Boy, I wouldn't want to be in your position.' It was just something that you realize is going to happen to you when you go into the program. From the eighth grade on up, you know this is going to happen."

He is six-four and powerfully built, not rangy the way the prototypical star quarterback is. Powlus played forty-two straight games in high school, and he passed for 7,339 yards and sixty-two touchdowns. In his senior season, the Bulldogs were 15–0. They were the quintessence of what Curry has constructed: solid, tough and ineffably Berwickian. Powlus's favorite receiver was Bo Orlando's younger brother, Chris.

After arriving at Notre Dame, however, Ron was dogged by misfortune. That first spring, in 1993, Coach Lou Holtz said that Powlus would be his starting quarterback, only to have Powlus break his collarbone twice during the following two months. Ominous rumbling arose about him in the larger Notre Dame community— rumbling that was stilled only when Powlus tore up the early part of Notre Dame's schedule this past September, throwing four touchdown passes against Northwestern in his first college game, and then leading a touchdown drive in the final minute against Michigan that might have lived forever in Irish football lore had Michigan not won the game on a last-second field goal. Ron Powlus probably bought himself a career with those two games. Notre Dame football is not unlike Berwick football, except the stakes become mortal there.

There are rumors flying in the Bulldog Lounge, interrupting Dan McGann and John Strenchock in the middle of one of their several ongoing arguments. McGann went to Notre Dame and Strenchock attended Penn State, which is the basis of several of their ongoing arguments. "I'll root for Notre Dame for four years," Strenchock says, "as long as Ronnie's there."

"We're thrilled," says McGann.

Today, though, it seems that the grapevine has receiver Mike Bennett, Berwick's most coveted player, signing to play at Penn State. The previous weekend, Bennett visited the school, which somehow has been translated into a commitment to go there. Ironically, Penn State never has done well recruiting Berwick players. There are numerous and arcane theories as to why this is. Most of them center on some sort of spat between Curry and Penn State coach Joe Paterno, and Strenchock is tired of hearing all of them, anyway. If Bennett were to go with the Nittany Lions, at the very least John Strenchock would get to tell some people to shut up. McGann suggests that Bennett is going to have a fine career at Penn State—as a linebacker.

McGann believes that Joe Paterno would look at Meryl Streep and see a linebacker.

"Oh, shut up," Strenchock says.

"They play the game through us," says Mike Bennett, an ebullient young man despite the fact that he was shown on *Nightline* last year with a football whistling through his fingers. "It's a little strange, but it's also fun. We have players who know how to work through that, and they teach the younger kids. Like Ronnie Powlus really helped me with it when I was a sophomore. From what he taught me, I'm teaching the younger guys."

Mike's father, John Bennett, is a machinist at a plant outside of Berwick. He's hoping for more than that for Mike. "He plays well and gets the good grades, he can get a good job," he says.

Together, father and son face the central conundrum of Berwick football. The town invests itself in the efforts of its children so that those children one day will have the opportunity to leave it. As so many of the other young people of Berwick have, the players rise together and scatter, like the steam clouds—over the mountains and gone. Behind John Bennett, in the field house, the weights ring out like the old muscular factory music once did. Mike Bennett catches a pass, and the old men cheer, and the night falls on the valley, hanging there sweet and red on the two great goalposts in the sky.

GQ **November 1994**

Danny Nee's War

It was only one voice in a raucous Kemper Arena, but it was as clear as the bells on victory morning. It was a voice draped in bunting. It was a voice with yellow ribbons flying behind it. It was a voice you could hear over the din and clamor of a skintight Big Eight quarterfinal because it was a voice that was coming from someplace else. It was a voice—one single voice, clear as the bells on victory morning, calling from out of the national mood.

"Hey, Danny. Howja like the war now?"

Danny Nee, the basketball coach at the University of Nebraska, had come walking across the floor to check on one of his players, who had gone down with a leg injury. Earlier this year, when American troops began flooding into the Middle East, but long before the first shots were fired, Nee had expressed the hope that no American soldier would spill blood in the sand. He had also said he would protect his own son with all his might from the horrors that Danny Nee had seen in his own war, the one he had fought when he was very young. Now, from the perspective of this latest war, his words were being flung back at him in contempt and in self-congratulation by a nation in love with itself.

"Hey, Danny. Howja like the war now?"

You fight in a war, you own the war. That's the rule. For good or ill, it belongs to you. It belongs to you because of the fear and the death and the blood, and it belongs to you because you left an arm, a leg or a part of your soul there, and it belongs to you because of your friends who never came back, and it belongs to them, too.

Loud and fat with satisfaction—this voice was not talking about Danny Nee's war.

This voice was not talking about a kid from Brooklyn who joins the Marines and goes to a place called Vietnam because part of what made his family finally feel American demanded that he join the Marines and go to Vietnam. It was not talking about that same kid, who takes a job as a doorway gunner in the helicopters that transport wounded soldiers—a job in which you deal out death in order to save lives, and a job with a life expectancy in combat that was measured, coldly, in minutes. The kid takes this job so he'll be less likely to step on land mines and lose his legs and never be able to play basketball again.

Danny Nee's war was not quick. It was not successful. It was not a neat little technological whiz-bang of a thing. It was not universally applauded. It was not greeted at its outset with a festival of right-eousness and it was not toasted at its conclusion by an orgy of self-congratulation. It was not an occasion for the stifling of dissent or the knuckling of the press.

Danny Nee's war was hard and brutal, and it left such awful wreck-age behind it. Heroism, once clean and strong, was bent and twisted and left as debris. One very good man who fought there once told his friend, "You never ask anyone who was in Vietnam whether or not he killed anybody." And, while it belongs ultimately to those who fought it, the war marked everyone. It defined generations. Michael Herr, whose journalism is the finest that war produced, concluded a collection of his work with the line, "Vietnam, Vietnam, Vietnam. We've all been there." But, unlike most people, and unlike virtually all of his colleagues among the nation's basketball coaches, Danny Nee actually was.

"He tells us when we're tired, 'Hey, you don't know what tired is,'" says Clifford Scales, Nee's rock-solid co-captain at Nebraska. "Tired is not sleeping for four or five nights because that's the way you stay alive. It gives you an appreciation of where he's coming from."

Which is not to say that Nee wears his war as a badge, or makes a habit of using it to give facile lessons. He respects it too much to treat it as cheap currency. He has had a life for himself, more of one than have had most of the cookie-cutter college coaches who have fought no harder fights than The Battle of the Prospect's Living Room.

He was a poor kid in New York, where he once got thrown out of Power Memorial High School because he got in a gang fight that began when somebody threw an epithet at a teammate named Lew Alcindor. He was one of Al McGuire's first recruits when McGuire was starting out at Marquette. Al romanced Nee's parents over tea and soda bread, and Patrick Nee told Danny that Marquette would be where he'd be going, even though Danny Nee had no idea where the place was. He was an assistant to Digger Phelps and a head coach at Ohio, and now for five years at Nebraska, where it all has turned around for him this year. And, once in his life, Danny Nee became a soldier, and he went to war.

And, when the latest war began—the war that owes so much of its own definition now to Danny Nee's war, because George Bush told the nation that his war would not be Danny Nee's war, by God—Danny Nee looked at his war and said some things that were contrary to the prevailing political and cultural mood. The words came from his heart, which had seen too much when it was much too young, and people didn't want to hear them. Once the war began, Danny Nee got behind the effort, but that is somehow not enough today.

Nee is far from the first or last victim of the demagogic victory-drunk fever now epidemic in the nation. We have heard much hoo-ha about the evils of "political correctness," as people spring to the defense of every drunken frat boy who yells "nigger" on a public street. But there was not much concern shown by these same people when Nee was widely denounced—and Seton Hall player Marco Lokar was actually run out of the country—for not adhering to the current politically correct attitude on the Persian Gulf war. Many Nebraskans were angered by him. Many more Nebraskans were puzzled, even those who were marveling at the wonders Danny Nee had wrought in their university's basketball team.

On this night, that team is playing Oklahoma in a quarterfinal game in Kemper Arena. Scales has fallen down and hurt his leg, and Nee has come across the floor to check on his player. He gets booed—a coach's reception, nothing more. Then comes this one voice—a voice that sounds like goalposts being torn down, calling in a voice that sounds very much like gloating. Wartime, it seems, doesn't end just because the war does.

"Hey, Danny. Howja like the war now?"

Danny Nee says nothing. He gives no sign that he's even heard. Perhaps he hasn't. But he's felt the spirit that sets the voice to calling. Felt its chill. Felt it too close to him. He learned something a long time ago. He learned it because he is Irish, and as a race the Irish may have learned this lesson before anybody else. He learned it in Vietnam, because there it was the final truth. "There are no guarantees," he says. If you know that hard lesson, if it's there in your blood and in the life you have made for yourself, then you do not gloat. Because to gloat is to tempt something bigger and better than yourself—something that is capable of a terrible revenge.

Patrick Nee came to New York from Boston and Nova Scotia, and, ultimately, from a little fishing village nestled among the cliffs near Galway. To support his wife—and, eventually, his two sons—Patrick took a job as an elevator operator in a men's store across the street from the New York Public Library. "I don't think he ever made more than $100 or $125 a week," his son, Danny, says today. "He got up every day, sick or not, and he went to work. He worked that elevator, and he did what he's supposed to do, and everybody in the neighborhood liked him." New York was different, then. There were neighborhoods. There were parishes. There were little connections that had little to do with the formal structure of a society. "I don't think New York is even a city now," Nee says. "I don't know what it is."

Among the Irish who came to this country when Patrick Nee did, there was a drive that came from their bones—and from the reception that they got from established society, which was not a warm one—to become the best Americans that they possibly could, and that was defined by taking full part in the country's institutions and patriotic rituals. At its best, this gave us some of the people who fought our fires, and many of the best of our cops. At its most successful, it gave us the political machines that ran the Eastern cities. At its worst, it gave us Joe McCarthy, and Father Charles Coughlin before him, and it gave us the people who bought the poison they peddled. But of all these avenues of cultural validation, the most compelling was the one presented by the military, if only because the military's call was so simple that it was amplified in the popular culture. "It was that John Wayne mentality, you know?" Nee says. "Patriotism. George M. Cohan. Yankee Doodle Dandy. All these things were a part of my life. I can't tell you why. I just thought [joining up] was the right thing to do."

After captaining the freshman basketball team, Nee dropped out of Marquette in 1967 and enlisted in the Marines. He did not do so in order to keep Quantico, Va., safe from the Viet Cong. "I was going to go into the Marine Corps and I was going to go to Vietnam," he says. "I wanted to go. Then I got to Parris Island, and I realized as the process was taking place that this was very serious. I realized that this wasn't no goddamn basketball game. You had to control your fear and work at just getting through the day. I heard the guys in the bunks at night, crying.

"And this was just Parris Island, but at least it gave you a shot at being prepared for Vietnam."

He was attached to the First Marine Air Wing, and his unit kept moving farther and farther north, which was not the safest direction to be moving in that part of Indochina. Nee burned off the leeches. He watched the rats. He heard the shellfire. His helicopter brought out the wounded and the dying. One time, just before a mission, he changed seats with another crew member, and the soldier sitting in Nee's seat was killed. His life was thick with death. He stayed alive.

"There was a soberness, a solemnness to it," he says. "I don't think anybody ever thinks they're going to die." He carries that with him today. He does not tell his war stories easily, and some he never tells at all. "Never ask someone who was in Vietnam if they killed anybody," a good man once told his friend.

"From what I understand," says Dr. John Stark, a Lincoln psychologist who has worked extensively with Nee's team during the past two seasons, "Danny went through as much personal agony as anybody went through over there at the time. In terms of some of the things that happened to him, it was absolutely terrifying."

Eventually, he began to bleed internally, and he was medically evacuated from the combat zone, and honorably discharged in 1968. By then, he'd lost nearly 60 pounds. He wound up back in New York, loading trucks for a paycheck and hating it. "I took the uniform off and I never put it back on," says Nee. "And I knew it was time to get my [life] together."

The GI Bill took him to St. Mary's of the Plains College in Dodge City, Kan.—a small school that oddly had become an enclave for gypsy Brooklyn athletes, largely through the efforts of a football player named Donnie Kent who started a recruiting network in the old neighborhoods. Nee graduated from St. Mary's and went on to get a master's degree in health, phys ed and recreation from Kansas State.

He coached high school ball in New Jersey and, in 1976, he hooked on with Digger Phelps's staff at Notre Dame—at the time, a great incubator of future head coaches. Two years later, while he was scouting a game at Marquette, Nee collapsed again, bleeding into his belly. This time, the doctors found a huge ulcer that had been hidden by scar tissue from a childhood operation. Nee nearly died, but it was not simply the ulcer that was killing him. It was the war he'd thought he'd put behind him. You fight the war, the war belongs to you. "I got physically sick," he says simply. "And it was all Vietnam."

Nee worked for Phelps for two more seasons, and then he went on to be the head coach at Ohio. He was enormously successful, putting up a 107–67 record in six seasons. That brought him to the attention of the administration at Nebraska, which had been stunned in the spring of 1986 when coach Moe Iba walked into a postgame press conference at an NCAA Tournament game and quit on the spot. Nee took the job and came to Lincoln, which is pretty far from Brooklyn on the map, and even farther from it in the mind.

"I can honestly say that I never felt out of place," Nee insists. "It was natural and, honestly, I'd been un-Brooklyned for a long time. I wasn't looking for New York. I mean, Lincoln's not a farm town. It's a medium-sized Midwestern city." Nevertheless, he found what little bits of Brooklyn there that he could—including an airy joint called Barry's Cafe, which reminded Nee of the taverns his father used to visit in the old neighborhood, when neighborhoods mattered. He has been known to hold postgame court in Barry's, win or lose. Until this season, it was the latter case more than the former.

He was 61–64 in his first four seasons, intense as ever, burning with frustration. Hard enough to win at basketball at a football school, but last year's team disintegrated. There was backbiting and dissent, and Nee couldn't break through to many of his older players. The town sank into apathy. Nobody wanted to drag themselves to Devaney Arena in the middle of February, through the winds that begin in northern Manitoba, to watch a losing, dispirited team. One night in their own building, the Cornhuskers had Kansas beaten, but one of them picked up a technical foul, and the game got away. "That was the one that did it," Nee says. "We lost six or seven in a row after that. You've coached your best. The players have played their best. Everything's going your way, and you lose anyway. You wonder then."

It ended, bleakly, at 10–18. "Losing like we did permeates your whole life," says Nebraska center Rich King. "It feels like it comes down on every aspect of you. Your social life, everything."

"I started questioning a lot of things," Nee admits. He set himself back to work reconstructing his players' better natures. Dr. Stark, who'd previously worked with the Nebraska football team, already was working with the basketball team during the middle of the miserable 1989–90 season, and he stepped up his efforts. "Last year, which was my first year, I was just getting to know the people," Stark says. "I told Danny that all the stuff I was working on would start to show up next year."

Stark, who believes that psychological "coaching" is going to be in the '90s what strength-coaching was in the '80s, put all the players and coaches through a battery of tests. There were individual meetings and there were group meetings. "We were looking to change the patterns of behavior from last season," Stark explains. The coaches were not exempted. It was then that Stark began to see glimpses of the marks left by Nee's experiences in Vietnam. "I saw someone with incredible mental toughness," Stark says. "Most people would have wilted last year. He just said, 'Jack, I know how good I am.'" The trick was to get the players to realize that same thing. Then, early this season, King came to Stark and said, "Do you know how good we *can* be?" That was the question Stark had been waiting to hear.

The running joke in the Big Eight has been that everybody knows how good Nebraska is—except Nebraska. The Cornhuskers are a big, robust lot. King is a solid 7 foot 1, and co-captain Beau Reid, who followed Nee from Ohio to Lincoln, is 6-8 and 220 pounds, and there's a lot more Bo than Beau to his game. These were the people who went through last season angry and confused, asking, in essence, "How good are we?" This year, the team's seniors decided that they were fed up with the way things used to be.

"These seniors finally got to be leaders," says Reid, who is one of them. "We've had seniors here who didn't have their best seasons when they were seniors. It was really bad."

That changed swiftly at the beginning of this season. The Cornhuskers got off to a 15–0 start. They crushed Illinois 100–73 in the second game of the year, and Reid drained a jumper to beat Michigan State a week later, a signifying win that got them noticed nationally for the first time.

While Nebraska had been moving to the top of the polls, however, American troops had been going on station in the Middle East. Naturally, Nee was asked about the situation. After all, hardly any other basketball coach's opinion would be relevant. "I pray every night that not one kid loses a drop of blood," he told *Sports Illustrated*. "I have a son who's 13, and the police would have to pull me off of him before I'd let him go through what I did." That differed little from what Nebraska Sen. Bob Kerrey—himself a Medal of Honor winner in Vietnam—was saying in Congress. Only Nee said it better.

What Nee said rang with sincerity and carried more credibility than anything said on the subject of combat and soldiers by most of the TV talking-heads, or by the vice president of the United States, for all that. It was deeply personal to him, and it reflected the turmoil Nee felt when he watched another generation go climbing into the transports.

"There were times in the past few years when my experience [in Vietnam] would resurface," he says. "Not often, because, I mean, that's 25 goddamn years ago now. But it resurfaced over the past three months more monumentally than it ever has before."

Then the bombs began to fall on Baghdad, and Danny Nee found his patriotism under severe attack. There were angry letters from the VFW posts. There were phone calls. Nee called a press conference to try and point out that what he had said before the war shouldn't be used to bludgeon him now that the United States had launched the war itself. He tried, but he was so angry that he couldn't keep the profanity out of his voice. Dammit, Patrick Nee had given him his patriotism as a birthright. He had treasured it enough to have fought for it in a place where life and death were often a simple matter of changing your seat. Who were these people to come and question it now?

It intensified as the war was prosecuted more successfully, something Nee publicly and sincerely applauded—and the national mood of self-satisfaction fed upon itself. Danny Nee found himself the victim of what passes for Red-baiting in the early 1990s and, somehow, the credentials he had earned, the credentials that had nearly cost him his life, didn't matter much at all. Wartime, it seems, doesn't end just because the war does.

A few days before his team made its remarkable run in the Big Eight tournament—coming from 11 points down in the final three minutes of its opening game against Oklahoma, then overcoming an early 31–18 deficit to beat Kansas—Danny Nee was talking about his father and he was talking about fishing, and he sounded a lot like Al McGuire. Because they are both Irish and from Brooklyn, they do sound alike, but the similarity doesn't end with the accent. Nee coaches like McGuire, relying on communication and the individual relationships he has with his players rather than a heavy concentration on strategic minutiae. McGuire knew his players so well that they regularly shouted at each other without the slightest regard for their respective stations, and, on one memorable occasion, McGuire challenged a player to hit him, and the player complied. "I'm coachable," the player later explained.

Nee works in much the same way, although he has yet to initiate a brawl with one of his charges. "I think I coach more like Al than anybody else," Nee says. McGuire and Nee share more than a coaching style, though; both went closely through the primary traumas of their generation—in McGuire's case, the Depression, and in Nee's, the Vietnam War. You cannot help but be changed by that. So, when Danny Nee talked about his father and about fishing, he sounded like Al McGuire because the genuine peace in his voice had been so dearly bought.

"He'd go out on Sheepshead Bay to watch the boats and to fish, and I'd go with him," Nee says. "You know, [Nebraska football coach] Tom Osborne gets a lot of credit around here for fishing, but I've been known to get out to a lake myself. Of course, I'm a city fisherman. My idea of fishing is you get a folding chair, some sandwiches and a couple of beers and you put on the suntan oil and you sit there for a while."

The letters from the VFW posts eventually stopped flooding the Nebraska basketball office. The furor died away, but that which fed it was still alive. Sen. Kerrey, a Democrat who is immensely popular in the state, has heard from some of the same voices that came calling for Danny Nee, and there has been a lot of talk about a Republican Senate in 1992, swathed in yellow ribbons. The feeling is now made most manifest in the sports arenas in which Danny Nee will finish out this, his finest season as a basketball coach. "What happened to me was very tiny compared to everything else that was going on," he says now.

Before the Big Eight final game with Missouri, the first such final Nebraska had ever made and a game the Cornhuskers eventually would lose, there was the now-customary patriotic pageant, featuring not only the national anthem, but Lee Greenwood's "I'm Proud To Be an American," which is rapidly becoming the "We Will Rock

You" of the new world order. There will be more of it as the troops come home, and as the NCAA Tournament progresses over the next month. Nebraska is a fine team, capable of beating at least five of the top eight seeded teams in the field. Danny Nee's doubts about his coaching have disappeared. And Danny Nee, who went off to a different war once, long ago, is what Patrick Nee wanted so much to be when he came to Brooklyn—a good American, which never has been as simple as the dumb brute crowd would want it to be.

In March of 2000, after a 13–17 season, Danny Nee was fired as head basketball coach at the University of Nebraska. On the other hand, Saddam Hussein is still in charge in Iraq.

The National

The Survivor

On February 18, 1993, a bomb blew up the car of Jonathan Owens, a freshman football player at the University of Idaho, in Moscow. A week later, another bomb went off, in the second-floor men's room of Gault Hall, the dormitory outside of which Owens had parked his car. It set everyone on edge, all up and down the highways winding through the great sweep of wheat fields that the people in eastern Washington and western Idaho call, with justifiable grandiosity, the "Inland Empire." Law enforcement went on edgy alert. They have been nervous about guns and bombs in the Inland Empire ever since various white-supremacist groups took to the hills and the forests and the wheat fields to await their own peculiar Armageddon. One man, named Randy Weaver, had felt it coming down on him ahead of schedule. Weaver was awaiting trial for killing a federal marshal when the bombs went off in Moscow, so up and down the Inland Empire, police and federal authorities went still and cold—and slit-eyed serious.

Route 270 connects Moscow to Pullman, Washington, where Washington State University sits on a high, round-topped hill, dominating the landscape the way it dominates the life of the little town below. When "Wazzu" is in session, 24,000 people live in Pullman. When school is out, the population dwindles to 10,000. Pullman is a knobby place, built on buttes and valleys, the wheat fields around it spread like great rumpled quilts over the queer topography of the land.

Spring came early in the hills this year. By April, Pullman's Grand Boulevard was alive with students. The front door was open at the Sports Page, the jocks' saloon. Breezes swirled in, cool and fresh and alive. Nobody had been arrested yet for the bombs in Moscow. Randy Weaver was now on trial. Every cop along Route 270 still had winter in his eyes. And flush with the fullness of springtime, two Washington State football players decided to make a bomb.

The previous season had been a good one for the Cougars. They had defeated the University of Washington for the coveted Apple Cup, one of those ancient college-football totems beloved of old grads and women who still wear camellia blossoms. This warmed the heart of that half of the state that considered U-Dub an impossible passel of sanctimonious bullies—and cheaters, besides. (This latter belief was fully justified this past summer, when the Huskies acknowledged that players had been granted a rather Rostenkowskian latitude with regard to unsecured loans.) The Cougars had also gone to the Copper Bowl, where they'd beaten Utah, 31–28. They had a gifted quarterback in Drew Bledsoe, whom everyone believed would be the top pick in June's NFL draft.

And, on April 10, at the end of spring practice for the 1993 season, a walk-on defensive player named Buddy Waldron won a scholarship for his final year of college.

It had been a long road for Waldron, a 22-year-old from Bellevue, in the western part of the state. As a freshman, he had been arrested for breaking and entering, allegedly trying to liberate a friend's stereo from the home of the man with whom she'd been living. As it turned out, the guy was home—and was an alleged drug dealer, as well. He'd capped off a few rounds at Waldron, and then had pressed charges anyway. Waldron spent a few nights in jail and began his college days on probation.

At Wazzu, he soon became known as a good-hearted person who liked living on the edge. He was the first one to skydive, the first one to bungee-jump. After college, he planned to become a Navy SEAL before trying to land a job with the Drug Enforcement Administration. He was moving toward that shadowland of the federal government where khaki fades to pinstripes and the bad guys are easily marked. One day that first season, on the practice field, he met another walk-on, a linebacker named Payam Saadat, the son of Iranian émigrés now living in Santa Monica, California. Saadat was best known around town for driving an old postal-service Jeep that he'd bought at an auction and painted black and referred to as the "Stealth Jeep." The two became training partners, matching each other on the weights until one or the other collapsed from exhaustion.

Beyond football and the weight room, however, they saw little of each other. Except that, in April of this year, Waldron rented *Under Siege*, the Steven Seagal potboiler in which the hero makes a bomb out of a microwave oven. He bought a book and asked Saadat if he'd like to make a bomb. "We were sitting around," Saadat says. "You know, you're in Pullman. You're bored. I was, like, 'Yeah, let's do it. Let's see what happens.'

"If anything, I should've said 'This is a real stupid idea, let's abandon it.' But it wasn't like that. I really wasn't second-guessing it at any time. I was, like, 'Yeah, let's do it.' Like it was a normal thing. I wasn't taking the perspective that this was an actual bomb—that it could hurt, that it could do damage. I didn't look at it that way."

According to Saadat's account, they made it on the kitchen table in his apartment. The bomb was an eight-inch section of galvanized pipe stuffed with smokeless powder. They attached a cheap plastic clock for a timer. After finishing the device, they had begun working on another when they decided to test the first bomb. Waldron said that they should drive out to the middle of a wheat field and detonate it. They left in such a hurry that they forgot to unplug a soldering iron on the table. They set the bomb and then took Waldron's 1978 Dodge Ramcharger truck and drove down into the valley and then up again.

They turned up Irving Street, into a residential neighborhood covering a butte just northeast of downtown. Irving Street dead-ends in Sevdy's Trailer Court, which is considered by the Pullman police to be the nearest thing they have to a high-crime area. At Sevdy's, one must turn right, into another residential neighborhood. In fact, this area is perhaps the only one for about thirty miles from which no wheat field is accessible at all. The truck slid around the corner onto the NW 300 block of Irving Street, and it stopped. It was about 10:45 on the night of April 19. Waldron wanted to check the bomb, which Saadat was holding across his lap. Payam Saadat heard a soft, insistent buzzing, and then he knew.

Residents said later that it sounded like dozens of garbage cans being slammed together at once. The truck careened into a parked car, and then stopped. The windshield was blown out. So was one of the side windows, and a piece of the roof. One man staggered out of the vehicle and collapsed on a nearby lawn. The sirens came then, dozens of them, police and fire. There were more of them than anyone had ever heard. After a while, they screamed away, rising and falling and finally dying in the deep valleys. The only sound left on Irving Street in the strange and shattered night was that of a dozen cops, talking in low voices about all they didn't know.

Harvey Waldron couldn't leave his den. A week earlier, he'd agreed to pay off a deal he'd made with his son, Buddy. If Buddy won a football scholarship for his last year at Wazzu, Harvey would take him scuba diving anywhere in the world. Typically, Buddy wasn't satisfied to collect coral in the Caribbean. They were going to Australia, to dive with the great white sharks. On the night of April 19, Harvey called Buddy at his apartment in Pullman. Buddy said that he was busy but that he would call back later. Harvey went down into his den to do some work on his computer.

"It was kind of weird," Waldron says. "Historically, he always called me by ten or eleven. When he didn't, suddenly I started feeling very uneasy. I stopped working, and I kind of sat there. I couldn't sleep. I couldn't go upstairs. I felt very odd. A little after 2 A.M., the phone rang, and I knew I had lost my son."

It was a doctor from the Sacred Heart Medical Center, in Spokane. Buddy had taken the blast full in the face, and he was on life support. There was no hope of survival. While Harvey Waldron was on the phone with the doctor, he took another call. This call was from Mike Price, the head football coach at Washington State. Price is a lifer who worked his way back to his alma mater through jobs at Missouri and at Weber State, in Utah. He is a gentle, calming presence, not at all the fire-breathing martinet so common to his profession. In fact, until Price and Bledsoe took the Cougars to the Copper Bowl, there was some loose talk around the Sports Page that Price perhaps was less inclined to the whip hand than he should have been.

"It was not a great call to make," Price says. "My boy's on the team, and I've got another boy in graduate school. I know that those calls are the worst calls a parent can receive. You know, in the middle of the night, the phone rings. 'Oh, boy,' you say. 'It's one of the kids.'"

Waldron made arrangements for his wife to fly to Spokane later that morning. He jumped into his car for what is normally a five-hour drive. He got there by six-thirty that morning. "I met the doctor," Waldron says. "He showed me Buddy's CAT scan, and he told me what the injuries were. He indicated that Buddy would never recover." Waldron agreed that Buddy could be left on life support long enough for his body parts to be removed for transplants. Then he and the rest of the family, which had gathered by this time, visited Buddy one last time before the doctor shut off the machines.

Saadat, who'd lost his left hand in the blast, had been flown by helicopter to Harborview Medical Center, in Seattle. Price went there, too. On April 21, Saadat told him about the accident, that the two of them had just wanted to blow up their bomb in a wheat field. Price arranged for a steady stream of Washington State alumni, especially former players, to come and visit Saadat.

Back in Pullman, the Cougars were angry and confused. They were furious at the news media, which had dragged up Buddy's burglary bust in an attempt, they thought, to make him out to be some sort of campus wild man. However, it was more than that. Pullman is a small town. It hadn't seen anything like this since a local man had died during the Tylenol poisoning scare in 1982. The local police launched an immediate investigation. So did the federal Bureau of Alcohol, Tobacco and Firearms, still smarting a bit from the twin fiascoes of Randy Weaver (whose wife and son had died at the hands

of ATF) and David Koresh. Given that the area's police forces generally had been edgy ever since the bombs had detonated in Moscow
two months earlier, this latest inexplicable pipe-bomb explosion,
only a few miles up the road, sent everyone quivering into red alert.

The police in Idaho quickly dismissed the notion that the explo-
sions there were connected to the Pullman bomb. However, from
the start, it became clear that the Feds found Saadat's explanation at
least partly implausible. After all, sources argue, the two men had
lived in Pullman for more than three years. If they wanted to get to a
wheat field, they would have known how to get to a wheat field, instead of turning the truck into the tightly packed residential area
around Irving Street. "Like they say," says one law-enforcement
source, "you can't get there from here."

Rumors flew thick and fast, cluttering the investigation more than
helping it. It was revealed that Saadat had collapsed on the lawn belonging to Laurel Holth, a graduate assistant in whose laboratory
Saadat worked. Soon, people were calling the police to tell them that
Holth and Saadat had been having an affair, and that the two players
had gone over to blow up Holth's husband. (Laurel and Allan Holth
were not available for comment.) "There was no substance for that
one at all," says a source close to the investigation. "How're you going to keep an affair like that secret in Pullman?"

More intriguing was the possibility that Waldron and Saadat were
going up to the trailer park to perform a kind of vigilante raid on
some drug dealers said to be living there. After all, Waldron's previous run-in with the law involved being shot at by an alleged dealer,
and the police suspected that Buddy had decided to begin his career
with the DEA a little sooner than was wise. All the inquiries were
concluded by the end of July, and both the Pullman P.D. and ATF
handed their results over to the United States attorney in Spokane
for possible prosecution.

There was a funeral for Buddy Waldron in Seattle and a memorial
service for him in Pullman. Afterward, Harvey Waldron went home
to Bellevue to mourn. It was a long summer. "We had planned on
doing so much this summer," he says. "So every week, there's some
reminder of something we won't be doing. There's no way I could've

been closer to my son that I was. We lived our lives together. You can't explain what it's like to lose your blood that way. It's like I haven't gotten off the ground yet. Like last night, right? We were watching that movie *The Last of the Mohicans*. There's that scene at the end when the father kills that guy who killed his son. That hit me right between the eyes."

The police were respectful, and so were the federal authorities. Then, one day, a reporter from the *New York Post* called. The reporter jived Harvey Waldron a little. "Payam?" the reporter asked. "Is that Italian?"

"I told the guy to give me a break," Waldron says.

The reporter obviously had been clever enough to make Payam Saadat as Islamic. Eventually, the reporter got around to asking Waldron, quite nicely, if Buddy had helped bomb the World Trade Center.

The black Jeep sits in the late-August sun on Main Street, in front of a cappuccino bar just west of Grand Boulevard. The students are coming back in great bunches now, greeting one another raucously all over downtown. There is talk of summer jobs and distant romances. There is talk of the upcoming football season, and about how Drew Bledsoe will do with the New England Patriots, the doom-struck NFL team to which he has been indentured. Occasionally, someone will stop on the sidewalk and point at the black Jeep. At those moments especially, Pullman is a very small town.

"The hardest thing has been coming back here to face the music," muses Saadat. "Most people wouldn't come back to the place where their lives almost ended. Definitely, I know what people are thinking. Regardless of how many people come up and shake my hand, I know there are a few people who are, like, 'What was this stupid kid thinking about, building a bomb?' But none of those people have come up to me, and that's the way I prefer it.

"I mean, I'm known here. My house. My car. I'm known in this town. Before, it was because I drove an old mail truck. Now, it's because I almost blew up the freaking town or something. My way of fighting all that is to come back to town, to come back to play."

Saadat says he remembers everything clearly. The little buzz the bomb made before it blew up in Buddy's face. The truck's sudden surge into the parked car. He remembers staggering out and collapsing on Laurel Holth's lawn, and the urgent voices of the people who worked on him. "I knew what was happening," he says. "I saw my left hand, and I knew it was gone. Then everyone showed up. Policemen were with me first, and then the paramedics were there. One guy was over me for a good long time, holding my vessels because I was bleeding pretty badly. After that, it felt like the whole world was up there." He was conscious through the helicopter ride to Seattle. "I was thinking about what the rest of my life would be like without a left hand," he recalls. "I was thinking about Buddy. I was thinking about whether I was going to live, whether the next breath would be my last. I was thinking about my parents, the pain I'd be causing my parents with the phone call they were probably getting right then." He finally passed out, just after landing.

At Harborview, the first doctor who talked to him told him how lucky he was. After all, Saadat had been holding the bomb when it went off. "He was the one who told me that Buddy had passed away," Saadat says. "Then he told me, 'Look, I've treated a lot of people in situations like this.' He told me, 'You could've lost your right hand, too. You could easily have lost your left leg, your eyes.' I was blessed to be in the hands I was in."

His parents flew in from Santa Monica the night after the explosion. While Payam and his sister were born in this country, the family returned to Iran to live for a year, in 1978. They came back to the United States just ahead of the ayatollah's revolution, and Payam's father landed a job as a government accountant. His mother, particularly, was overwhelmed by the attention paid to her son by Cougars past and present. "I think that's when she got a whole different feeling for what her son was a part of," says Mike Price. "I mean, the chemistry or biology teacher doesn't fly right over and spend three days."

Saadat spent eleven days in the hospital and almost three months in occupational therapy learning to use the prosthesis that occasionally takes the place of his missing hand. Buttoning his coat has become a chore; tying his shoes, almost an impossibility. "My therapists really opened my eyes to what my problems are going to be," he says. "They said, 'Your frustration is going to hinder you. If you feel yourself getting frustrated, just put it down and do it later.'" More often, he leaves the device behind. His left arm ends just below the elbow. His right hand is thick with scar tissue from his burns, and there is a red patch on his right thigh.

The Pullman police questioned him extensively, as did ATF agents, who were rather less gentle. He's heard all the rumors, especially the speculations inspired by his heritage. Neither Saadat nor his sister was raised in the Islamic tradition, but he is Iranian, and there was a bomb, and that was enough for some people. "I heard about them hearing from New York. I heard about them trying to hook me up with something in Idaho, but that's their job," he says. "They have to look at the whole picture. I can't do anything except keep telling my story. They've got to go after what they got. They hear 'Payam Saadat,' they hear 'Middle Eastern.' They got to open those doors, too."

It is unlikely that the local authorities will charge him with anything. They appear to have handed the whole matter over to the U.S. attorney. If Saadat is charged, it will be with a federal crime—a felony. "Back then," he says, "I was kind of worried about it. Now I'm less worried. Now it's like, 'If you're going to give me something, give me something. I know what I did. If you guys want to charge me, charge me. Charge me federally, charge me state. Just do it.'

"They can't accept that it was just a tragic accident. They can't leave it at that. I'm just upset that it's taking so long. If you're going to do something, do it now. Let's get this whole thing over with."

He is doing some coaching this fall, working with the Washington State linebackers, and he is trying to get ready to play again next season. "My job is to make plays," Saadat says. "I'll worry about the ball coming straight at me when it happens."

He is back in the weight room at dawn again, alone these days. "I won't get over it," he says. "It's a part of me now. It's a constant reminder of how quick I could get taken off this earth, a constant reminder of Buddy. The whole incident will always be in my head."

Buddy Waldron's heart saved a father of five; his liver saved a woman from Seattle. One of his kidneys has given life to a woman in Alaska, and the other went to someone in San Francisco. Burn victims have some of his skin, and his bones are helping several people walk again. These are the most distant reverberations of the explosion on Irving Street, which will echo with Payam Saadat the longest, faint but full, the way sound will as it rolls down the hills and into the valleys and across the wheat fields that spread like great rumpled quilts across the queer topography of the land.

Payam Saadat graduated from WSU in 1994. He is now an assistant football coach at Western Washington University in Bellingham, Washington. No criminal charges were ever brought against him in connection with the Pullman bomb.

GQ November 1993

Fade to Black

Still and cool, like a pool of chill water far up in the sun-pummeled Carolina mountains, Chuck Thorpe is looking at a two-foot putt for the tournament. This moment never changes, whether you're playing at Royal St. Andrews, or at the Buncombe County Golf Course in Asheville, N.C. Whether the putt will win you the British Open, or the 31st annual Sky View Open Pro-Am, the moment is stuck fast and timeless. You course like bright water through 18 regulation holes and three playoff holes, and you come up to this putt, and you gather all of that up in one spot, the way a mountain stream levels out into a tiny, icy pond. Framed tall against the Smokies, Chuck Thorpe looks at this putt, so cool that he almost seems to hiss in the fat, waveless air.

It's hard to hear The Golf Boom here on the third green at Buncombe County, as Chuck Thorpe and a man named Bobby Strobel play down for the Sky View championship, one of the few tournaments that is flourishing on the fading North American Golf Assocation tour. The NAGA, long the only place where talented black golfers could play the game, is losing ground because one generation of players has aged, and because there has been no following generation come along to take its place. It's hard to hear The Golf Boom at Buncombe County, where there isn't enough money to buy rotary blades for the lawn mowers.

In truth, The Golf Boom is a lot like the Economic Recovery of the early 1980s. Your perception of it depends quite vitally on where you happen to have been standing when it hit. The Economic Recovery looked great in Grosse Pointe, but not so splendid in southwest Detroit. Similarly, The Golf Boom sounds like Los Alamos, if you happen to be standing on the first tee at Congressional with Vice President Skippy—or, for that matter, inside the front gate to Shoal Creek, where some ignorant turkeyneck labors at the public resurrection of John C. Calhoun. Out here at Buncombe County, with the Sky View Open trying to hang on to what's left of a dying tour, The Golf Boom is damned near inaudible.

(And, lest you think the comparison a labored one, consider that David Hueber, the CEO of the Ben Hogan Co., and former president of the National Golf Foundation, recently told PGA Magazine that The Golf Boom will continue because, among college students, "We've had a pretty radical change from the '60s . . . Now, that college student wants a nice house, wants a job. Golf's a part of that fabric." Ah, it's morning in America. Unfortunately, some folks are lying five.)

But golf is not necessarily The Golf Boom. Golf is still you against the course, and those 14 miserable Iagos in your bag, and your own tremulous self. And if the fairways are baked into green slabs, and if the clubs are dinged and cranky from having been bounced around from tournament to tournament in the trunk of an aging gold Cadillac, the essential golfing self is still the same, despite how many corporate logos may or may not be hung upon it. The essential golfing self looks at a two-footer for the tournament and feels the ripples rising in that still, cool pond.

"Love of the game," says Billy Gardenhight, the NAGA national treasurer who was a pro on the circuit for 20 years, and who founded the Sky View Open. "If you're like me, and like a lot of other people, you sacrifice to keep doing what you're doing. You sacrifice a lot out here, because you're not getting the money that the other people are getting.

"You know, my head is hard. I've been beating it against the wall since the day I was born about stuff like this, and I'll keep on banging it because I've seen a little change. Some people say there was a lot of change, but that's bull. There ain't been too much of a change because you got the same people doing the same things they've always been doing."

Chuck Thorpe looks at his championship putt for a long time. Seconds before, Strobel had looked at the same putt from the other side of the hole and, the ripples in the pond rising into whitecaps, he had stabbed it off to the right. That handed Thorpe his chance.

He calibrates the putt with infinite care. He clears the line of tiny obstacles, some of which may actually exist. Bobby Strobel silently fumes at Thorpe's dilatory meticulousness. In fact, Gardenhight and Thorpe annually fuss at each other over what Gardenhight's believes is Thorpe's deliberately slow play. Finally, Thorpe bends over the ball. His putt takes a slice of the left lip of the cup. And spins out.

One more playoff hole. At least one more. One more chance to make the long, cool river tun straight and true. At least one more. Strobel and Thorpe, victims both, walk off toward the next tee, playing another hole of golf, enduring the damnable game a little while longer, for love and for whatever thin money happens to be left.

It all began on Mondays, early Monday mornings in the old South, the second old South, the one that began at Appomattox and ended at the Edmund Pettis Bridge in Selma, Ala. Early Monday mornings, bright with birdsong. There would be a country club, and all the members would be white men, and all the caddies would be black, and none of them would be called men no matter what age they were. On Mondays, the caddies would be allowed to play the course. Sometimes, there would even be a tournament.

The caddies played with whatever old clubs were lying about. No one ever had a full set. No foursome ever had a full set. They would throw the clubs to each other, back and forth across the fairways. Some improvisation was inevitably necessary. For example, a caddy named Bobby Bethea once had to putt an entire round with a sand wedge. Later, when he was a touring pro on the NAGA circuit and had grown wise in the ways of the world, Bobby Bethea met a man one day on the putting green. This man thought he could putt. Not only that, but it was his wallet that had convinced him. Fine, said Bobby Bethea, I'll putt you with, oh, this sand wedge right here.

"I aced him four holes in a row," Bethea says now. "You have to be in this game a long time."

There was a rich tradition of African Americans playing golf, but few of the caddies knew very much about it. In 1899, a black dentist named Dr. George Grant registered U.S. Patent No. 638,920, which only happened to be the tee. In the 1920s, Dewey Brown was the first black member of the PGA. And, in 1926, a group of golf-playing doctors from Washington, D.C., organized the United Golf Association in Stow, Mass., having been forced north to play by the Jim Crow laws that held sway in the nation's capital. Blacks also had opportunities to play at the black colleges, and in the armed forces.

The UGA represented the best black players, including Walter Speedy in Chicago, and Harold Wheeler, who hit everything crosshanded and looked on every swing as though he would break his arms off above the wrists. The UGA never represented a majority of the black golfers, but it managed to roll on for several decades.

Still, Jim Crow was positively negligible compared with the social and cultural barriers that loomed behind the legal ones. The Shoal Creek flap ought to illustrate that golf, especially tournament golf, exists in a context of privilege the institutions of which are peculiarly indisposed to change. This is hardly a new thing. In the 1930s, an unwritten PGA rule held that blacks were acceptable as caddies, but not as players. (This is also the decade in which Augusta National graciously employed boxing champion Beau Jack . . . as a bootblack.) By 1943, the PGA had adopted an amendment to its constitution that declared the organization to be the province of "the professional golfers of the Caucasian race." Five years later, in the face of a lawsuit, the PGA threw out the amendment, but a clear and public statement had been made, one that echoes all the way to Birmingham and the 1990 tournament of that same PGA.

The caddies grew up, and they stayed with the game, playing where they could. Tournaments sprang up, especially in the southeastern United States. The pros would play for whatever purse could be cobbled up from the entry fees—usually about $100 a man—and for whatever they could make on spirited side-betting. "Out here," says Chuck Thorpe, "you gambled, or you didn't eat." They bet low-medal, and they bet so much per side, and, if you were real lucky like Bobby Bethea was, you ran into someone who didn't know that, by being a caddy in the second Old South, there were some kinds of golf that you didn't learn on the clubhouse veranda.

"Those guys were great because they learned to shoot par golf on courses that the average good pro wouldn't even play on," says Billy Gardenhight. "I mean, no grass. Dirt. Snakes. Everything. Those guys were shotmakers because, some of them, they didn't even have a full set of clubs out there as pros."

It was a scuffling life. The pros traveled four to a car. "Back then," laughs Gardenhight, "cars had real trunks, so you could travel with four sets of clubs." There weren't always hotels that would take them in, or restaurants that would feed them, or gas stations that would let them use the facilities, this being the second Old South and all. "The older guys would tell the younger guys," says Gardenhight. "You'd get the word that this place was all right, and that you should stay away from that place."

There were legends among them, just as there were in the Negro Baseball leagues. Crosshand Wheeler was one, and the three Browns: Cliff, Pete and Lefty. And Ted Rhodes, who may have been the best of them all. "He was one of the best strikers of the ball who ever lived," explains Eddie Harris, a former pro who coaches golf at Johnson C. Smith University. "But he never got a chance to go around the world and prove it."

Finally, a cold, hard man named Charlie Sifford came out of this little circuit and broke on to the PGA Tour for good. "Charlie always said that what he did was harder than what Jackie Robinson did, because Jackie had a team around him and Charlie had nobody," says Eddie Harris. "See, Charlie was good enough, and tough enough, and especially *mean* enough to take the punch." Then, in 1975, a protege of Ted Rhodes's named Lee Elder went to Augusta and personally brought the Masters into the 1950s. A man can only do so much.

"The greatest pro I ever saw was Teddy Rhodes, and the next was Lee Elder," says Harris. "Now, Lee won. But, if Lee could've gone on that tour 10 years before they let him, you'd have seen the real Lee Elder."

For a time, and in its own way, this little circuit thrived. Some 60 or 70 pros made a marginal living at it, and many of them became bona fide celebrities. A tournament was more than simply a golf competition. It was a community event, and many of them culminated in the Presentation Ball, a dance party held after the final round.

In 1968, in Jekyll Island, Ga., a group of small golf associations that had run these tournaments throughout the southeastern United States banded together to form the North American Golf Association. The UGA, which always represented only the very top pros, had withered, and the NAGA is its most immediate successor. Which means that it is the NAGA that is trying to hold on against the pressures that may end the black golf tour once and for all.

Some of the forces at work are all too familiar. Black tournaments, and the pros who play in them, are often unable to find sponsors. There is a lot of barely controlled bitterness at this. "We'll go to a big grocery store and ask them for some money," says Gardenhight. "They'll give us a couple hundred dollars. But the club across town, the country club, they'll give them $25,000, and their tournament won't draw as many people as ours will, and it won't be as good a tournament. But they'll turn that money loose for the white folks."

"You'll hear a lot of guys out here saying, 'We can't get sponsored, but the white boys always get sponsored.' Which they certainly do," says Bobby Bethea. "You got to be a Calvin Peete to get one off of here."

Aside from all this, nothing has dealt a more serious blow to the NAGA tour—and to black golf in general—than has the development and popularity of the golf cart. More golf carts means fewer caddies, and caddying was the heart and start of golf among the last four generations of black players. As those players get older, there are fewer and fewer younger players coming along to take their place because nobody is playing on those bright Mondays any more.

"Now, without caddying, black kids aren't exposed to golf the way they used to be," says Gardenhight. "It's hard to get kids involved when they don't know anything about it. It's easy to get involved in football and basketball when you can play it every day."

The number of fulltime pros who play on the NAGA tour is now down into the low 20s. Age has taken some of them, and still more can't make ends meet, and not even hustling on the side helps any more. "The purses stay the same, or they drop," explains Joe Johnson, "but those motels keep going up." Of course, this accelerates a ruthless spiral. Because NAGA tournaments cannot get sponsors, their purses are dependent upon steadily rising entry fees, which in turn depend upon a dwindling number of pros who can afford them.

While Gardenhight proudly boasts that the Sky View never has had to cut its announced purse—$1,600 this year—many other tournaments award far less than had been advertised simply because not enough pros showed up to make the nut. On the weekend before the Sky View, the Green Turf Open in Knoxville announced a $1,500 first place prize. Winner Chip Oliver took home $1,050. Other tournaments simply have folded altogether.

Consequently, most of the pros on the tour now are "working pros," which means they hold down fulltime jobs elsewhere and schedule their annual vacations so they can play at least a piece of the NAGA tour. Bobby Bethea and Joe Johnson both work for the R.J. Reynolds Co. Jimmy Moore, who plays the way that Harold Wheeler did and is known as Crosshand Carolina, will retire in October after 30 years with the Lorillard Co. in Greensboro. Only then will he become a full-time pro on the NAGA circuit.

"I was lucky. I never had to live in no car, though I know some guys that did," says Bethea. "If I could put forth what some of those guys put forth, I might be on the tour myself some day. But I had a good job myself, at $35–$40,000 a year. I says to myself, when I go some place to play golf, I says, 'I already got mine when I get there.'"

This tour is almost out of stars. They can't afford it any more.

"Like Chuck Thorpe," says Crosshand Carolina. "I beat him last week in Florida. It kills him. We weren't in a tournament, but we was gambling, and that's the same thing."

He walks alone, swiftly moving away from his playing partners, and figuratively apart from the tour that's been his livelihood, but that's dying all around him. The rest of the foursome climbs into a cart, and they all drive out to the area where their tee shots have landed. But Chuck Thorpe almost never rides. After hitting his drive— which he has teed up on a mound of dirt, eschewing Dr. Grant's invention—Thorpe strides off straight down the fairway. Billy Jackson, who's caddied for Thorpe for 21 years, rides the cart far behind him.

"I could be bitter," Thorpe says. "But I learned a long time ago that that never helps. It was a hard lesson. Man, that was some hard schooling."

He is the oldest of five children born to a greenskeeper and his wife in Roxborough, N.C. All five Thorpe boys grew up on a golf course, and they all played professionally, starting on the NAGA tour. One of them, a big hitter named Jim, beat all the odds and became a solid player on the PGA Tour, where today he makes big money while curiously warping time for the readers of America's scoreboard pages ("JIM THORPE 71-70-72-70").

Chuck was up there for a while, too. But he lost his place in the big time. Some people say he wasn't good enough. Other people say he took to the nightlife too hard. Nobody quite knows why for certain, and Chuck's not talking. He is back in the NAGA, playing for entry fees. In Knoxville, he tied for second and brought home (officially) $630.

Nevertheless, he is an undeniable star out here. He's about the only player at the Sky View who had his own gallery, albeit one that fluctuated between 15 and about 40 people. He is affable enough around the clubhouse. Everybody he meets is, "Pro." As in, "Hey, Pro." Or, "What's up, Pro?" Or, "You hittin' today, Pro?" Once, it appears, Pro was the very nicest thing you ever could call somebody.

"There was pride to it," says Chuck. "You got called that, and you knew you made it."

There is about him, however, a singular aloofness, a core of impenetrable mystery. Some people say that he's carrying the hurt of his failure on the big tour. He is almost never where he is supposed to be, making appointments and then failing to show up. He even once suggested that some people meet him at a party in the Asheville motel where most of the golfers were staying. The people showed up.

Chuck never made it. Rare indeed is a man who no-shows his own party.

"You know Chuck," said one of the other golfers. "He's hanging out."

Pinned down briefly, he talks only in the broadest strokes, generally agreeing with whatever perception is tossed at him. "I got 140 tournament wins, all around the world," he says. "Guys like me, Teddy Rhodes, Bill Spiller, Zeke Hartsfield, all those guys, we all played 90 percent of the tournaments under difficult conditions.

"I came back down here, and I stayed angry all the time. Older I got, though, the more I figured it didn't matter. Things'd always get better. They always do."

He goes off to play—"Thanks, Pro"—and he looks for just a moment like the living embodiment of his whole sport. He will talk later, he says. He never will. He will go off and play golf, striding along the hard fairways as though he's the fenceline of his own private property. He's so good that he always tees off late in the day. When Chuck Thorpe walks apart and alone down the last fairway of the day, the sun usually is going down behind him.

He wins it finally on the fifth playoff hole. He knocks a 9-iron within four feet of the pin—inside 100 yards of the flag, Chuck Thorpe will make you a poor person very quickly—and, this time, he drops the putt right in the heart of the hole. He is the champion of the 31st Sky View Open Pro-Am tournament. He will make (officially) $1,500.

There is a palpable connection between these people and the history of their sport, whereas the PGA Tour has become opulently faithful to the present, and as false as blue money to its past. The primary appeal of the Seniors Tour is as a kind of living museum, a doubleknit Colonial Williamsburg. Affluent geezers aside, you probably could draw the connection between Mark Calcavecchia and Ben Hogan, but to what purpose? It's like tracing the links between the

New Kids On The Block and the Drifters. It doesn't illlustrate evo-
lution, just change. If the sport truly had evolved, they'd be playing
the PGA Championship at a different golf course this year.

But the past is all the NAGA has now, because the present isn't all
that different. Watching Chuck Thorpe, you can see the crossroads
where all the back roads meet. You can see Lee Elder and Charlie
Sifford, Ted Rhodes and Crosshand Wheeler, and a whole course
filled with caddies on a bright Monday morning, clubs flashing silvery in the air as they fly from hand to hand. The Golf Boom is distant and vain. Here, you play for what you can get—a new bag, a thin
check, somebody else's cash, and the chance to dance all night at the
Presentation Ball.

*In 1993, the African-American Golf Association was founded and estab-
lished a national tour with seven stops. The smaller tours survive as remnants. Somewhere, Chuck Thorpe is playing on one of them. Jim Thorpe
plays regularly on the PGA's Senior Tour.*

The National August 1, 1990

Junior Johnson
Has Left the Building

Fat with rain and veined with lightning, the gray sky presses down on the North Carolina foothills, squeezing out any little bit of spring that might have slipped into the valleys and hollows. The men out by the barn hurry to finish their work. They are moving the bent engine cover of a rusty old tractor, hoisting it onto the bed of a truck and trying to beat the rain and lightning that's past due from the silent western mountains.

One man stands in the truck bed, a gray Ford Motor Company ball cap on his head. He steadies the heavy chunk of corroded steel as they swing it up toward him, all the while looking far down the road, past all his strolling and stolid cows, watching for the rain. Junior Johnson is old now, but with a new wife, a new baby and a genuine mansion tucked away off old Route 421 in Yadkin County. He is no country squire, however. He is a working farmer, tending to his stock and to his fields, hoisting the odd chunk of metal when need be, alert and sharp because there was a time when being alert and sharp was all that kept him from a fiery, clattering death, when being alert and sharp was enough to keep him safe, and famous and rich.

He drove cars swiftly for a living. He ran the 'shine down the back roads here, and he did it so recklessly and so well that when a redneck dreamer named Bill France, Sr. decided in 1947 to make a professional sport out of moonshine running, Johnson signed right up. He drove those cars so recklessly and so well that he got legally rich and legally famous, and he became an authentic American legend— the Last American Hero, Tom Wolfe called him, so many years ago.

"I can't believe people still remember that story," says Johnson, whose life—it can be safely said—prepared him for many things but not for anthologies. "Come on in the barn; we'll talk."

He unfolds himself into a battered folding chair. He's portly and strong, and he moves slowly now, but his eyes haven't changed. They flicker like gunports, quickly and with serious purpose. They miss very little. That's how he saw all those government men lurking in the dark hollows at midnight in their slow government cars. That's how he saw Lee Petty or Ned Jarrett or old Ralph Earnhardt sneaking by him low on the track to steal his money at Talladega, or trying to take him high in turn four at North Wilkesboro, his home track in North Carolina, where they all helped build the sport that's made the sons of Lee Petty and Ned Jarrett and especially of old Ralph Earnhardt so spectacularly wealthy that the sport of racing stock cars has outgrown not only places like North Wilkesboro but perhaps the entire South as well.

"It's lost that old southern spirit, that's for sure," Johnson says. "You got people in California and New York and out in Phoenix, Arizona, involved now." The way he says "Phoenix, Arizona," rolling every syllable around like someone taking his first class in a foreign tongue, makes it sound as though he might as well be sitting in his barn talking about the moons of Neptune. "Phoenix, Arizona," he repeats softly, and his eyes move again into the distance. In the silence, you can hear the whine of a single powerful car running down the mountains ahead of the swift, slicing rain.

"You can say it's lost its soul," Junior Johnson says softly. "But it's making a lot of money."

NASCAR—the National Association for Stock Car Auto Racing— has always sold itself as a sport of the common man and, moreover, of the common southerner. But it is no more populist than is the PGA Tour, and it is no more southern than the National Hockey

League is Canadian. It trades on both these things, and it profits greatly in the process, but it is not *of* these things. Not anymore. Not in the way it was when Bill France was cutting sharp deals with every shitkicker pol, from county commissioners all the way up to his good friend the Guv'nah. It was Alabama's George Corley Wallace himself who gave France the land to build Talladega Motor Speedway so that France's cars could race each other someplace besides Daytona. France obliged by raising gobs of money for Wallace's various attempts to make himself our national gauleiter. (In 1972, with Wallace shot half-dead and George McGovern as the Democratic presidential nominee, Bill France shrugged off his party loyalties and raised money for Nixon.) Bill France was a one-man Southern Strategy.

From its founding, NASCAR was suffused with the backlash ethos of the 1970s—ambitious people in every field realizing there was money and power to be had in Wallace's astonishing discovery that (in many important ways) the whole country was southern. When the Guv'nah cracked that great secret of the American demographic code, Bill France's sport was already there on the track, idling heavily. Today, wildly popular and ludicrously profitable, it is nothing like it pretends to be. It is corporate connivance dressed up as populist celebration, careful contrivance masquerading as raucous authenticity. It has become, in short, simply another American sport, and the distance it has traveled is that same distance that got us from Huey Long to Newt Gingrich, from William Faulkner to John Grisham and from Patsy Cline to Shania Twain. How you feel about that pretty much depends on how much you like Gingrich's thinking, Grisham's writing and whatever it is that Shania Twain does besides looking like the most popular lap dancer in Dogpatch. How you feel about NASCAR pretty much depends on your individual tolerance for ersatz crackerism sanctified by the *Fortune* 500—which, come to think of it, is pretty much the formula that won the Republicans all those elections since Bill France turned his coat in '72.

There is little arguing with NASCAR's success. France's first flash of genius came when he realized that there was an audience to be gained by putting onto the track cars not dissimilar to the ones many of the fans would drive home from the stamping plant. Suddenly, there was a bit of the sleeping panther to the family Fairlane. That was the original connection made between NASCAR and its audience, and the connection remains solid today. Its fans remain fiercely devout and frighteningly informed—as regards the nuances of their chosen sport, NASCAR fans are the most sophisticated and knowledgeable in America, and nobody else is close. With the IndyCar circuit tied up in hopeless internal wrangling, and with Formula 1 still primarily the province of anonymous Brazilian astronauts, stock-car racing likely will remain the country's motor sport of choice well into the next century.

It is a massive business now. It costs almost $6 million to run a single team through a single Winston Cup season. A new speedway can cost up to $120 million to build, largely because the various corporate sponsors are beginning to require that luxury suites be included at every new track, just as they are required now at every new stadium and in every new arena.

As with every other sport, the fan must decide on his own how much charlatanism and fakery he is willing to tolerate before his internal bullshit receptor blows a gasket. There are moments within the NASCAR experience in which the pressure builds far past critical. Dale Earnhardt last year made more than $30 million just on the various gewgaws and trinkets bearing his name. That means that, without even getting into his car, he made more than ten times as much money in a single year as Junior Johnson did over thirteen years and 313 races. And still, the fiction that sells all those $20 T-shirts bearing his visage is that Earnhardt, like all of the other good-ol'-boy millionaires he chases around the circuit, is just one of us.

Moreover, NASCAR's panjandrums increasingly talk about the sport as though it were simply a marketing tool, commercials making left-hand turns at 117 miles per hour.

"We're more sophisticated," says Bruton Smith, who owns the speedways outside Charlotte and Atlanta and who's about to open the biggest one of all, outside Dallas. "We are dollar driven. When you see the *Fortune* 500 companies getting involved, what are they getting? Number one, they're getting exposure for their product.

We find that our fans are intensely loyal to the product. If there's a product on one of these cars and a product on the shelf next to it, our fans will pick up the product that's on that car.

"I think it's wonderful. A lot of the financial magazines are looking at our sport since we went to Wall Street. I took Speedway Motorsports Inc., public last year. That alerted the financial institutions. In fact, just thirty minutes ago, our stock hit an all-time high of 49 1/2." Bruton Smith looks very pleased. That is the way it is today. Speedways are on the Big Board.

What this means is that, when a NASCAR fan attaches himself to a driver, the fan is automatically linked to that driver's product. Those people in the T-shirts with Earnhardt's name also carry that of Mr. Goodwrench. A Jeff Gordon devotee covers himself in rainbows that shill for Du Pont. And Terry Labonte's fans find themselves thickly festooned with the Kellogg's rooster. To be a NASCAR fan is to be a voluntary public billboard. This also means that the driver is not simply a driver; he is a spokesman for a major corporation.

"I can't say that the drivers are better today," says Ned Jarrett, a former champion driver and a current ESPN analyst. Jarrett is a gentle soul who once drove like a demon and whose son, Dale, this year won the Daytona 500. "If you include the ability to represent his sport and represent his sponsor, if you include the fact that a driver is articulate, then they are better today. As for the physical ability to drive the race car, I don't see any difference."

What this means is that any interview with any driver invariably includes how good the (YOUR SPONSOR HERE) Ford/Chevy/Pontiac was running that day. That shameless plugola is a bow to the sport's present and to its future. And it goes on and on, driver after driver making sure the sponsor's name gets mentioned, talking big-money ragtime until hell won't have it. And do you know what it means?

I'll tell you what it means.

It means they all talk like golfers.

Lord, no.

It didn't take long to choose the Spam car.

It would've been easy to become just another conscript in the Earnhardt legions, but, hell, that would have been like rooting for the Cowboys. (In fact, it's exactly like rooting for the Cowboys. Anyone standing in the souvenir line who buys an Earnhardt product invariably gets booed by at least some of the people standing behind him.) It would've been easy to sign on with Gordon or Labonte, but I look stupid in rainbows and even worse in roosters. But Spam was intriguing—certainly more intriguing on a race car than it ever was in a sandwich. There must be a certain kind of courage that allows a man to drive a tin can with Spam written all over it at speeds in excess of a hundred miles per hour on a track with four dozen other well-financed maniacs.

The very presence of Spam on the starting grid made no sense to me at all. Some sponsors seem perfectly logical: It's hard to argue with race cars that advertise Mr. Goodwrench or Havoline Motor Oil. Some sponsors seem at least culturally appropriate, like Remington firearms and Skoal tobacco. Some of them simply seem inevitable, like MBNA bankcards and the Family Channel. Even so, Spam? The bane of servicemen and high school lunchrooms? *That* Spam?

Indeed.

I became a Spam man. Got me a Spam hat and everything. I did not pay much attention to the fact that Spam is made by Hormel, and that Hormel has a labor-relations record only slightly better than that boasted by the Ottoman Empire, an odd choice of partner for a purportedly populist sport. I became a Spam man anyway. Go, Spam!

Vroom.

The driver of the Spam car is a bustling fellow from Jackson, Mississippi, named Lake Speed, and I am not making that up, either. Speed is as much a self-made NASCAR driver as anyone else on the circuit. He made his first mark racing go-karts; in 1978 he became the first non-European to win the World Karting Championship. In the late 1980s, Speed came back to the United States and ran his own NASCAR team, buying his first race car secondhand from a guy in Chicago. "Shows you what I knew," he says. "If I'da been smart,

I'da bought a NASCAR car down in North Carolina. But I go to Chicago to buy one." He ran his team until his sponsor bailed out on him; then he went to work driving cars for Robert Yates after Yates lost Davey Allison in a helicopter crash at Talladega.

After that he hooked on with Ford, and he ran pretty well until he had a falling-out with his sponsor. Shortly thereafter, Speed got a call from Harry Melling, a veteran NASCAR owner who was looking to rebuild his team. Between 1982 and 1991, with Bill Elliott driving his cars, Melling had had ten fat seasons, winning thirty-four races and more than $10 million. Melling chose Speed not simply because of his record as a driver but also because he knew Speed had built racing teams from scratch before. In 1994 Speed and Melling found a sponsor, and Spam found a race car to bear its name. That is the way it is today. Speedways are on the Big Board, the drivers all talk like golfers, and Spam runs a race car.

Surely, I thought, Speed hears something from the other drivers. I mean, it's one thing to run a car with STP—or even Tide—on the side. It's quite another to run the word Spam up into a guy's dual exhausts at great accelerations. An unusually thoughtful man, one of the leaders in NASCAR's weekly chapel services, Speed ponders the question. "Not too much," he muses. "Everybody else in racing knows that if you don't have the money to race, you can't race. When it comes down to it, having a sponsor and not having a sponsor is the difference between continuing to operate and people having to go look for other jobs. So, no, it's not something most people laugh about. Most people inside racing take sponsorship very seriously."

He is in deadly earnest. Lake Speed has lost sponsors; he has scuffled to find a new one. He understands what stock-car racing has become; after all, last season, without finishing higher than sixth in any race, Lake Speed won $529,435, more than twice as much as in 1988, when he won the only race of his NASCAR career. NASCAR is not even necessarily about winning and losing. It's about consistency, about staying at the front of the pack, where the cameras are, about not bending the logo so badly in one of the turns that the folks at home can't read it. Lake Speed was in no position to be choosy about a sponsor in a sport in which the Cartoon Network runs a car with

Fred Flintstone painted on its trunk. This is the way it is in NASCAR today. Spam is no laughing matter.

God love North Wilkesboro. Junior Johnson's old swaybacked track even has a grandstand named after him now, and the grandstand looks far less solid and dependable than Junior does, truth be told. The track is tucked away in the foothills of the Appalachians, and there are actual people with actual houses built right up onto the fringes of the property. It carries that sharp tang of history the way Fenway Park does and the way the old Forum in Montreal once did. Needless to say, it likely will disappear from NASCAR in the way that we lost the Forum this season and in the way that we must lose Fenway sometime in the next decade. There is a brawl over its NASCAR dates now. Bruton Smith wants one of them for his new supertrack in Texas, and a man named Bob Bahre wants the other date for his track in New Hampshire. That is the way it is today. Speedways are on the Big Board, the drivers all talk like golfers, Spam runs a race car, and NASCAR can no longer run at North Wilkesboro because it has to run in New Hampshire.

Built in 1947, not long after Bill France started dreaming his dream, the North Wilkesboro track is a short one, a little more than six-tenths of a mile around. It cannot accommodate the larger fields that are the result of modern corporate sponsorship. "Tell you the truth," says Lake Speed, "I don't think we should run anywhere that can't accommodate a full field. It's not fair to the sponsors or the drivers or everybody else who works so hard to get ready for a race."

There is an authenticity to the place, though, a sense of finding something that is, increasingly, lost. Richard Petty still comes, angling through the garage area like a hawk through tangled woods. People wander up—NASCAR must hand out garage passes at Kmart—and they simply stand next to him while someone else takes their picture. Petty taxes even Elvis Presley for the pole position in the race for the right to be called the King. To chat with him means that you run the risk of appearing in every photo album south of the Mason-Dixon line. "Come on over here," Petty whispers. "We stand there, we can start getting in the way of things."

This fall Richard Petty will be the Republican candidate for secretary of state in North Carolina. This seems laudably public-spirited but strangely disproportionate. After all, this man is already Richard Petty, which ought to be enough for one lifetime. Why does he want to hitch all that wonderful lore and legend to a banal political office suited only to ambitious aldermen? Secretary of State Richard Petty? It rings false, like City Councilman Little Richard or State Auditor Iggy Pop. When you're already the King, why run with the courtiers?

"Well," he smiles, "I was a county commissioner for sixteen years. Then I stopped doing that, and I started what we called the Richard Petty PAC to help elect Republican candidates across the state. And 1994 was a good year for Republicans, as you know."

He says some more about politics and his life, but the conversation beaches itself on that one thing—that Richard Petty has a political action committee. At that moment, it becomes clear that Bill France's dream has come to true fruition—that sturdy symbiosis between conservative politics and big business within what would style itself a people's sport. NASCAR has not been transformed; it has been fulfilled. Speedways are on the Big Board, the drivers all talk like golfers, Spam runs a race car, NASCAR can no longer run at North Wilkesboro because it has to run in New Hampshire, and Richard by God Petty has his own PAC. It has come true, all of it, Bill France's golden dream shining on a bright day in the Carolina hills. He was no romantic, the old man. This is exactly where he meant his sport to go.

The race begins, that great tumbling roar with the high whine of machinery at its heart, like the hottest place in the center of a star. Kellogg's wins, beating Du Pont and Mr. Goodwrench to the line, but only because Miller Genuine Draft collides with Little Caesars and drops out of the lead toward the end. It is a fine, competitive race, likely the last NASCAR race ever to run in front of the Junior Johnson Grandstand. It will become a place of echoes now, drowned out by the roar in other, distant places. But the echoes will be there. Only old men will ever hear them.

The Man. Amen

OK. Golf joke.

Jesus Christ and Saint Peter go out to play golf. Saint Peter steps up to the first tee. He's got the sharp designer vines. Even got a brand-new yellow Amana hat. (Amana sewed up a sponsorship deal long before anyone else, and Nike couldn't even get in the door.) Clubheads that gleam in the heavenly light like stars on sticks. Takes out a golden tee. Puts down a fresh Titleist Balata. Smacks it down the fairway for a clean 265, dead center. Ball sits in the green grass like a distant white diamond. Allows himself a little smirk as he steps out of the tee box. Listens carefully to hear if a cock is crowing.

Anyway, Jesus up next. Old robe. Sawdust up to his elbows (somebody needed a coffee table finished that morning). Got a black rock tied to a cane pole. Got a range ball with a red stripe around its middle and a deep slice up one side. Hits the ball with the rock, and it goes straight up in the air. It is plucked away by a passing pileated woodpecker, which flaps off down the fairway toward the green. Stiff head wind blows up. Woodpecker begins to labor. Just over the front fringe of the green, woodpecker suffers a fatal heart attack. Drops the ball onto the back of a passing box turtle. Ball sticks. Turtle carries the ball toward the hole. At the lip of the cup, turtle sneezes.

Ball drops into the hole.

Saint Peter shakes his head.

"You gonna play golf?" he asks Jesus. "Or you gonna fuck around?"

Is this blasphemous?

Is it?

Truly blasphemous?

Truly?

And what would be the blasphemy?

And what would it be?

The punch line? That Saint Peter is said to be using a curse word as regards his Lord and Savior?

No, ma'am. Sorry. Please consult Matthew 26:73–74.

> And after a little while, they came that stood by, and they said to Peter, "Surely, thou art one of them, for even thy speech doth discover thee."
>
> Then he began to curse and to swear that he knew not the man.
>
> And immediately the cock crowed.

Peter was forgiven.

And what would be the blasphemy?

And what would it be?

That our Lord and Savior would play golf?

That He would do anything within His admittedly considerable powers to win?

No, ma'am. Sorry. I believe that Jesus would play to win. I would not want Jesus in a $1,000 Nassau, not even with four shots a side. I do not like my chances at that. No, ma'am, I do not. I believe Jesus would take my money. I believe that He would take it and give it unto the poor, but I believe He would take it. I believe that Jesus would focus. I believe that His ball would not find the rough. I believe that there would be sudden windstorms. I believe that He would find no water, but that if He did, He would walk out and knock one stiff from the middle of the pond. I believe that He would go for the stick on every hole. I believe that the Redeemer cometh and He playeth to win, or else He'd have wound up as merely one of the foremost carpenters in Nazareth. I would not want Jesus in a $1,000 Nassau, not even with four shots a side.

Is this blasphemous?

Is it?

And what would be the blasphemy?

And what would it be?

That there is divinity guiding the game of golf? That the hands of God are on a steel shaft, the fingers of God overlapped and strong, and that the hands of God bring the steel shaft up brightly in the heavenly light—but not past parallel; never past parallel—and then down, hard, to smite the sinful modern world?

Is this blasphemous?

Is it?

In the limo, fresh from a terribly wearisome photo shoot that may only help get him laid about 296 times in the next calendar year, if he so chooses, the Redeemer is pondering one of the many mysteries of professional sports.

"What I can't figure out," Tiger Woods asks Vincent, the limo driver, "is why so many good-looking women hang around baseball and basketball. Is it because, you know, people always say that, like, black guys have big dicks?"

Vincent says nothing right off. Vincent is cool. Vincent played college ball at Memphis State under Dana Kirk, and that is like saying that you rode the range with Jesse James or prowled the White House with Gordon Liddy. Straight outlaw street creds, no chaser. Vincent is sharp. Vincent got into computers back when computers meant Univac, and that is like saying you got into navigation when navigation meant Columbus. Vincent is cool and Vincent is sharp, but Vincent is stumped here for an answer.

He and Tiger have already discussed video games. Tiger likes fighting games. He has no patience for virtual skateboarding. "I get fucking pissed when I've got a station and no games to play on it. It's frustrating," Tiger said. He and Tiger have also discussed the various models of Mercedes automobiles. The day before, Tiger won himself a new Mercedes automobile at a golf tournament outside San

Diego. But it was such an ordinary, respectable Mercedes that Tiger gave it to his mother. Tiger likes the more formidable model of Mercedes that Ken Griffey, Jr. drives. "That is a great fucking car, man," he enthused. Vincent agreed. But then Tiger came up with this question about why all the good-looking women follow baseball and basketball, and he came up with this theory about black men and their big dicks, and Vincent is not ready for the turn that the conversation has taken.

So I step in. It is said to be the case, I begin, trying to give Vincent a moment to regroup, that women follow baseball and basketball closely because those two sports put them in greater proximity to the players.

"What about golf then?" says Tiger, and now I am stumped for an answer.

Vincent finally tells him, "Well, what Mr. Pierce back there says is right, and what you said, well, there's probably some truth to that, too. And the other thing is that there is so much money involved in those two sports that that probably has something to do with it, too." Tiger seems very satisfied with the roundness of this answer. He says nothing for a moment. He looks out the window of the limousine, and he watches the failed condominium developments go passing by.

One day earlier, he had won the Mercedes Championships at the La Costa Resort and Spa. La Costa was the place into which the Mob plowed all that money from the Teamsters pension fund. La Costa is now owned by the Japanese. Jimmy Hoffa must be spinning in the Meadowlands. The Mercedes Championships used to be what the PGA Tour called the Tournament of Champions. All things do change. Still, only golfers who have won a tour event during the previous season are eligible to play in this tournament, which annually kicks off the new tour season. In 1996 Tiger qualified for the Mercedes by winning two of the eight tournaments he entered after joining the tour in September.

At La Costa on Saturday, he birdied the last four holes to move into a tie with Tom Lehman, the 1996 PGA Tour player of the year. On Sunday, however, La Costa was drenched by a winter storm out of the Pacific, and it was determined that Lehman and Woods would play a one-hole play-off for the championship, the $296,000 first prize and the brand-new Mercedes. The official chose the par-three seventh hole, which ran off an elevated tee down to a green bounded by water on the left side. Hundreds of people scurried down through the rain, a great army moving behind a screen of trees, a bustling little loop of humanity shivering under bright umbrellas.

Lehman hit first. He caught his shot fat. It landed on the far bank and hopped backward into the pond, scattering a flock of American coots. (These were genuine American coots—also called mud hens— and not the other, more visibly affluent American coots, some of whom were lining the fairway.) Now, there was virtually no way for Woods to lose the tournament. He could reverse pivot and line up the clubhouse veranda, and he'd still be better off than poor Lehman, who had to function amid the ragged and distant hosannas of Tiger's partisans cheering Lehman's misfortune. Instead, Woods took out a seven-iron. As he followed through, a raindrop fell in his eye, partly blinding him.

The ball damned near went in the hole.

The crowd—his crowd, always his crowd now—did not cheer. Not at first. Instead, what the crowd did was . . . sag. There was a brief, precious slice of time in which the disbelief was sharp and palpable, even in the pulping winter rain. Then the cheers came, and they did not stop until he'd reached the green. He tapped in for the championship, the check and the car, which he gave to his mother.

"All right, here's what happened," Tiger would explain later. "If I hit it toward the middle of the green and my natural draw takes over, then I should be right at the hole. If I hit the iron shot I'd been hitting all week, which was kind of a weak-ass shot to the right, then it should hold against the wind and make it dead straight.

"So I turned it over perfect. I finally hit my natural shot."

And how long did all this calculating take?

"A couple of seconds. Of course, if he'd have hit it close, I probably would've been more aggressive."

The next morning—this morning—a limousine picked him up at his mother's house, and it took him to a photo shoot for the magazine cover that is only going to get him laid 296 times in the next year, if he so chooses. He gave the photographer an hour. One single hour. Sixty minutes, flat, in front of the camera. In the studio, which was wedged into a Long Beach alley behind a copy store and next to Andre's Detailing Shop (if you happen to need an Aztec firebird on your hood in a hurry, Andre's your man), Tiger was dressed in very sharp clothes by four lovely women who attended to his every need and who flirted with him at about warp nine. Tiger responded. Tiger told us all some jokes.

This is one of the jokes that Tiger told:

The Little Rascals are at school. The teacher wants them to use various words in sentences. The first word is *love*. Spanky answers, "I love dogs." The second word is *respect*. Alfalfa answers, "I respect how much Spanky loves dogs." The third word is *dictate*. There is a pause in the room. Finally, Buckwheat puts up his hand.

"Hey, Darla," says Buckwheat. "How my dick ta'te?"

He was rolling now. The women were laughing. They were also still flirting. The clothes were sharp, and the photographer was firing away like the last machine gunner at Passchendaele. And Tiger told jokes. Tiger has not been 21 years old for a month yet, and he tells jokes that most 21-year-olds would tell around the keg in the dormitory late on a Saturday night. He tells jokes that a lot of arrested 45-year-olds will tell at the clubhouse bar as the gin begins to soften Saturday afternoon into Saturday evening.

This is one of the jokes that Tiger told:

He puts the tips of his expensive shoes together, and he rubs them up and down against each other. "What's this?" he asks the women, who do not know the answer.

"It's a black guy taking off his condom," Tiger explains.

He tells jokes that are going to become something else entirely when they appear in this magazine because he is not most 21-year-olds, and because he is not going to be a 45-year-old club pro with a nose spidered red and hands palsied with the gin yips in the morning, and because—through his own efforts, the efforts of his father, his management team and his shoe company, and through some of the most bizarre sporting prose ever concocted—he's become the center of a secular cult, the tenets of which hold that something beyond golf is at work here, something that will help redeem golf from its racist past, something that will help redeem America from its racist past, something that will bring a new era of grace and civility upon the land, and something that will, along the way, produce in Tiger Woods the greatest golfer in the history of the planet. It has been stated—flatly, and by people who ought to know better—that the hand of God is working through Tiger Woods in order to make this world a better place for us all.

Is that blasphemous?

Is it?

There is no place in the gospel of the church of Tiger Woods for jokes like this one:

Why do two lesbians always get where they're going faster than two gay guys?

Because the lesbians are always going sixty-nine.

Is that blasphemous?

Is it?

It is an interesting question, one that was made sharper when Tiger looked at me and said, "Hey, you can't write this."

"Too late," I told him, and I was dead serious, but everybody laughed because everybody knows there's no place in the gospel of Tiger for these sorts of jokes. And Tiger gave the photographer his hour, and we were back in the car with Vincent and heading back toward Tiger's mother's house. "Well, what did you think of the shoot?" Tiger asks, yawning, because being ferried by a limousine and being handled by beautiful women and being photographed for a magazine cover that will get him laid 296 times in the next year, if he so chooses, can be very exhausting work. "The key to it," he says, "is to give them a time and to stick to it. If I say I'm there for an hour, I'm there, on time, for an hour. If they ask for more, I say, 'Hell, fuck no.' And I'm out of there."

Hell, fuck no?

Is that blasphemous?

Is it?

And what would the blasphemy be?

And what would it be?

Can he blaspheme against his own public creation, his own unique role, as determined by his father, his management team and his shoe company? Can he blaspheme against the image coddled and nurtured by the paid evangelists of his own gospel?

Hell, fuck no?

And what would the blasphemy be?

And what would it be?

Can he blaspheme against himself?

God willing, he can.

Two days earlier, while Tiger's father was greeting passersby behind the ninth green at La Costa, Tida Woods was following Tiger around the course. She is a small, bustling woman who occasionally is forced to take a little hop in order to see over the spectators in front of her. On the fifteenth hole, Tiger left his approach shot short of the green.

"Well," Tida said, "Tiger will chip this one in, and we'll go to the next hole."

Tiger chipped the ball, which bounced twice and rolled straight into the cup.

"That boy," said Tida Woods. "I told you he would do that."

She walked on. I stood stunned under a tree for a very long time and wondered about what I had just seen. I think there are pilgrims at Lourdes who look like I did.

This is what I believe about Tiger Woods. These are the articles of my faith.

I believe that he is the best golfer under the age of 30 that there ever has been. I believe that he is going to be the best golfer of any age that there ever has been. I believe that he is going to win more tournaments than Jack Nicklaus won. I believe that he is going to win more major championships than Jack Nicklaus won, and I believe that both of these records are going to stand for Tiger Woods longer than they have stood for Jack Nicklaus. I believe he is going to be rich and famous, and I believe that he is going to bring great joy to a huge number of people because of his enormous talent on the golf course. This is what I believe about Tiger Woods. These are the articles of my faith.

I believe that he is the most charismatic athlete alive today. I believe that his charisma comes as much from the way he plays the game as it does from the way he looks and from what he is supposed to symbolize. I believe that his golf swing—never past parallel—is the most perfect golf swing yet devised. I believe that he is longer off the tee than any good player ever has been, and I believe he is a better player than anyone else longer off the tee. This is what I believe about Tiger Woods. These are the articles of my faith.

I believe that Tiger Woods is as complete a cutthroat as has ever played golf. I do not want Tiger Woods in a $1,000 Nassau, not even with forty shots a side. I believe he would take my money. I believe I would leave the course wearing a barrel. I believe that the shot that won for him at La Costa was not completely about beating Tom Lehman on that afternoon, because Tiger could have used a lemon zester to do that. I believe that shot was for a couple of weeks or a year from now, when Lehman is trying to hold a one-shot lead over Tiger Woods down the stretch in a major tournament. This is what I believe about Tiger Woods. These are the articles of my faith.

This is what I do not believe about Tiger Woods. These are the theses of my heresy.

I do not believe that Tiger Woods was sent to us for any mission other than that of "being a great golfer and a better person," as his father puts it. After all, this is the mission we all have, except for the golf part. (No just and merciful God would demand as the price of salvation that we all learn to hit a one-iron.) I do not believe that a higher power is working through Tiger Woods and the International Management Group, even though IMG once represented the incumbent pope. I do not believe that a higher power is working through Tiger Woods and the Nike corporation:

Tiger, Tiger, burning bright
Selling shoes for Philip Knight

This is what I do not believe about Tiger Woods. These are the theses of my heresy. I do not believe the following sentence, which appears in one of several unauthorized hagiographies: "I don't think he is a god, but I do believe that he was sent by one." This sentence presumes, first, that there is a God and, second, that He busies himself in the manufacture of professional golfers for the purpose of redeeming the various sinful regions of the world. I do not believe this about Tiger Woods.

I do not believe what was said about Tiger by his father in the issue of *Sports Illustrated* in which Tiger Woods was named the Sportsman of the Year: "*Can't you see the pattern?* Earl Woods asks. *Can't you see the signs?* 'Tiger will do more than any other man in history to change the course of humanity,' Earl says."

I do not believe that Earl Woods knows God's mind. I do not believe that Earl Woods could find God's mind with a pack of bloodhounds and Thomas Aquinas leading the way. I do not believe that God's mind can be found on a golf course as though it were a flock of genuine American coots. I do not believe—right now, this day—that Tiger Woods will change humanity any more than Chuck Berry did. This is what I do not believe about Tiger Woods. These are the theses of my heresy.

Is that blasphemy?

Is it?

In the beginning was the father.

"I said," Earl Woods insisted, "that Tiger had the ability to be one of the biggest influences in history. I didn't say that he would be. I am not in the business of predicting the next Messiah, nor do I feel that Tiger *is* the next Messiah. That's stupid. That's just stupid."

Earl Woods was a tired man. He had walked the back fairways of La Costa, where he was treated by his son's galleries the way that mobsters used to be greeted by the doormen at this place. But he'd forgotten his folding chair, and he'd forgotten his CD player on which he listens to his jazz music while Tiger plays. He was a month away from bypass surgery, and he was beginning to get cranky about it.

"I'm a terrible patient," he said. "I'm one of those people who say, 'I don't want to be here.' And then I make such an ass of myself that people let me go. They don't have any reason to keep me."

The story of Earl and his son is worn nearly smooth by now. How Earl fought in Indochina as a Green Beret alongside a South Vietnamese named Nguyen Phong, whom everyone called Tiger. How Earl returned from the war with a Thai wife named Kultida, and how they had a child whom Tida named Eldrick—"Fathers are just along for the ride on that one," Earl explained—but upon whom Earl insisted on bestowing his old comrade's nickname. How Earl would take the toddler with him when he went to hit golf balls. How the little boy climbed out of the high chair and swiped at the ball himself, showing superlative form. And how everything came from that—the appearance on television with Mike Douglas when Tiger was only 3, the superlative junior amateur career, the three consecutive U.S. Amateur titles, the explosion onto the PGA Tour at the end of last season.

And it was Earl's apparently limitless capacity for metaphysical hooey and sociological bunkum that produced the gospel that has so entranced the world, the golfing press and large conglomerate industries. Separated into its component parts, Earl's gospel is predestination theory heavily marbled with a kind of Darwinist Christianity and leavened with Eastern mysticism. Simply put, the gospel has it that while Earl Woods was wandering through Indochina, a divine plan was put in motion by which Earl would one day have a son who would win a lot of golf tournaments and make a lot of money because it was his karma to do so, and that, through doing this, the son would change the world itself.

"I think that the *SI* article went a little too deep," Tiger muses. "As writers go, you guys try to dig deep into something that is really nothing." Well, perhaps, but Earl certainly said what he said, and Tiger certainly has profited, because the promulgation of Earl's gospel is as much at the heart of Tiger's appeal as is his ability to go long off the tee.

There is a dodgy sense of transition around Tiger now, a feeling that the great plates on which he has built his career have begun to shift. In December, for example, he and his father fired John Merchant, Tiger's longtime attorney. Moreover, there is a sense among the other people on Tiger's management team that Earl has pushed his own celebrity far beyond the limits of discretion, particularly in his comments to *SI* concerning Tiger's place in the world. At La Costa, after Tiger's round on Saturday, his swing coach, Butch Harmon, dropped by the press room to cadge a beer.

"Earl," he said with a huge sigh, "is getting out of control."

This is not something anyone would have dared to say even a year ago.

It is perhaps understandable. By his play and by the shrewd marketing that has surrounded his career almost from the time he could walk, Tiger Woods is now an authentic phenomenon. Golf tournaments in which he plays sell more than twice the number of tickets they would if he did not. With Michael Jordan heading toward eclipse and with no other successor on the horizon, Tiger Woods is going to be the most popular athlete in the world for a very long time. The old support system worked splendidly as he came up through the amateur ranks. But there are unmistakable signs that it has become seriously overtaxed.

Consider, for example, the persistent rumors that Earl and Tida have all but separated. At La Costa, they were not seen together on the course at all. Tida commuted to her new house, while Earl stayed at the resort. (At the time, IMG insisted that any rumors of a split were not true.) There was no evidence in his room that she had been there at all. There was only Earl, alone in the room, suffused with a kind of blue melancholy, an old man now, and tired besides.

"I'll be satisfied if he's just a great person," Earl says. "I don't give a shit about the golf."

Ah, but he does. He has given up a lot for it. He left another wife and three other children. He has devoted his life, a lot of his energy and a great deal of surpassing bullshit to creating something that may now be moving far out of his control. "I'm not worried now," he says. "Obviously, I will not be here to see the final result. I will see enough to know that I've done a good job."

On the first day at La Costa, Tiger was paired with David Ogrin, a veteran tour pro who'd won the previous year's Texas Open, his first victory after fourteen years and 405 tournaments. Ogrin is considered one of the tour's most enlightened citizens despite the fact that he looks like a rodeo bouncer and is the owner of one of America's most genuinely red necks. The two of them reached the ninth tee. Tiger had the honors. He absolutely scalded the ball down the center of the fairway, yards beyond anyone else who would play the hole that day.

"Hey," said David Ogrin in awe and wonder. "Eat me."

It was Butch Harmon's time of day. The son of a Masters champion and the brother of three other PGA pros, Harmon was stalking the practice tee at La Costa in the mist of the early morning. He explained how much of Tiger's power comes from his longer musculature—"almost like a track athlete," he said. "Tiger was born with a beautiful natural flow to his swing. It enables him to come through the ball almost like the crack of a whip. Add to that the fact that he was taught well early, because Earl had a real good concept of the golf swing." And then he said something else—something beyond mechanics, but just as important.

"You know, you can get so wrapped up in this game that you have no fun, and as soon as you know it, your career is over and you never had any," he said. "It's a game you can get so serious on that you can't . . . *play.*"

It is the golf that is the sweetest thing about Tiger's story. It is the golf that is free of cant and manufactured import. To the untutored, Tiger Woods is an appealing golfer because he is young and fresh, and because of the distances he can carry with a golf ball. To the purist, he is appealing because his swing is the purest distillation of Everyman's swing. Unlike John Daly, who approaches a golf ball with a club in much the way Mel Gibson approached English infantrymen with a broadsword, Tiger has a swing that is both controlled and clean. "I never go past parallel," he says. "I think people look at me and say, 'That's the way I want to hit the ball.'"

There was resistance to him on the tour at first, because he had come so far so young. But what overcame that was Tiger's manifest hunger to compete. It is not artificial. It is not feigned. It is real and genuine and very formidable. There is a difference between getting up in the morning to win and getting up to *beat* people. Tiger's gospel says that he has more of the first kind of days than he has of the second. The reality is far less clear. He didn't have to go after the pin on Lehman. But he did. "It's nice to know you're out there with somebody whose sole goal isn't to make third on the money list," says Justin Leonard, a gifted young pro.

"I just love to compete," Tiger says. "I don't care if it's golf or Nintendo or in the classroom. I mean, competing against the other students or competing against myself. I know what I'm capable of.

"You know, the prize money, that's the paycheck. That's the money I earned for myself. All the other stuff, my Nike contract and Titleist and now the All Star Cafe, to me, that's a bank account, but it doesn't really make me as happy as what I earn through blood, sweat and tears on the golf course. That money, I have the sole responsibility for earning that. Just me, alone. All the other stuff can depend on how good your agent is."

It's the gospel that has complicated his life. He can commit minor faux pas that become major ones because they run counter to the prefabricated Tiger of the gospel. Soon after he announced he would leave college to turn pro, Nike featured him in a commercial in which he said, "There are still courses in the United States that I am not allowed to play because of the color of my skin," and the world exploded.

The racial aspect of Tiger's gospel has always been the most complex part of it. At first he emphasized his multiracial background— after all, he is as much Thai as he is American, and Earl is an authentic American ethnic stew. At the same time, Tiger and his management team were pushing him as a racial pioneer along the lines of Jackie Robinson, Muhammad Ali and Arthur Ashe, none of whom considered themselves "multi-ethnic." The Nike commercial pointed up the dissonance of the two messages. One prominent gasbag of a pundit challenged Nike to find a course that Tiger couldn't play.

It was an interesting case study in the practical application of the gospel. In the first place, if you dressed Tiger up in ordinary golf clothes—an outfit, say, without thirty-three Nike swooshes on it—

I'm willing to bet you *could* find a course in this great land of ours that wouldn't let a black man play. However, the gospel insists that Tiger came to heal and not to wound. There is no place in journalism whiter than sports writing, and there is no sports writing whiter than golf writing, and generally it is the received wisdom that to be great any great black athlete must be a figure of conciliation and not division. Witness, for example, the revolting use of Muhammad Ali in this regard, especially now that he can't speak for himself. The imperatives of the gospel held. The spot was pulled.

There is little question that Tiger has brought black fans into the game, and that he is part of a modern continuum that reaches back to Jack Johnson. Johnson was a hero generally among black people not far removed from *Plessy v. Ferguson.* Later, Joe Louis served much the same function, except that Louis was far less threatening to white people and thus had an easier time of it. (It was with Louis that we first saw white people using a black champion to prove to themselves how broad-minded they'd become.) Jackie Robinson was a hero to those black people who came north in the great migration to work in the factories in places like Brooklyn. Arthur Ashe came along at a time when the civil rights movement had begun to create a substantial black middle class. And now that America has begun to wish for the appearance of the great racial conciliator, along comes Tiger Woods.

"The reason is the timing of it," he says. "Other guys, like Charlie Sifford, they didn't get the publicity, because the era was wrong. They came along when prejudice reigned supreme. I came along at the right time."

I believe that Tiger will break the gospel before the gospel breaks him. It constricts and binds his entire life. It leaves him no room for ambiguity, no refuge in simple humanity. Earl and Tida can't break up, because the gospel has made their family into a model for the "unfortunate" broken homes that produce so many other athletes. Tiger can't fire his lawyer, because the gospel portrays him as a decent and caring young man. Tiger can't be an angry black man—not even for show, not even for money—because the gospel paints him as a gifted black man rewarded by a caring white society. Tiger can't even tell dirty jokes, because the gospel has no place for them, and they will become events if someone reports them, because, in telling them, he does it:

He blasphemes against himself.

I believe in what I saw at La Costa, a preternaturally mature young man coming into the full bloom of a staggering talent and enjoying very much nearly every damn minute of it. I watched the young women swoon behind the ropes, and I believe that Tiger noticed them, too. There was one woman dressed in a frilly lace top and wearing a pair of tiger-striped stretch pants that fit as though they were decals. I believe that Tiger noticed this preposterous woman, and I do not believe that she was Mary Magdalene come back to life.

"See her?" said one jaded tour observer. "Last year she was following Greg Norman, and there were sharks on her pants."

It is not the world of the gospel, but it is a world I can believe.

Hello, world.

The seventeenth hole at La Costa is a 569-yard par-five that the locals call the Monster. Legend had it that no professional had ever reached it in two. Back up in the tee box, Tiger was getting ready to drive the hole. He had birdied the previous two holes, hurling himself at Tom Lehman, who was still leading the tournament by two strokes. As I walked from tee toward green, I noticed a young couple standing alone, far ahead of the mass of the gallery. They had established a distinct position under a gnarled old jutting tree. The tee box was invisible back behind the crook in the dogleg. A few yards in front of the couple, a browned footpath bisected the fairway.

"This," the man explained, "is where John Daly hit it last year."

The roar came up the fairway in a ragged ripple. And I saw the heads swivel all the way back along the fairway, swivel back and then up, back and then up. And then forward, still up. Forward, still up. I found myself caught up in it, and I saw the ball passing overhead, passing the point where the couple had decided to stand, passing the point where John Daly had once hit a golf shot that no longer mattered.

The ball dropped on the other side of the little brown path. The crowd did not cheer, not instantly. The crowd simply . . . sagged.

Then they cheered, and the crowd came tumbling after Tiger along the sides of the fairway. He had hit the ball past everyone's expectations.

Tiger had a birdie in his pocket, unless he jerked it over the flock of genuine American coots and dunked it into the designer pond in front of the green. All he had to do was lay it up, pitch the ball close and sink his short putt. That was the safe play. That was what he should have done.

Tiger took a wood out of his bag.

The gallery erupted.

It has been a long time since any golf gallery cheered someone for removing a club from his bag. The ovation was not about redemption or about inspiration. It was not about the metaphysical maundering of theological dilettantes. It was about courage and risk and athletic daring. Its ultimate source was irrelevant, but I do not believe this golden moment was foreordained by God while Earl Woods was stumbling around Indochina trying not to get his ass shot off. To believe that would be to diminish God.

And that would be the blasphemy.

And that's what it would be.

He needs so little of what is being put upon him. I believe in the 21-year-old who tells dirty jokes and who plays Nintendo games, and only the fighting games at that. I do not believe in the chosen one, the redeemer of golf and of America and of the rest of the world. I hope he plays golf. I hope he fucks around.

I believe he can blaspheme himself. And I hope to God he does.

These are the theses of my heresy.

"Hey, Darla. How my dick ta'te?"

And I hope the jokes will get better.

It was a savage and wonderful choice that he made, the choice of a man who competes and who knows the difference between those days when you want to win and those days when you want to beat people, and who glories in both kinds of days. The choice he made to hit the wood was a choice he made not only for that day but also for a hundred others, when other golfers will be playing him close, and they will remember what he did, and maybe, just maybe, they

will jerk it over the coots and into the pond. If that is the hand of
God, it is closed then into a fist.

"Because the lesbians always go sixty-nine."

They will get much better.

He took back the club—never past parallel—and it whistled down,
and I could hear Butch Harmon talking softly about the crack of the
whip. I heard no sound at contact. The ball rose, gleaming, into the
soft blue sky. Tiger followed the flight of the ball, stone silent but
smiling just a bit. The gallery began to stir as the shot easily cleared
the pond and rolled up onto the green no one had ever hit in two before. The smile never made it all the way to his eyes.

This is what I believe in, finally. This is the article of my faith. I
believe in that one, risky shot, and I believe in the ball, a distant
white diamond in the clear heavens, and the voices that rose toward
it, washed in its wake, but rising, rising still, far above the profane
earth.

I believe in the prayers of the assembled congregation assembled.

"Youthemanyouthemanyouthemanyoutheman.

"God! You the fucking MAN!"

Amen.

*At one point, Earl Woods told an interviewer that he hoped that this story
wouldn't completely derail his son's career. The consensus among experts is
that it has not.*

GQ April 1997

The Blessed Fisherman
of Prosper, Texas

And so it came to pass that the land was redeemed.

And the land was called Prosper, and it was north of Dallas, and it was a place of desert and scrub weed and tall, thirsting flowers that did wave in the breathless air. And there was sin in the land. Jezebels and Delilahs all, they did come to Prosper to set up shop, for Prosper was unincorporated, and north of Dallas, and beyond the law. And the sinful did come to Prosper and did spill their seed in the various and lubricious chalices who did wink and wave and tempt the weak from the front porches and parlors.

But then there came upon the place the godly, the righteous, and the upper management, looking for homes from which they could journey back into the city with joy in their hearts, and with a minimum of fuss and bother, except on the weekends, when traffic was hellish. And the good land did come to be valued by them (at $50,000 an acre), and the sin was squeezed out of the place, and a town beloved by its people did grow in Prosper, and prosper they did. And so it came to pass that the land was redeemed, and a pilgrim did come here to build a great house by a fishpond:

"Two seconds," says Deion Sanders. "I give that fat one out there two seconds."

A little ways out from the shore, a big old F-16 of a grasshopper is floundering, trying to swim back to shore. There is a stirring in the water beneath him, then a swift flash of bass and the grasshopper is gone. We are walking his property, and Sanders is flushing out great clouds of grasshoppers toward the water. Some of them fall in and get eaten, thereby fattening the bass that Sanders plans to catch as soon as his house is finished, the great pile of a place that is rising even now at the top of the slope that begins at the far bank of the fishing hole. Scripture, of course, tells us that grasshoppers are plenty good eating; John the Baptist liked his with honey. The pond comes alive with hungry fish.

"You want to describe me?" Sanders asks. "Call me a fisherman. I always fish."

Since 1989, when he came out of Florida State as a rookie cornerback, a neophyte center fielder, and a full-blown celebrity, Deion Sanders has produced as eccentric a body of work as that produced by any athlete. Having signed this season to play for the Washington Redskins, Sanders is now on his fourth stop in the NFL, which means he has played for exactly as many professional football teams as he has professional baseball teams. He is the only man ever to play in the Super Bowl and in the World Series. He's the first two-way starter in the NFL since 1962. As he grew older, he left baseball behind, and he transformed himself into one of the great defensive backs in the history of the league, but he has remained a full-blown celebrity.

He conspired in creating his own image. He admits freely that he deliberately fabricated "Prime Time," his gold-encrusted *nom d'argent*, which had its official public debut in a *Sports Illustrated* profile that was practically written in blackface, to help himself get rich. His entire career has been an exercise in trying to control the personality that he created. If it weren't for Prime Time, maybe he wouldn't have been associated willy-nilly with the *I, Claudius* atmosphere surrounding the Dallas Cowboys, when, in fact, the worst trouble with the law that Deion Sanders had ever had was a glorified traffic wrangle with a stadium security guard in Cincinnati and a trespassing bust that occurred when Sanders was discovered on private land where he'd gone to . . . fish.

If not for Prime Time, then, maybe the divorce wouldn't have been so ugly, and maybe he wouldn't have been there in Cincinnati contemplating, he says, putting an end to all of it. And maybe it was Prime Time who drove Deion Sanders to Jesus and drove him then to a new life with a new wife and a new baby and a new team and a new house here in Prosper. Anything's possible. Life's strange, and that's what's kept Scripture interesting all these years.

"They never give athletes credit for knowing who they are," he says. "As an athlete, you're in business. And I knew how to market my business. The Lord intended me to be different. He intended everyone to be different. I never tried to emulate anyone, ever. I was the first Deion Sanders, and I'll be the last Deion Sanders.

"I created something that could command me millions of dollars, and it served its purpose. But I was playing a game, and people took it seriously." He took it so seriously, if you believe him now, that he needed to be rescued in one of the oldest ways of all.

He says he's Saved—capital-S Saved—from when he used to chase around and dance the hootchy-kootchy. In fact, he says they're both saved, Deion *and* Prime Time. Saved from the world. Saved from each other. Saved for a good woman and a baby and for his other two children, too. Saved now for the Redskins, for whom he'll lock up the best receivers in the league the way he did for the Falcons, 49ers, and Cowboys. (Daniel Snyder, the Redskins' owner, has hurled money at veterans like Sanders and Bruce Smith in order to buy himself an instant Super Bowl.) Saved, says Deion, to go to Washington and play for the endless dollars of a profligate child.

This might be an act. Might just be the Prime Time shuck again, the gold covered up now in choir robes. (Sanders's spiritual guide, the charismatic preacher T. D. Jakes, is not long on vows of poverty.) But watch him walk his land, stirring up the grasshoppers, admiring the fish, and there is a peace, an ease, a kind of steady grace that might be theological and might not be.

"I'm blessed," says Deion Sanders. "God's blessed me well."

The steady hammering drifts down the hill through the heat of the afternoon, and isn't that the damnedest thing, too? The gospel turned on its head—a bunch of carpenters come out into the desert to work for a fisherman.

All right, so it got in the way. A $30,000 golf cart will do that to a fellow's image, especially when the golf cart has tinted windows, an ice machine, and a mist dispenser, and especially since the fellow who owns it doesn't play golf. If Deion Sanders got defined as a heedless spendthrift, it's only because he moved through most of his life a walking cloudburst of wealth, flashing gold and diamonds, his professional antecedents not Emlen Tunnell or Night Train Lane but Little Richard and the Reverend Ike.

"Just being a cornerback wasn't enough," he explains. "Being a cornerback wasn't looked on as being a *showstopper*. And you've got to understand, I sat in my dorm room at Florida State and created that whole thing in my imagination. I just created a persona with the nickname, but you had to back it up with substance, and I think that once the media got hold of [the fact] that it was all a game for me, they got upset and tried to take things too far.

"I mean, you don't think Eddie Murphy's *Eddie Murphy* at home. Do you think Jim Carrey acts like a darn fool all day? I don't think John Wayne sat around the house with a gun all day, and I don't think he shot the mailman when he cam through the door."

He is a bigger man than he appears on television, all sinewy angles and not inconspicuous strength, a sprinter gone bigger. But the first thing that registers about Deion Sanders—besides the fact that at thirty-three he is still youthful and handsome—is that he is disconcertingly slow to speak. He is not bubbly or bright or glib. An interview is a conversation conducted in paragraphs. But by creating Prime Time and, more important, by *selling* Prime Time as effectively as he did, Sanders placed at the heart of his career an intractable personal dissonance.

He played the same way. That was the odd thing about it. The gold came off and the diamonds went into the locker, but the bandanna came on and Deion Sanders lit up the football field with his talent. People who saw only the high-stepping final yards of a touch-down return missed the controlled intelligence that got him there. "If you watch him," says Dave Campo, the former Cowboys defensive coordinator to whom Jerry Jones handed the head-coaching job this season, "you will see this guy do things that nobody else can do. Nobody."

It is quite possible that Sanders is the best pass defender who has ever played the game. As fast as he is down the field, he is even faster at those five- and ten-yard sprints needed to close on the ball. His matchups with the 49ers' Jerry Rice were breathless, electric things, the finest man-to-man confrontations the NFL had seen since Sam Huff rang hats with Jim Brown back in the dim times before Chris Berman. He is smart and he is canny. He will bait quarterbacks by laying off receivers just enough, then close the distance like a swooping hawk. And if he doesn't hit hard enough to suit the NFL's broken-nose lobby, he is still one of a very few players who can change a game all by himself. That he is also a brilliant and enthusiastic returner of punts means that all doubts regarding his courage are rendered moot because, if Sanders is reluctant to hit, he is clearly willing to *be* hit on what is arguably the most dangerous play in the game.

And yet—and there always is an "and yet" to this guy—as tight a rein as Sanders claims to have had on the Prime Time persona, it became his public definition. Baseball, for example, never got it, largely because baseball is the institutional equivalent of your Aunt Gertrude, who collects both balls of string *and* Winslow Homers in her attic because she never quite mastered the difference between that which is classical and that which is simply old.

"One thing about baseball is that the guys who have played a few years get to thinking they're the authority on this and that," Sanders explains. "They're quick to throw their years in your face. Football isn't like that, because I don't care if you play ten, twelve years, a rookie will come in and knock your head off and you're going to respect him, you know? That's why I didn't relate to that part of baseball."

Baseball did not welcome Deion Sanders, whom it saw as a speedy dilettante who did not respect Our Game the way that Our Game respects itself. Baseball did not welcome Prime Time, whom it saw as a space alien. Sanders didn't help himself, either. He got into an on-field wrangle with Carlton Fisk, which is rather like arguing socialism with the heads on Mount Rushmore. Once, after broadcaster Tim McCarver upbraided Sanders for playing a football game and a baseball game on the same day, Sanders responded by dumping a bucket of ice water on McCarver's head. As promising a player as he was—in 1992, as an Atlanta Brave, Sanders hit .533 in his only World Series—baseball was not a context within which the subtle interplay between Deion and Prime Time would ever work.

In fact, by 1996 it had become clear that Sanders was losing control of the balancing act that had been his entire public life. He was a solid citizen by the standards of the Cowboys—which were hardly rigid—but his life was coming apart. His marriage dissolved swiftly and in rancid fashion. (Once, in court, when asked whether he'd committed adultery, Sanders replied, "Are you stating before the marriage of 1996 or after?"—which is pretty clearly not getting the point.) While he insists that it was the public that would not let his Prime Time persona go and that it was that ol' devil media that kept the public hungry, Sanders was clearly dependent upon it himself. If it was a fabrication, then it had become real—a doppelgänger that Sanders was not secure enough to shake.

Today, he says the pressure was enough to make him contemplate suicide—most seriously three years ago in Cincinnati. That he did not follow through with it, he says, is because he heard the Word. And maybe he has. Of course, maybe he's a heretic, too. Nobody—not even Carlton Fisk—ever called him that.

"If there's a heaven, there's got to be a hell, too," he says. "Think on that."

God, you've got to love sportswriting when it draws you into third-century theological disputes. Hey, Saint Athanasius, you da man!

Anyway, long about A.D. 200, a doctrine arose that held that the members of the Trinity were not three distinct personalities but only successive modes through which one God manifested himself. It became known as modalism and, later, Sabellianism, after Sabellius, an ancient Christian theologian who adopted the controversial doctrine as his own. Needless to say, this notion ran so contrary to the essential trinitarianism of Christianity—three persons *in* one God, and not one God acting through three successive agents—that all hell, you should pardon the expression, broke loose.

The Sabellians were given the gate from the early Christian church. The doctrine, however, was a stubborn one, persisting so durably into modern Pentecostalism that in 1916, it caused a split that divided the church into two distinct sects. It is now called the Oneness Doctrine, and it is the main problem that many modern Pentecostals say they have with Bishop T. D. Jakes, who, Deion says, brought him to the Word and the Word to him. Call him a modalist. Call him a Sabellian. Call him a heretic. Deion doesn't care.

"He's the only man I've ever called Daddy," says Sanders, who never really knew his biological father.

Since coming to Dallas from West Virginia in 1996, Jakes has built an empire out of his Potter's House church. His television show is one of the hottest on the television-preacher circuit, and his books sell in the millions. He drives a Mercedes and lives in a $1.7 million lakefront home next door to H. L. Hunt, and he is so wired into the world of Texas celebrity that he is likely to become the Billy Graham in a possible Bush Restoration. (Governor Dubya regularly uses Jakes in his outreach to minority communities.) Unlike many of his more judgmental colleagues, Jakes has involved himself conspicuously in ministering to battered women and gay people. There is nothing of the Christian bluenose to him. He is very much a man of this particular sinful world. Consider, for example, his views on the theology of satin sheets, taken from his book *The Lady, Her Love, and Her Lord*:

"You see, ladies, satin might be pretty, but it destroys all semblance of balance and leaves you grabbing for the bedpost and groping for handfuls of mattress just to turn around in the sack, much less try an acrobatic feat of passion."

And, well, amen.

Sanders came to Jakes with his first wife, Carolyn, as they tried to rescue their marriage. Jakes was the perfect person to minister to

Sanders. From the start, Jakes saw the effort that Sanders was making to reconcile the person he was with the person he'd created. "I found him to be, though outwardly a flamboyant person, inwardly very sincere," Jakes says. "I was able to separate the character he plays on the field and who he really is.

"One thing I've not found him to be is somebody who says things he didn't mean. When he wasn't into it, he wasn't into it, and everybody knew it. I have 50 percent of my church like that, and it's wonderful, because they've learned not to be religiously fraudulent."

It was Jakes who baptized Sanders in 1997 and Jakes who officiated when he and his new wife, Pilar Biggers, were married in the Bahamas two years later. Somewhere in there, for whatever reason, Deion made his peace with his own creation and, possibly, with everyone else's, too. After all, the Father's house has many rooms, and there are some nice ones down here, too, but you still have to live with yourself somewhere. If that's heresy, he's making the most of it.

The Potter's House church is coming loose from the earth. The Wednesday-night Bible study is shaking the place. A camera on a crane swoops above the whole congregation like the Divine Eye as Deion Sanders comes bouncing down the aisle toward where I'm sitting. "Thanks," he says, the gleam of righteous transport in his eye. "Thanks for coming."

It is a huge and theatrical place, rows of pews rising in arcs and layers away from the pulpit. Two huge screens hang from the ceiling; a video of the service will be projected on them, as will whatever Bible verses Bishop Jakes chooses this night for his lesson. Deion flows easily into the enthusiastic congregation, one of many and nobody in particular. The band—pushed by an organ and a gorgeous bass guitar—reaches a long and sustained peak before the introductory prayers. There is a moment of soft and palpable anticipation before Bishop Jakes rises to speak—a gathering of the drama. Deion, who has been swaying to the music, goes still and silent. Worship falls on the place all at once.

Jakes dives into the Gospel of John, and he's talking about how Jesus and the disciples went outside the camp to pray. "They said, 'We don't need your controversies and your factions and your de-nom-in-*na*-tions,'" he thunders. "And they went. . . *outside the camp*."

"Preach, Daddy," says Deion. He's an enthusiastic celebrant, underlining his Scripture heavily and, when truly moved, waving his left arm in a huge flapping motion. They make the altar call, and a battalion of well-dressed deacons appears, each with a box of Kleenex in his hands, and people come down from all corners of the huge tabernacle. As the service winds up, we all join hands for the benediction, an old woman to my left, me, and Deion, and something feels as though it's cutting the side of my hand, and I look down, and I realize that it's the diamonds on his watch. At the end, he catches me in a sudden embrace.

"Welcome to my world," he says.

And it is a whisper.

Esquire October 2000

The Brother from Another Planet

This is some pale stuff out there on the wing. All the other basketball players, Celtics and Pacers alike, have cleared the side, and they have left two of their own all alone. This is the isolation play, an offensive maneuver as simple as milk, yet responsible in large part for the wild and unruly success that has overtaken professional basketball in the past decade. It is out of this alignment that Michael Jordan is cleared for takeoff, and it was out of this alignment that Magic Johnson ground up the hapless on his way to the low post, and it is out of this alignment that Charles Barkley is freed to do both, often on the same play. It is a wonderful set piece—a scorer and a defender, alone with each other, the center of all focus. It is a prideful moment for both players—the Ur-matchup of the American game. One-on-one.

Anyway, this is some pale stuff out there. Larry Bird has the ball cocked high and waiting. He is guarded by an Indiana Pacer named Detlef Schrempf, a blond German with a brush cut who makes Larry Bird look like Sam Cooke. Bird has Schrempf on a string now, moving the ball just slightly, faking with his fingertips. Other Celtics heckle the Pacer forward from the bench. More tiny fakes, and Schrempf is hearing imaginary cutters thundering behind him toward the hoop. His eyes cheat a bit over his shoulders. Finally, with Schrempf utterly discombobulated, Bird dips the ball all the way around his opponent's hip. Schrempf half-turns to help defensively on the man to whom he's sure Bird has just passed the ball. Bird pulls the ball back, looking very much like a dip who's just plucked a rube's gold watch from his vest pocket. He throws up that smooth hay-baler of a jump shot from just above his right ear, and it whispers through the net. The play draws cheers and laughter, and even Bird is smiling a little as the two teams head down the court again.

A few days earlier, Connie Hawkins was nominated for the Basketball Hall of Fame, the final vindication of what poet Jim Carroll has written about basketball, "a game where you can correct all your mistakes instantly, and in midair." Hawkins was a glider and a soarer. A legend in Brooklyn long before he was twenty, he fits snugly between Elgin Baylor and Julius Erving on the path of the game that continues upward to (for the moment) Michael Jordan.

Hawkins's best years were wasted in exile on the game's fringes; his innocent involvement in the point-shaving investigation of 1961 truncated his college career and put him on an NBA blacklist until 1969. He will go into the Hall of Fame only because some people saw him do something wondrous and they told the tale. It is a triumph for the game's oral history, for its living tradition. There is a transcendence about Connie Hawkins and about his legend. It resides out of time and place, floating sweetly there in the air above all convention and cavil.

In large part, of course, this living tradition is an African-American tradition. In reaction to it, basketball's overwhelmingly white establishment assailed the skills of legends like Connie Hawkins, deriding their game as "playground basketball," the result of some atavistic superiority that must be controlled by (predominantly white) coaches for the greater good. Black players were innately talented, of course, but they were lacking in the Fundamentals, which virtually always were defined in a way that brought the game back to earth and removed it from the largely black custodians of its living tradition.

Withal, both sides were talking past each other. The game's white establishment was talking about strategy and tactics. Black players were talking about the psychology of defining oneself as a person by what one did on the court. From this emphasis on psyche came the concept of Face—a philosophy of glorious retribution by which you dunk unto others as they have already dunked unto you, only higher and harder. It's this competitive attitude that makes the Fundamentals interesting. And it's this guilty knowledge that made basketball's white establishment so determined to minimize its obvious importance. Soon, these views ossified into the attitudes by which black players are praised for their "athletic ability"—code for the Super Negro not far removed from William Shockley's laboratory—while white players are usually commended for their "intelligence" and their "work ethic." Both sides internalized these notions, and they were irreconcilable.

By the late 1970s, the NBA, having expanded far too quickly and recklessly for its own good, was floundering. Competition had vanished. So had most of the fans. There were some drug busts, common enough in all sports. At the same time, the league was perceived as becoming blacker; by 1979, 70 percent of the players were African American. People made the usual foul connections. There were the nods and the winks in the executive suites. Disillusioned fans drifted away, and pretty soon the NBA found its championship series being broadcast on tape delay.

In 1979, Larry Bird and Magic Johnson began their careers with the Boston Celtics and the Los Angeles Lakers, respectively. There was a frisson of expectation as soon as they went around the league. By season's end, Bird had been named the NBA Rookie of the Year, and Johnson had propelled the Lakers to the title, scoring forty-two points against the Philadelphia 76ers in the seventh game of the final series. Over the next decade, the two of them played so well and drew so many fans that they are now given undisputed credit for saving professional basketball. Neither one ever evinced eye-popping athletic skills; Bird may be the only great player in history more earthbound than Magic. Their importance lies in the fact that the two irreconcilable halves of the game found in them—and, especially, in Bird—a common ground.

The most fundamental of the traditional Fundamentals is that a great player must make his team greater. Thus does a whirling dunk count only the same two points as a simple layup. Both Bird and Magic pass this test easily. However, the game's living tradition demands that this be accomplished in a way that ups the psychic ante, that forces the cycle of payback onto the opposition. Neither man has ever shrunk from this imperative. What Bird did to Schrempf, he did not do merely to score two points for the Celtics but to break his opponent's will, just as once in a championship game, he looked down to see where the three-point line was, took a conspicuous step back behind it, and then sunk a coup de grace through the Houston Rockets.

In short, the NBA has succeeded because it has become the world's premier athletic show. Playground ball has triumphed completely. It's hard to imagine now that college basketball once thought it was a good idea to ban the dunk, or that former UCLA coach John Wooden *still* thinks it's a good idea. Wooden, supreme guru of the Fundamentals, now sounds like a hopeless crank. What Bird and Magic did was difficult, and damned-near revolutionary—they made the Fundamentals part of the show. They did it by infusing the simple act of throwing a pass with the same splendid arrogance that so vividly illuminated Connie Hawkins midflight.

"What you've got to understand about Larry is that he plays a white game with a black head," says Atlanta's Dominique Wilkins. "If he could do a three-sixty dunk and laugh at you, he'd do it. Instead, he hits that three, and then he laughs at you."

"There's no doubt about it," adds Indiana's Chuck Person, who has enjoyed a spirited rivalry with Bird. "Larry's a street kid."

It comes from his life—a lost, lonely kid whose father was an amiable drunk who one day called Larry's mother on the phone and, with her listening, blew his brains out. There was grinding poverty. There was hopelessness. Compared to this life, Magic Johnson had it easy, as did Michael Jordan. Compared to this life, Spike Lee, who uses Bird as a cartoon foil, was one of the Cleavers. Instinctively, Larry Bird understands the country's most pernicious division as one of class and not of race—a distinction that a decade of public demagoguery has done its damnedest to obscure.

"The poorer person," he muses, "the person who don't have much will spend more time playing sports to get rid of the energy he has." And anger and desperation? "Yeah, them too. Why go home when you got nothing to go home to?"

All his life, he has resisted the notion of being anyone's great white hope, because it never seemed logical to him. "I've always thought of basketball as a black man's game," Bird says. "I just tried to do everything I could to fit in."

Long ago, Indiana was a demographic fluke. Unlike the other midwestern states, it was settled from south to north rather from east to west. It was flooded with refugees from Tennessee and the Carolinas. They brought with them so much of the Old South that, by 1922, the Ku Klux Klan was virtually running the state. An Indiana town called Martinsville is famous for being the home of two institutions—John Wooden and the modern Klan. When Jerry Sichting, a former NBA player and now the Celtics' radio commentator, left Martinsville to go to Purdue, his black teammates shied away from him. "I said I was from Martinsville, and I got that look," Sichting says. "It's still out there, no question." Larry Bird is from French Lick, which is thirty miles down Highway 37 from Martinsville. Thirty miles south.

Bird seems to have grown up remarkably free of prejudice. Throughout his career, he has managed to stay admirably clear of those who would make him a symbol through which to act out their own fears and bigotry. He has called Magic Johnson his role model, and he referred to former teammate Dennis Johnson as "the greatest player I ever saw." He even delighted in bringing NBA pal Quinn Buckner home to French Lick and into the worst redneck joints in town. "Yeah," recalls Buckner. "He took me to some places that I might not have gotten out of in less than three pieces if I went in alone. But Larry truly doesn't look at it that way. He doesn't want any part of that great white hope stuff. He never did."

"Just the other day," Bird says, "a guy come up to me and says, 'Here, sign this. Put on it that you're the greatest white player to ever play the game.' To me, that don't mean nothing. The greatest player ever to play the game. That means a helluva lot more."

Unfortunately, Bird has been a lightning rod. The Celtics, whose historical record on racial matters is positively revolutionary, have been forced to carry the weight of Boston's abysmal history in the matter of race relations. They were criticized for lightening up their roster in the early Eighties, although it's difficult to make the case that it's immoral to draft Bird and Kevin McHale, or to concoct a roster that won the NBA title three times in the decade. However, on a larger scale, the Eighties were generally a decade of reaction in racial matters. Bird's first season coincided with the ascendancy in culture and politics of the shibboleth of the Oppressed White Male. A society that could straight-facedly equate Allan Bakke with Rosa Parks evolved easily to one that could see no metaphorical distance between Clarence Thomas and the Scottsboro Boys.

Those comforted by the prevailing reactionary zeitgeist were looking for a hero, and Larry Bird and the Celtics qualified. Those revolted by it were looking for a villain, and Bird and the Celtics qualified there too. Thus, when it became fashionable to make Larry Bird into the greatest player of all time—certainly an arguable proposition, particularly up until about 1986—few people were objective about it anymore.

In 1987, after losing to the Celtics in a conference playoff series, Isiah Thomas blurted out the problem. Defending statements made by rookie Dennis Rodman, he said, "If Bird were black, he'd be just another good guy." The comment was graceless and ill-timed, but it was also the truth. Had Bird been black, his physical abilities would've been emphasized at the expense of his intelligence and his diligence at practice. Thomas's statement was excoriated for being racist, which it certainly was not. To identify a racial problem is not racist. One might as well call a black man racist who points out that white people are rather heavily involved in redlining his neighborhood.

By downplaying the comments and refusing to respond, Bird got Thomas out of the situation so deftly that Thomas later credited Bird with saving his public career. Bird would not have been able to do that had he not effectively defused the issue among his peers by connecting with the game's psychology. While he passed and rebounded and got praised for his mastery of the Fundamentals, he exhibited such cutthroat competitive flair that the dunkers sensed a kindred spirit.

"I always said that Larry was one of the most creative players I ever saw," says Celtic center Robert Parish. "That same kind of thing that makes people do a dunk makes Larry throw that touch pass over his shoulder."

Neither was Bird blind to what was happening elsewhere. Just last fall, Celtic rookie Dee Brown was thrown to the ground by police in the chichi suburb of Wellesley because some clerk thought Brown "looked like" the man who had recently robbed the bank.

"It's still a scar," Bird says. "You hear that Boston is a tough town for blacks. I don't know. I can't speak for them because I'm not black. I've seen some incidents, though. Dee Brown. Robert Parish got stopped a couple of times. Just for being black, you know."

Joe Bird's son never talked about him. It was part of a past buried so deeply that when a writer from *Sports Illustrated* mentioned Joe's suicide in an article, some of the boys from French Lick were said to have gone looking for him. But the son talked about Joe Bird this year. Talked freely, if not easily. Talked because a black man, a friend in L.A., was threatened by a fatal disease, and suddenly there was a connection between an amiable and self-destructive white man in a hard little town in Indiana and an amiable and doomed black man in the fastest lane of all. The son of the first saw the connection there between his father and his friend, and he saw it clearly, far beyond the cold balm of convenient banality.

"I thought about when my Dad passed away," said Larry Bird on the night after Magic Johnson announced that he had tested positive for HIV. "I thought about how I wandered around for a week, just numb. That's what this is like."

He said it in that light little twang, the one that the people in southern Indiana brought with them from Tennessee, the one that made even Elvis sound modest in conversation. In truth, Bird has grown up remarkably unmarked by the benefits of his celebrity. "Larry doesn't care about being a famous white player," says Dave Gavitt, the Celtics CEO, "because Larry doesn't care about being famous, period." Indeed, as far as commercial endorsements are concerned, he falls well behind Johnson and Jordan. He has, however, consciously worked to change the racial debate in a way not easily done. He has proven himself in his way on someone else's terms.

It would have been easy for him to grow up hard in the native bigotry of his place. Once grown, he could have easily sensed in his bones that that bigotry is general throughout the land and exploited it shamelessly. If there are people who would make him the best player ever simply because he is white, then that's their problem. If the Celtics became white America's team, then that's white America's fault. Larry Bird, as an individual basketball player, has defined his enormous abilities in an African-American context, and he has triumphed within it.

In his play—and, therefore, in his life, because the two are inextricably bound—he has declined to profit from the advantages that spring from the worst in our common culture. There are politicians, men infinitely more powerful than Larry Bird, who have proven unable to resist this same impulse. One of them plays horseshoes in the White House now.

They say that basketball's greatness is in its ability to bring people together, but that's a lie. Glib and facile people say that about every sport, and yet sports are as riven by class and race as any other major institution of this culture. Those people are closer to being right in basketball, though, than they are in any other sport. Basketball, much more than baseball or football, unites and makes whole two cultures, and it obliterates the artificial divisions created by faceless, fearful men who cling to their own pathetic advantages. Those who would turn Larry Bird into a symbol useful to that vicious endeavor—and those who would use him as a straw man against whom they could fight back—are all blind to his true genius. They are frightened of the best possibilities of America.

On this night, before he talked about his father and Magic, Larry Bird began the game by throwing a floor-length, behind-the-back pass that nobody could recall having seen Bird ever throw. But everyone on the floor knew it for what it was—an homage, extended in high style and in the game's truest and most precious currency. Everyone who ever had dunked on a man, or had defied both aero-dynamics and orthopedics to drop a shot full of life and music, iden-tified it immediately. Dominique Wilkins, trailing the play, saw it for what it was—an entertainer's play, but a bounce pass sure enough, with the arm extended right through to the fingertips, following through just the way that Clair Bee and Nat Holman and all those other guys wrote it down years ago, before the game moved into the air for good. The Fundamentals, but Showtime, too, beyond all measure.

"Larry," said one of his coaches, "was just saying goodbye."

Esquire **February 1992**

The Magic Act

At the corner of Washington and Ionia streets, in the city of Lansing, Michigan, there was a grand old movie house called the Gladmer Theater. Growing up on Middle Street, in a small auto-boom frame house, temple of the tiny dreams, you lived in a world that extended north as far as the freeway and south as far as the Oldsmobile plant. But slip off to the side, down Logan to Washington and into the Gladmer, and the world seemed to crack open. There in the dark, you could curl up in the balcony's deep shadows and feel the place come alive in bursts of golden wonder. You could tuck in at noon and stay the whole day. Early Seventies movies—Godzilla taking down Osaka, and the new black cinema of the day. Richard Roundtree and Billy Dee. Jim Brown and Ron O'Neal, *Superfly* so very sharp. You'd be sharp, too, if Curtis Mayfield did your music. New stars but the same old dreams. They were selling the old Hollywood there, and if you bought it, you bought it right down to your bones. Life as performance. Performance as life. Walk into the Gladmer and your life didn't dead-end at the Oldsmobile plant anymore.

Earvin Johnson, Jr. would save up the money he earned cleaning yards and shoveling snow and helping Earvin senior on the garbage truck. He'd buy his ticket and stay all day, walking blinking out into the summer twilight or wide-eyed into the winter gloom. "They didn't kick you out until five o'clock," he recalls today. "You could stay and watch the movie two or three times. But those were the times, man. And that was why I wanted to meet these people, to get to know them." He bought the old Hollywood dream, not knowing that it was a dream straight out of movies that had played the Gladmer long before he was born. Old musicals and Tinseltown melodrama. Kid, some day, all this will be yours.

According to popular belief, Magic Johnson was created when a sportswriter named Fred Stabley thought that Earvin Johnson, Jr. wasn't a sufficiently respectful nom de hoop for the effervescent young player at Everett High School. Truth be told, though, Magic Johnson was born on those afternoons long ago when Earvin Johnson, Jr. tucked himself into the balcony shadows and watched his dreams explode like skyrockets around him. It is the esssential dichotomy of his life. It will one day be the essential dichotomy of his death.

"I wanted to be a part of that," he muses. "There was Earvin, but it was Magic who wanted to be a part of that Hollywood life. Magic is the side where you go to Hollywood and live that Hollywood life and so forth." They were not compatible, Earvin and Magic. Not even in the same person. Where Earvin was eager to be loved, Magic throve on adulation, which is not the same thing at all. Earvin was the happy one, the joyful child who had worked so hard to be the conciliator within his family when his mother threw herself into a new and unyielding religion, the teenager who had made the best of being bused to the predominantly white Everett High, far across town. Magic did the premiers and the clubs. He hung with Eddie and Arsenio, and he signed autographs for the pretty people who came to the Forum to see the Los Angeles Lakers play.

They were coming for him. That was the marvel of it. There were Thirties-style Hollywood parties, but with the heedless edge of Eighties consumption. There were fine women and more than enough opportunities, and Magic Johnson was one of the biggest stars in town. "I'm living a dream," he remembers. "I'm from Lansing, Michigan. I mean, here I am in Hollywood, and so I was living not just for myself but for a lot of my friends back home, 'cause I would always tell them, man, I met Ali. I met Stallone. I met, you know, Richard Pryor. I know Eddie. I would always call back, and they were living through me. Man, I'd tell my friends that so-and-so talked to me. I said, 'Wow!' They would run over and ask me for my autograph. That's what shocked me the most. I was in awe of the movie stars sitting on the court."

In his mind, Earvin watched it all unfold before him as though he were at once the audience and the actor, as though he were still in the Gladmer, still curled up there deep in the balcony shadows, an odd and lingering distance now come between himself and the movie that his life had become. The movie rolled through the five NBA titles with the Lakers in the 1980s, picking up supporting characters along the way: Larry Bird; teammates like Kareem Abdul-Jabbar and James Worthy; sudden, intense rivals like Michael Jordan. Eddie. Arsenio. Luther Vandross, singing just for him. It was as though Magic were another John Shaft, another Superfly. Performance as life. Life as performance. Earvin watched as his life was hijacked by its own public creation.

"Don't call me Magic," Johnson once told a woman. "Only people who don't know me call me Magic. People who really know me call me Earvin."

It could not go on, this bow-tight interplay between two incompatible personas. Earvin could not function credibly as a kind of freefloating alibi for Magic's life-style, and Magic was not willing to submit to Earvin's control. The knowledge that the other existed made each of them insecure. In basketball, for example, it was Magic who threw the blind passes and orchestrated Showtime, that resolutely L.A. phenomenon that owed far more to the Village People than it did to James Naismith. But Earvin was the solid player, schooled so truly in his own unique fundamentals that he could see the game three or four moves ahead. Earvin was serious. Earvin had goals. Earvin was going to be a businessman—a tycoon, really. In a town full of players, Earvin was going to be respected as a Player.

There was a terrible pulling and hauling, an awful straining beneath the shallow artifice of celebrity, and an unstated demand that Earvin be taken more seriously than he could be within the glittery caul that was Magic's life. They could function within the context of the NBA and within the context of pure fame. But they were not prepared, either of them, to work together in the consuming crisis of their lives.

It is a vast story now, sliding inexorably toward the epic. When Johnson announced on November 7, 1991, that he had contracted the human immunodeficiency virus, the apparent cause of AIDS, he first let Magic do the talking. It was an up performance. He even spoke vaguely of beating the disease, which is plainly impossible. "BELIEVE IN MAGIC," said the T-shirts. And at the start, it seemed that it might work. Society appeared to suspend briefly the malicious notion that there are guilty and innocent victims of this disease. When it was rumored that the various companies whose products Johnson endorsed were considering dropping him from their commercials, the ensuing public outcry seemed like a benediction.

Society has allowed itself its AIDS saints—Elizabeth Glaser, say. Or the late Ryan White. But both of them had contracted HIV in a socially acceptable manner: to wit, accidentally, through tainted blood products. Since Johnson openly admitted that he'd become infected through unprotected sexual congress, the early, positive reaction to his announcement suggested that he would be the AIDS saint who could eliminate this final stigma. He would be more than merely an example. His life with the virus would be his witness, his public testimony. Performance as life, and life as performance.

Forgotten for the moment was not only the long history of how the world reacts during times of plague but also the recent, sorry history of how the world has reacted to this particular one. Forgotten was the fact that the lives of saints are not the rosy, sanitized versions that make it into the prayer books and onto the movie screen. Saints are terribly inconvenient. They often make trouble. They often make people look very foolish. After all, Ryan White first became famous because some people in Indiana tried to keep him from going to school. Nevertheless, it was contended that Magic's inimitable persona would be enough to crack open the formidable collusion between unreasoning fear and moralistic stupidity that had attended this epidemic. So loud and universal was this contention that a number of uncomfortable personal truths were swept aside—most notable, that his attitude toward women caused him to treat them as (at best) a disposable commodity.

The performance closed quickly. Magic went on *The Arsenio Hall Show*, and he was loudly applauded for declaring himself "far from being a homosexual." Gay activists threw that back in his face, and a dying AIDS patient named Derek Hodel read him off at a meeting of the national AIDS commission in January 1992. Johnson was learning on the fly about the ambiguities of the disease he had contracted. He did a kids' show about AIDS for Nickelodeon, a gentle, Earvin-like show that was very well received. He played in last year's NBA All-Star Game, and his smile on the victory stand remains the enduring image from last summer's Olympics.

What remained plain, however, was the fact that he never understood the public ramifications of his condition. "It's funny," he says. "I didn't know what was going to happen. I didn't know how people were going to react. I didn't know until you actually got into it and really saw how people were treated who had the virus, or who already had AIDS." It was out there, however, waiting for him, the human reflex that was born on the day Genghis Khan introduced the flea-bitten rats of East Asia to those of the Balkans. A decade later, a third of Europe was dead, and the survivors were blaming the Jews and burning them alive in their synagogues.

Not quite a year after his upbeat press conference, there was another one, and Johnson wasn't even there. He is gone from the game for good now, his comeback aborted by those same forces that the public witness of his life was supposed to eliminate. Players spoke openly of being afraid to guard him too closely, even though they are at far greater risk of dying every time they climb on the team plane. There were renewed rumors about how he had acquired the virus. He wrote an autobiography, in which he discussed his baroque extracurricular sex life, and then undertook a huge publicity tour, on which it seemed he was defending himself against charges of bisexuality by pleading satyriasis.

The woman to whom he had once said "Only people who don't know me call me Magic" was suing him for $2 million, alleging that it was Johnson who'd passed the virus on to her. That Johnson did not attend his second retirement is not surprising. The comeback had been a performance by Magic, a headlong dive for the spotlight, and it had become plain that Magic now scared people. Too many of them had been living Magic's life themselves—still are, truth be told—and they didn't need him out there as the great golem of antibody roulette. That would be just too frightening. So Magic wasn't wanted anymore, and Earvin had the good sense to stay home.

"It would have been good, but not great," he says of his attempt to return to play. "Because if I was Magic Johnson, it would've been great, see? That's the difference. To show that somebody with HIV could not just play, because I can play. I can go back now and play. But I'm talking about somebody that did it and did it the way it's supposed to be done. To be Magic Johnson, the guy that I was. You know, he's a lot. He's a lot of roles in one."

There is a *gravitas* to him, pure Earvin-ness, and there is much more substance than perhaps even he has ever allowed. The smiles do not come as quick and as easily as they do on television when Oprah is billing and cooing and asking to see new pictures of the baby. Blue notes ring behind his words. "I lost the fun of it," he says. "Fun makes me be Magic Johnson, the enthusiasm. That's a big part of my game, and then that was taken away. I couldn't use all my energy to play the game because I was using it all to explain myself." He cannot be Magic the way he was, but he also cannot be Earvin, either, because Magic gave Earvin a fatal disease. Magic will want to go to Heaven while Earvin does the time in hell. It cannot work anymore.

Ultimately, he asked for too much and for too little. He wanted his normal life back, but his normal life is performance, and performance is life, and there was no part left for him. He forfeited the only role that was left for him to play, AIDS saint, because saints—even real ones—need constituencies as much as politicians do.

In *Making Saints*, journalist Kenneth Woodward chides the Catholic Church because, in choosing its saints, the Church forces itself "to exclude . . . any evidence of human failure; in doing so, [they] omit what is truly exemplary in the life of a saint—the struggle between virtue and vice or, in a wider scope, between grace and nature." The real world is even less forgiving. Magic Johnson has not been what the world wanted him to be, and the world cannot seem to accept Earvin Johnson, Jr. for who he is. Our grace and his nature have gone to war.

"He who dies of epidemic disease is a martyr. When you learn that an epidemic disease exists in a country, do not go there; but if it breaks out in a country where you are, do not leave."

—Muslim proverb

According to Thucydides, a plague fell upon the Athenian Army during the first Peloponnesian War. Soldiers refused to bury the infected bodies of their comrades, and as the conventional religion of the day failed to provide either an explanation or relief, the men turned from the priests of the gods and sought intercession themselves, or else they turned away from the gods entirely. They ran riot, engaging in all manner of sensual excess. The living gave themselves up for dead. "Already a far heavier sentence . . . was hanging over a man's head," the historian reports. "Before that fell, why should he not take a little pleasure?"

Boccaccio writes that during the height of the Black Death in Europe, fathers would abandon their sons. Jews were suspected of poisoning the wells. In 1878, when yellow fever broke out in Memphis, people caught fleeing the city were hanged on sight by the hysterical residents of the surrounding towns. Today, there are undertakers who refuse to bury those whom AIDS has killed, and the disease has been variously described as God's (or nature's) revenge against the carnal and the wicked. When Earvin Johnson announced that he was HIV-positive, he was stepping into the middle of the inglorious history of human intolerance.

Of course, at the time, he knew less about the history than he knew even about his disease. By his own admission, he went through the 1980s unconcerned about AIDS. "I thought it was a homosexual thing," he recalls. "It wasn't even close to my mind. We knew it was out there, but I never thought it could affect me. In the circles I was around, it was oblivion." Considering that those circles came to encompass the Hollywood show-business community, which was hit hard in the early stages of the epidemic, this is a formidable bit of denial, but not an uncommon one.

His professional success, however, was immediate and remarkable. It is now beyond cliché to say that Johnson (along with Bird) helped resuscitate professional basketball, which nearly drowned in the late 1970s, due to public apathy and a spate of nasty drug scandals. When Johnson entered the game, in 1979, he was a fresh and vibrant presence. In Johnson's Lakers debut, Abdul-Jabbar won the game with a lordly hook shot, only to be seized in an ungainly embrace by the enthusiastic rookie guard. Pictures of the moment show the cool and elegant center looking quite amused, as though someone had just handed him a mackerel. What Johnson did for Abdul-Jabbar, he did for the Lakers and, ultimately, for the entire NBA. Competitively, his Lakers and Bird's Celtics were a matchup for the ages, and one that providentially took place in two large television markets. Moreover, before anyone else did, he saw the genius in the NBA's attempt to market itself as a league—as a single entertainment entity. This succeeded wonderfully; the NBA was able to sell a largely black sport to a largely white audience, even during a decade in which racial relations worsened. Magic Johnson became a crossover hit.

By the time he got to the NBA, he had set the corporate class as his goal; he claimed to idolize Michael Ovitz, Hollywood's king fixer, and now he employs him. Johnson himself has always sought to make things work, to cast the movie of his own life. In 1981, when he engineered the dismissal of Lakers Coach Paul Westhead—a good move, as it turns out, since it resulted in the hiring of Pat Riley—he was simply firing the director in order to get the story to come out right. He had learned quickly and well.

As the Lakers prospered, Magic became one of the town's most vivid performers. Academy Award winners paid him court. He'd made it at last. His life was performance, and performance was his life. Magic Johnson was the next best thing to a movie star.

The good life was a perquisite of his new station. At first, liberated L.A. amazed him. "I mean, you had women with no panties. Women with women," he recalls. However, he soon lost whatever inhibitions he had brought with him, or (more likely) he simply parked them with Earvin and let Magic be Magic. The Lakers became notorious around the NBA, the Forum coming to be known as the league's primary pleasure palace. Games at the Forum were glamorous affairs, forty-one Hollywood premieres a season. Lakers officials noted how often the same women's names appeared on the list of complimentary tickets left by the players. In 1990, forward James Worthy was caught in a police sting operation while attempting to solicit two women from a Houston escort service.

By all accounts, Johnson was central to everything that went on. He helped entertain visiting players, showing the rookies the (you should pardon the expression) lay of the land. In his recently published autobiography, *My Life*, he claims that he once had sex in an elevator, another time in a boardroom, and he has also confessed to *ménages à trois, quatre* and *six*. At one point, sources say, the Lakers became so alarmed at Johnson's sexual escapades that the team asked the league to step in. Through it all, though, he maintained his relationship with Earleatha "Cookie" Kelly, whom he had met in college, at Michigan State, and whom he eventually married, in September 1991.

He veers between caution and candor while discussing all of this. For example, he claims never to have slept all night with any woman except Cookie, as though that mitigates whatever guilt he may feel. He also seems to excuse promiscuity on the basis of good conversation.

"I think when you talk about [having] a lot of women, people think that's all you're doing," he says. "I wasn't, like, numbers, like a Wilt Chamberlain and thousands of women or whatever. It wasn't even close to that. People don't realize that I was *friends* with these women, not that I just went out and picked one up and that was it. See, I talked to them because I wanted to know what's up here and, see, people are not getting that, so I guess they think it's one night here and one night there and that was it, and it wasn't like that at all.

"When it was time for them to go . . . because I'm a man, I couldn't sleep with any of them. I couldn't sleep with nobody but Cookie. So I said, you know, 'You got to go,' because I was, like, I didn't trust them, you know? So they was, like, 'Oh, you kicking me out?' I said, 'Yeah, you know I told you that before.' So they didn't understand." It's almost as if Magic picked up the women and left Earvin to do the explaining afterward. Later, when he was touring to support his book, he was roundly criticized for revealing as much as he did.

When Johnson announced his HIV status, in November 1991, the NBA shook briefly in its success. There is still that sub-rosa fear that white America responds unwillingly to a largely black sport and that any scandal would bring that odious dynamic back into play. Uncontrolled black male sexuality is one of this culture's most durable racist myths. Indeed, it was the psychological underpinning of the whole system of segregation. The NBA and its new corporate pilot fish wanted no part of a sex scandal to rival the drug scandals of the late 1970s.

Hence, the league was relieved when Johnson seemed to be granted a conditional public pardon, contingent upon his properly performing the bestowed role of AIDS saint. That lasted all the way through the Dream Team summer of 1992. Public opinion began to turn only last August, when Johnson started dropping broad hints that he would like to return to the Lakers full-time. But there were whispers throughout the league, and for the first time, Johnson felt himself losing a part of his most basic constituency: the players.

On October 12, columnist Dave Kindred wrote in *The Sporting News* that if Johnson planned to return to active NBA competition, he should "tell the whole truth about how he acquired the AIDS virus," intimating that Johnson could have become infected during unprotected gay sex, an accusation Johnson has repeatedly denied. The charge was the first overt indication that there were people in the NBA who found Johnson's return unsettling. It began a media frenzy, and the publicity tour for his book, including a graphic interview on ABC's *Prime Time Live*, only fanned the flames.

Meanwhile, Phoenix Suns President Jerry Colangelo spoke out about the alleged risks that Johnson posed to his players. Utah Jazz star Karl Malone, an Olympic teammate of Johnson's, expressed similar concerns to the *New York Times*. Oddly enough, a controversy that began with the opinion that "the odds" were against Johnson's having attained the HIV virus through heterosexual sex had evolved into one that assumed as credible the even-longer odds that he could somehow pass the virus along to another player during a game. In the Lakers' last 1992 exhibition game, in Chapel Hill, North Carolina, Johnson, playing badly, scratched his arm, and the photograph of Lakers trainer Gary Vitti bandaging the barely visible wound flashed all over the country. Clearly, Johnson's position had become untenable. On November 2, he retired again.

Perhaps Johnson thought he could finesse it. Perhaps he thought Magic could smile and wave and somehow beat the collective fear that has risen up in the face of epidemic disease over the past 2,500 years. But he was an uneasy saint. People could relate to Elizabeth Glaser, as a mother struck by vicious happenstance. They now looked at Johnson and saw somebody who took sexual risks, especially when he came out and told them just how blatant those risks had been. That was too threatening, particularly if you're out there yourself. He *had* to be gay, because then straight folks could feel less threatened by their condom-less Saturday nights. Besides, he'd performed well at the Olympics, and the sick are not generally loved until they become pitiable.

"People are real strange animals," Lakers General Manager Jerry West muses. "Everyone has great compassion for people, until it cuts into their livelihood. I think it's a shame because this could've been a remarkable story. If it would've progressed in a normal way, I think it would've quieted a lot of people's fears."

Caught between the hysteria that attends any epidemic and his admitted flouting of sexual convention, Johnson had come to a place where his diplomatic skills were of no use, a place where he could not broker a peace even between Earvin, who needed to be loved, and Magic, who needed to be adored. There was a conflict in the plot to which there was no resolution. He had violated the old Muslim proverb. He had left the country of the epidemic, and he was out there all alone.

They have known each other for years. That's what her friends say. She met Earvin Johnson when they were both students at Michigan

State. For some reason, friends say, she was able to touch Earvin when all anybody else wanted was to be touched by Magic. She got married to someone else, had a daughter and then got divorced. In March 1990, she says, she was in the Palladium club in Los Angeles, and she saw him again. On June 22, she alleges in her suit, they made love at her apartment. She says that she asked him about using a condom. She says he declined to use one.

A year later, she discovered that she was HIV-positive. She says she spoke with Johnson by phone in July 1991. She says she wrote him a letter about it on August 29, 1991. She says she found him on September 12 of that year playing basketball with his friends at Jenison Fieldhouse on the Michigan State campus. She says he didn't believe her, that he was too healthy to have AIDS. Finally, last October, she sued him for $2 million.

Among other things, the suit alleges that Johnson knew that he was HIV-positive seventeen months before he admitted it publicly. If her facts are correct, that makes him more than simply oversexed. It makes him willfully reckless. In the dichotomy of his life, it would be the final triumph of Magic over Earvin. It would make him a villain. Johnson will not comment on the lawsuit, saying only that "they have no case, so they have to attack my character."

The woman in question—a 31-year-old health-office worker—is being advised by one Armstrong Williams, a close friend and a conservative Washington, D.C., media specialist whose business partner is Stedman Graham, Oprah Winfrey's fiancé. Theodore Swift, the plaintiff's Lansing attorney, refers all calls to Williams, who was Clarence Thomas's press officer when Thomas was the head of the Equal Employment Opportunity Commission. During the stormy hearings before the Senate Judiciary Committee, Williams worked the halls, drawing for reporters a portrait of Anita Hill as a frustrated and bitter ex-employee.

Williams is shell-mouthed on the whole affair, declining to comment for the record. He has been busy, however. A source familiar with the case insists that it was Williams who orchestrated the steady stream of leaks about the case to Frank Deford of *Newsweek*. Ever since the first story about the suit appeared, Johnson's lawyers have charged that the plaintiff was promiscuous herself and that Johnson may have contracted the virus from her. "I don't know why they have to say that publicly," says attorney Swift. "I haven't been running around calling him a whoremonger." However, since Johnson's defense will undoubtedly involve impugning the plaintiff's character, there is no little irony in the fact that it will be Armstrong Williams's job to keep Earvin Johnson from doing to his client what Williams worked so hard to do to Anita Hill.

Once a portion of the text of the August 1991 letter appeared in *Newsweek*, last November, it became plain that the woman's allegations contradicted not only Johnson's claims at his original retirement press conference but also his autobiography, in which he writes "Of the women I talked to, nobody has tested positive . . . thank God for that." Further, if the woman's story is true, then the past two years of Johnson's life are open to serious revisionism, and his moral claim to leadership on the issue of AIDS education becomes perilously threadbare. In addition, the revelation of the lawsuit prompted inquiries into whether, married or not, Johnson is still carrying on, something that would sink his public image entirely and forever. Last November, *The National Enquirer* ran a purported account of Johnson's weekend trip to Las Vegas to see the heavyweight championship fight between Evander Holyfield and Riddick Bowe, during which, the tabloid alleges, Johnson propositioned anything that moved, except, possibly, the white tigers at the Mirage.

"That whole Vegas thing is a farce," Johnson says. "I can't do anything about it. If they want to follow me, they will. I know the truth of it."

He says he has broken the habit of promiscuity. "Gradually, you take yourself out, and that's what's happened to me," he says. "You're gradually taking yourself out of the club-type atmosphere where all the single people are who want to meet people. And I think it's made it easier to me that I'm not playing.

"As a man, you know, you're always going to say 'There's a beautiful woman.' Now, if a guy says that he can't see a beautiful woman, that's lying. Let's be up-front about it. There's nothing wrong with saying 'That's a beautiful woman.' What's wrong is acting on it."

That is clearly Earvin talking, but it was Magic who went alone to Vegas, which is not exactly taking oneself out of that atmosphere he's talking about. See Magic at ringside, smiling in the spotlight, adored if not loved, and you think of Thucydides and his Athenians, who got drunk on their own private religions because they didn't have anything to lose, and even the gods had given up.

He has an office in Century City, not far from the one Ronald Reagan keeps. He goes there after he works out. There is remarkable bulk to him, so much so that one of his friends wonders "Do you really think he knows what he's in for? I don't. We see him all big and strong, but what happens when he gets sick? What will we see, and will we even want to?" In a sense, then, he is buying time, building a kind of public monument to himself while he is still strong enough to do so. Over the course of his career with the Lakers, more than 150,000 people died of AIDS in the United States. He says he's not afraid that one day he will die a very public death.

"If you're truthful with yourself, you can sleep good," he says. "You don't have to worry about anything or any skeletons in [the] closet. I'm not worried about any of that stuff. I've never been a worrier, you know? If something's going to happen, it's going to happen, you know? I keep praying at night, then everything'll be all right. If I eat right. If I get enough sleep. Everything's going to be all right because people can live with this for twelve, fourteen, fifteen, years. So I'm thinking, Why can't it be like this for fifteen years?"

He can look out from his office into the hills above Hollywood. There are a hundred things that could've happened. He could've got cancer, and nobody would care how or why. He could've been drafted by Indiana or Cleveland. "I'd be married for years," he says, "with a lot of children." But he bought Hollywood long ago, bought it in his bones and in his soul, and Hollywood delivered. Tonight, he will go on television with his friend Arsenio, and they will laugh and joke and there will be warm applause and a serenade in his ear from saxophonist Kenny G., and it will be a long way from Lansing, Michigan, and the little road that dead-ends at the Oldsmobile plant. He will be back there in a week, home for Thanksgiving and for a book-signing that will be more restrained than the one at the Manhattan bookstore where a woman screamed "Magic!" and fainted backward into an aisle marked "FANTASY."

No, the people will line up, all decorous and stolid, Christmas carols ringing out of the walls behind them. The signing will be at a suburban bookstore, just up the block from an eightplex movie house that is not a theater, not by a damn sight. "I'm just glad to be home," he will tell the local press, who love him. "Here, I'm just Earvin, you know?" Downtown, the stores are shuttered, the great blank-staring bones of the auto industry. There is a little public park where the Gladmer Theater was. It is a cold and empty place, and it has no stories to tell.

GQ **February 1993**

The Last Good Shot

The last good shot was a fairway iron. It rose in that odd flat way that golf shots have of rising if you're looking at them from about 180 yards downrange, which is where the spectators were sitting, huddling under trees to stay out of the fat, sweet-smelling rain that was falling on the Atlanta Country Club. The shot seemed to go straight up in stages, finally hanging way up there in the rain, and the spectators who had followed it up watched it hang, not realizing that the ball was moving, not realizing that it was eating up 180 yards of fairway because their eyes were in the sky where the golf ball was, and not on the ground where the golfer was. The sound of it trailed the shot—a sharp, cracking sound that seemed detached from the event of the last good shot itself, which was still in the air, but coming down now, coming down faster than it had risen before.

Golf is a game of many horizons. They change as you walk the course, one to another. They rise and they fall, often on the same hole. You reach one, really sting the ball, and then there's another, far in the distance, drawn now with water, perhaps, or lined tall with trees and thick with people. They change as you walk the course, one to another, and you hit toward them, one by one, each horizon as it comes, false or true.

For one extraordinary weekend last June, all the horizons were broad and true for Mike Donald, a 34-year-old journeyman professional golfer from Florida. He hit the ball from one horizon to another, each of them in turn as they rolled up at him from the Medinah Country Club in Illinois. Until that weekend, Donald was known only as a man willing to go anywhere to play—in 1989, he played in 35 of the 42 PGA Tour events—and as a likable playing partner whom his fellow pros regularly elected to the Tour's Policy Board. He has a broad, red face, and a little bit of a gut on him, and he looks like everybody that's ever clipped you for a $10 Nassau. Except that, in the 1990 U.S. Open, he nearly hustled the biggest game of them all.

He was tied for the lead after three rounds, and he made a one-shot lead stand all through the fourth, even when he bogied the 16th. Unfortunately, Hale Irwin birdied five of the last nine holes, draining a 60-footer on the 18th to catch Donald and force a playoff. They took Sunday night off and came back on Monday.

By then, Donald was a celebrity—Everyman in spikes. His mother was watching him, and she was a celebrity, too. On the morning of the playoff, after the emotion of the whole thing got to him and he cried a little, he saw three reporters standing around in the locker room. "I'll bet you're waiting for me," he said. He talked to them briefly, and then he went out to try to win the U.S. Open.

He didn't fold. He and Irwin both shot 74s, but Irwin birdied the first genuine sudden-death hole in Open history and won the championship. "God bless Mike Donald," Irwin said. "I almost wish he'd won." Irwin was a good story himself, an old pro steeped in confidence, but he'd won two of these already. Mike Donald had not. In 11 years on the Tour, Mike Donald had won only one tournament: the 1989 Anheuser-Busch Open, which is not steeped in much of anything, except hops. He had the gallery, all the way around the horizons of Medinah, one last time. That night, the U.S. Open runnerup went out and had a pizza.

"It's funny, but whenever you do something like that, you look back and say, 'That wasn't as hard as I thought it would be,'" Donald says today. "Even when I finally won, that was my reaction, that it wasn't as hard as I thought it would be. I'd been out here 11 years, and I hadn't won, and when I did win, it was like winning wasn't any harder than losing had been."

It's Friday at the Atlanta Golf Classic now—"Moving Day," is the way the pros put it. What that means is that you hit a certain score, or else you move on to the next stop, on to the next set of new horizons, on to the next last good shot. The spectators under the trees—the ones that aren't still in the sky with the ball and shouting, "Legs!" or "Come down!"—look out toward the nearest horizon, the top of a small rise in the center of the 18th fairway. Mike Donald is standing there, a lump of brown on the little green hillside, the shaft of the club sliding silvery through his fingers. He's in the sky, too, watching the last good shot fall toward the horizon tall with trees and thick with people.

A month after last year's Open, Donald tied Fuzzy Zoeller for second in the Buick Open, and, since then, nothing much has gone right for him. His mother died in January, after lingering for a time with complications after heart bypass surgery. Emotionally, Donald was spent by the time he finally rejoined the Tour this year, a month late. Coming into Atlanta, he was 141st on the Tour's money list, having earned $28,969, barely breaking even on his expenses for the season. The defending U.S. Open runnerup was in clear danger of having to play his way into tournaments throughout 1992.

But, though he's lost a few places on the money list, he's lost none of the good will that his play at Medinah engendered. Nowhere is the gulf between athletes and their fans more vividly wide than in golf. The Tour has sought the same kind of uniformity in its players that it seeks in its golf courses, and it thereby has rendered its players very little more than a set of interchangeable automatons. One blond head bobbing in the distance is the same as any other. Consequently, when a Mike Donald came along, with his red face and his belly hanging over his belt, a guy who was only 12 years removed from delivering flowers for a living, the galleries responded the same way Huey Long's used to when he'd show up in galluses and brogan shoes. The Kingfish was no redneck, and Mike Donald, whose career earnings exceed $1 million, is no Saturday four-ball hacker. But something there is in both of them that touches the common soul.

"So many people have come up to me and told me that they were rooting for me to win the Open," says Donald. "They told me how they watched the Open, and how great it was, and how much they enjoyed it."

The last good shot at the Atlanta Golf Classic is the 77th shot Mike Donald has struck this day, and the 152nd he's struck during this tournament. The Atlanta Country Club is playing soft this week. The rain has turned the greens into gentle cushions, and the pros are being allowed to "pick and clean" in the soggy fairways, meaning that they can place their golf balls in the spot where the ball may be most crisply struck. Given the skills of the average professional golfer, this is akin to allowing them to play Putt-Putt for the purse; all the Atlanta CC needs to do further is construct a little windmill on each of the greens. Nevertheless, the last good shot is coming down, and it's the 152nd that Mike Donald has struck in this tournament, and that means that today is Moving Day for Mike Donald.

It has been a horrible, aggravating round—bad golf played very slowly. Donald's threesome has been on the course since 1:15 P.M., and 5 o'clock's gone by already. Donald has been all over the course with his driver, and he has had to wait several minutes between each bad shot. On the seventh hole, a black dog retrieves tennis balls that spectators toss into the creek, and the dog is having a better time than Mike Donald is. It's raining again, too.

Finally, he gets to 18, and he drives it down the middle, and he hits the last good shot. Standing on one horizon, Donald hears the cheers rippling toward him from the other one. The last good shot has landed on the softened green, nestling gently three feet from the cup. Mike Donald steps off the far horizon and walks toward his most immediate future.

In a very real sense, the drama that was the 1990 United States Open began at the Doral Open of 1969, one of the 30-odd stops along the Tour that were, and are, totally indistinguishable from each other. A Doral might as well be a Western as it might as well be a Greensboro or an Atlanta. They all lead toward the Open, but they are of a totally different order of being. They are like all those tiny Nevada towns that choke all night on the dust kicked up by the traffic pouring into Las Vegas.

That day, the first one of the 1969 Doral, the game had gone all treasonous and sour on a pro named Bob Murphy. He came off 18 knowing full well that he was not going to make the cut, that the next day was going to be Moving Day for him. Kids stood in an unwieldy clot around the gate that led off the course, and they clamored for any faintly magical talisman, even one that had been so vividly accursed that day as to be attached to Bob Murphy. One short kid stood in the crowd near the gate. Murphy spotted him. Murphy looked at his golf ball. The logic that afflicts all golfers great and small came upon Murphy, who looked at his golf ball and saw every vicious thing that it had done to him all day. He looked back at the short kid. He tossed him the golf ball. "Here, pard'ner," said Bob Murphy. "Maybe you'll have more luck with it."

"You know," says Mike Donald, now 35 years old and the defending U.S. Open runnerup, "I've still got that stupid golf ball." He took up golf because he was too small to play baseball. The Christmas when he was 12 years old, Mike Donald's parents gave him his first set of clubs and that was it. "I distinctly remember when I was 13, shooting 60 for nine holes," he says. "I got a few lessons, and I was 14 when I broke 90. I got better pretty quick." He came from working people—his father was an auto mechanic, and his mother did several jobs, including opening her own ceramics shop—and so he had to chase the game harder than a lot of kids his own age did. Golf got him to Broward Community College, and thence to Georgia Southern, where he played one year and lost his scholarship. "The coach there tried a power play on me, basically," Donald recalls.

What happened was that the coach asked how much the Donald family could afford to pay. The elder Donald responded by asking the coach how much scholarship money was available. The coach called back and told the Donalds that he had none left. Mike Donald left school. He hung around the house doing nothing for two weeks, and then his father told him that he could move out, or he could get a job. Mike went to work for Bunny's Florist Shop in North Miami Beach, delivering happiness and allergies for a princely $90 a week. "That," he says, "was brutal." Consequently, when Georgia Southern replaced his old coach, Donald fairly flew back into school. His mother took his old job with the florist.

He turned professional in 1978 and spent a year hacking around the mini-tours. He qualified for the big Tour a year later. He loaded up his 1978 Cougar with this new life of his, and he proceeded to see parts of North America heretofore unexplored since the demise of Lewis and/or Clark. "When you're young," he explains, "you're so hungry. You want to play so badly that, man, nothing's that tough." Once, he drove from Atlanta into Canada, played one practice round, proceeded to blow qualifying, and then drove straight to Memphis in order to try again the following week. In 1982, he was driving from Florida to Arizona in order to catch the opening events of that year's Tour. He ran into a storm, and wound up spending New Year's Eve snowbound in Fort Stockton, Texas. "I couldn't wait to get up the next morning and get on the way again," he says. He retired the Cougar later that year. It had over 200,000 miles on it.

He never changed, not even when his earnings crawled gasping over six figures for the first time in 1986. Nobody on the Tour loves the Tour life the way that Mike Donald does. For others, there are family obligations. Mike Donald never married, and, up until this year, he lived at home with his mother. For others, there were stock portfolios, and courses to design, and whiskey to drink with rich people. For Mike Donald, there was next week. Always next week. Iron Mike, the pros called him, chuckling.

"This is play," he says. "Really. It all depends on how you look at it. When you realize how nice the people treat you—I mean, they treat you like you're doing something special, like you're curing cancer or something. Any time you think it's tough, you realize that some people have to go to work for 50 weeks a year. Me? Even when I play 35 of 37 events, I'm still getting 17 weeks off. Most people would die for that."

Anyone can say that. However, there is in Mike Donald a sense of absolute authenticity in those words. Elsewise, they wouldn't have responded to him the way they did at Medinah last year. He played four marvelous rounds, parring the course to death, adamantly refusing to crack. Irwin caught him with a monumental rally, but Irwin never caught the crowd, and he knew it. "It was probably the contrast," Irwin says. "The player that's done just a little more than the other guy. The lesser-known player against the better-known player. The underdog, if you wish, against the favorite."

Some followed him simply because he was the underdog. However, most followed him around because he looked like he had walked out of their lives. It was as if they had driven every one of those 200,000 miles themselves, splitting the driving and chipping in for gas. It was as if they'd hit every one of those thousands and thousands of practice balls, and delivered every one of those flowers, sweating and exhausted on Easter, and on Mother's Day. It was as if Mike Donald's mom, who followed him around Medinah on what was supposed to be the final day, was the mother to them all. Mike Donald had paid all his dues into their own hands, and they held them there as if they were the most precious gold.

"It was like everybody I walked by was yelling words of encouragement," Donald says. "You almost have to semi-ignore it because, if you don't, you'd be so damned excited that you couldn't do anything.

"For me, I'd been playing golf for almost 25 years and working on my skills, and to get a chance to test it against the greatest pressure. Oh, man—to play that well and to hit that many great shots, it makes you realize that all the time you spent was worth it."

Which brought him to the locker room that Monday, chatting with reporters as though he weren't going out to try and win the United States Open. He walked to the practice tee, and he saw some friends of his from Florida who had flown up and bought tickets to the biggest day in his life. He greeted them, talked for a while, tried not to cry, and then he walked into the playoff round for the championship. The Cougar was rusting somewhere behind him, and they were probably watching in the hotel bar in Fort Stockton, Texas, watching Hale Irwin and Mike Donald, the only two men still on the golf course.

They paced each other as the first of the many horizons rose and shifted and fell away. Gradually, though, Donald pulled ahead. He walked up to the 16th tee with a two-shot lead. The little short rise to the tee had brought Mike Donald as close as he would come to the very top of his sport. "So many things happened that made it look like he was destined to win," Donald muses. "I got a two-shot lead with three to play for the Open, and I play the last five holes at par and I lose. That's not supposed to happen."

He was done in by a long Irwin birdie putt on 16, and by knocking his own approach into a bunker at 18 when all he needed was a par to win. Instead, the two went into sudden death and Irwin beat him with a birdie on the first extra extra-hole. Mike Donald soaked in all the cheers, collected his $110,000 runnerup check, and he moved on. To Westchester. New horizons. Next week. Always next week.

She'd had heart trouble for quite a while. She'd always worked. A waitress now, then a bookkeeper. She worked for an advertising agency, and she took the job at Bunny's when Mike went back to school. Finally, she took to making pottery and, ultimately, she opened up her own store. She'd worked hard and now she had heart trouble. So they told her all the risks, and they did the bypass operation, but she didn't get any better. Last January, after lingering for five weeks, Mike Donald's mother died.

Of all the lovely moments during last year's U.S. Open, she had provided the loveliest. "I got letters from people telling me how much my mom reminded them of their mom," recalls Donald. "It was like we had a lot of people in my family all of a sudden."

For the first time since he began playing for a living, Donald was in no hurry to get to the Tour. He stayed with her until the end, missing the year's first four events and playing very little at all. He's not yet caught up. "Not to make excuses," he says, "but I missed that whole month and, when I finally got [back to the Tour], I hadn't played any golf for about 40 days." Moreover, after an understandably miserable start, Donald took a two-week vacation prior to the Atlanta tournament. There are unmistakable signs that Iron Mike is slowing down. Not many, mind you, but some.

"For me, I'd like to play for as long as I'm able to," he says. "I'll probably be one of those guys they finally have to boot off. I'll probably be one of those guys that hangs on too long."

It's not difficult to see why. His was always a solitary life, even by the gypsy standards of the Tour. Unmarried, all of his social life revolved around his work. Two of his best friends out there, Lance Ten Broeck and Bill Britton, have curtailed their playing careers. Now, he's getting old; at 35, he's well beyond the median age of the people against whom he plays. The charm of that old Cougar and the romance of the open road may be dimming somewhat.

"Is it lonely?" he asks. "That's a tough one. I've been dating this girl for a couple of years, and she hasn't been able to travel as much this year as she did last year, so I've spent a lot of time alone, but I don't really get lonely, I don't think. If I was doing something I didn't like, that would be different. I don't know. I just finished an 11-week trip, and it got to the point where I was frazzled. Two weeks at home really helped me."

He's at the point where he's supposed to be very full of age and wisdom, but so much of his knowledge of who he is came over those five remarkable days last June that it's hard to know now where his Open ends and he begins. It's as though all the affection he earned as he walked Medinah has stayed with him, defining who he is as a man and as a golfer. If, as Tennyson said, self-knowledge and self-reverence are two of the keys to absolute power, then Mike Donald became very powerful. Now, for better or worse, he will live the rest of his days with it. You see a great deal when you're standing at the top of your profession, however, briefly you may be there. All the horizons spread themselves before you, false and true.

"I think a lot of being successful has to do with how you perceive yourself," he says. "If you don't perceive yourself as somebody who can win tournaments, then you probably won't. When I get into contention now, I can see myself hitting shots. I realize that I don't have to play my best golf all the time to win. I used to think you had to be perfect. I don't believe you have to be perfect any more."

He has walked along to Atlanta's last horizon, following the last good shot right to the spot where it landed, three feet away from the hole. There is some applause from under the trees. Mike Donald knocks in his birdie putt, and then he'll go on to Muirfield in Ohio for the Memorial. Far away, up on that little rise that marks the far horizon of the 18th hole, back up there whence Mike Donald has just come, three more golfers appear, walking through the rain like the very ghosts of him.

Mike Donald is still coming over the hill. He lives in south Florida and plays on the satellite tours and, every now and then, he gets a sponsor's exemption into a PGA Tour event.

The National

Abe Lemons

Oklahoma Route 74, going north. Crescent coming up now. Hometown of Globetrotter Geese Ausbie, whom Abe almost recruited once, but the times were against any black kid playing basketball at Oklahoma City University—or anywhere else hereabouts, for all that. Also hometown of Gary Duncan. Abe did recruit him, and now he cuts hair here at the Captain's Chair. Duncan once shaved the head of Abe's manager as a prank, and Abe had to discipline him. Made all the pranksters shave their heads, too. Crescent coming up now, and Abe is talking about dressing for success.

"When I started coachin', and I went out recruitin', the first thing I did was go out and buy me a $65 suit. I bought that $65 suit, and I bought me that diamond ring. Bought me some alligator shoes. I looked . . . prosperous. I'd go visit some kid somewhere. Then I'd come home, hang that suit up, put them 'gators in the closet. I still got them 'gators, got 'em to home in the closet still. They gotta be 35 years old. For sentimental reasons, I guess. If you look at a memento, or at a picture of something, it gives you a flash of other days. That's why you keep pictures of things, I guess. I wished I kept more accurate records of all the things I done, all the places I've been. But I always thought that, if I keep records, we might get captured or something. Might find out what I been up to."

Crescent going by now.

Mark Twain wrote: "The humorous story is a work of art—high and delicate art—and only an artist can tell it. But no art is necessary in telling the comic and witty story; anybody can do it . . . The art of telling a humorous story—understand, I mean by word of mouth, not print—was created in America and has remained at home."

Storytellers are going out of our lives now. There is no time for them. They lend themselves neither to soundbites nor video. They are out of step with an impatient age—an age that now does not allow them even the time to entertain, let alone educate. An age that believes that sophisticated humor means Candice Bergen dancing to Motown. An age that believes that a funny basketball coach means Jim Valvano, playing the buffoon to an audience culled from the semifinalists in the National Chest Hair Competition in Bayonne, N.J. An age that no longer has time for Abe Lemons, that moves too fast for the stories he has to tell.

For example: "Basketball always was fun to play. We played out back behind my house. Whippy Jones lived out there. Had an outdoor toilet. Had a hydrant out there so you could get yourself a drink of water. There's a guy across the street. His Daddy preached for the Indians. Had him that little brown church out there. I don't know whatever happened to Rollin Gilbert, but he had two goals. Everybody else only had one. His Daddy was a mean man. Wouldn't let Rollin play ever. Had him studying or something. We always tried to get Rollin because he had two goals.

"You stay out there. Stay out there and stay out there. Shoot that basketball. Then, in the evening, everybody's mother's calling. You can hear 'em down the road."

The funniest line in that story is, "His Daddy was a mean man." It does not read funny. It does not even sound funny, unless Abe Lemons is telling the story, and always is pronounced "allus," and "hydrant" takes a couple extra seconds to roll on out there, and then "His Daddy was a mean man" is as funny as whistling fish for no other reason than it gets put in there next to the Whippy Jones, the Indians, and the little brown church. There is a kind of reverence for detail that you get when you grow up in the Short Grass Country of

Oklahoma in the 1930's when nothing, not even the very land beneath you, is guaranteed to be any kind of permanent.

That is what leaves the game when Lemons retires this spring after coaching basketball for 34 years. With him go all those mothers calling, calling in the twilight. He has won almost 600 games. He has won at Oklahoma City, at Pan American, and at Texas, and back at OCU in the NAIA which, he explains, "is like Alcatraz. Ain't nobody ever got out. Some have tried. We found the bodies washed up on the beach one morning."

It doesn't matter that he has coached all these years and that he has won all those games. It doesn't matter that he is old now, and stooped, and that the Parkinson's makes his right foot shake. What matters is that voice—like dark bourbon and worn leather, as flat as the winter sunlight. A voice that takes you through the little stories that make up the big ones, the ones that are all tangled up like field wire and that take time to untangle and tell.

"It wasn't what he said that was so funny, but the way he said it," says LaSalle Thompson of the Indiana Pacers, who played for Lemons at Texas. "You could say the same stuff, or I could say it, and it wouldn't be funny at all. But he'd come out with that, 'Ahh-dam,' and you'd be on the floor."

Ahh-dam, without that voice, there's one less storyteller to tell the stories. They fall flat, sheet music on a dusty floor. When Abe Lemons retires this spring, it's the end of something very much like history.

"Everybody'd go to bed. You slept about four to a bed, or on pallets," he says, remembering Walters, Okla., where all the stories begin for him. "Kids'd go to bed, then everybody'd tell stories. Y'know, everybody that come out of the Depression is pretty much a storyteller. There's nothing much else to do."

Lamont coming up now.

A bus carrying the Medford Cardinals takes a corner wide. Uniforms swing in all the windows. The bus kicks up dust around the L&M diner, where Abe has stopped to ask directions from a woman in a mud-crusty green Buick. She points on up the road where the bus came from. Lamont coming up now, and Abe is talking about basketball players.

"It's like, I was watching on television, and everything is whether or not you're going to be a lottery pick, or whether or not you're going to play small forward, or be a 3-man, whatever the hell that is. I'd like to hear one of 'em say, 'I'm gonna get a job. When I get out, I'm gonna be a manager at a Pizza Hut. When I get out, I'm gonna be a real smart gas-pumper and, maybe after 20 years, I'll get a station and a couple of pumps of my own.'"

In his car, next to a package of cigars that is every bit as permanent a part of the console as the stick-shift, Abe Lemons keeps a 1935 newspaper clipping of a picture taken in 1922. The picture is of the center of a small town in Oklahoma, and there is a gigantic black cloud rising high in all directions. Pieces of Oklahoma and pieces of Kansas blowing high in the sky. A signifying, biblical cloud. "I keep it with me to remind me that it ain't ever going to get that bad again," he says. "You can always go to sleep on the steps of the bank, and they'll have to come getcha."

Like most of Oklahoma, Walters was blowing all over the place when Abe Lemons was a child. Walters threw itself around in great clouds. Walters got in your eyes. It got in your nose. While Abe slept, his mother would put a wet cloth over his face so he could breathe. All the neighbors went to California, taking Highway 51 west until it reached John Steinbeck and Henry Fonda. The Lemons family stayed in Oklahoma because they didn't have a car. Abraham Eldridge Lemons, a butcher by trade, took what jobs he could find to feed his growing family.

There were eight children, and the youngest one they named A. E. Just A. E. It didn't stand for anything. It wasn't long, however, before people just naturally dropped that "B" in there, and called the youngest after his father. Which was fine with him. "I got a cousin named R. D., and that don't stand for anything, either," Abe Lemons says. "It's hard gettin' by just as an initial."

He remembers his family as "scramblers," and he did a fair amount of it himself. He and his brothers swept piles of Oklahoma and Kansas off the streets. He even went so far as to be a professional athlete once.

"When I was 12, I weighed 75 pounds, and Roy Peck was getting up a group to go over to Lawton to the Ritz Theater. They had a boxing night. Nobody was trained or anything, and you'd wind up fighting some trained guy from Fort Sill. I told my Dad that I was going over. Now, nobody ever went to Lawton. I told him I thought I'd go over to Lawton to fight. He said, 'Well, why?' So I told him that I get a dollar and a hamburger. He said, 'Well, go ahead if you think it's worth it.' It was really kind of scary. I went up there three times. I remember I knocked one kid down three times and they called it a draw. Pretty damned scary there, though, looking over at that big old guy and realizing your limitations. He always looked bigger, and he usually was. One Friday, I was hanging around the house, and my Dad said, 'Ain't you going to Lawton?' I told him, no, it wasn't worth it any more. He said that was all right."

He was held back a year in eighth grade, which he reckons today as a turning point. The year off let him grow partway to 6–3, which helped him improve his basketball, and which eventually got him a scholarship to Southwestern Oklahoma State University in Weatherford. He also was dating a girl from Temple named Betty Jo Bills, who was every bit a match for him, and who has been known over 44 years of their marriage to tell him after tough losses, "Sometimes, I wished you passed eighth grade."

"When I first met him, I did not like him at all," says Betty Jo, two daughters and four grandchildren along. "Plus the first time we went out, we all went to a movie, and he arranged to have us sit next to each other, which I did not like at all."

At Southwestern, Abe lived in a dormitory built from bricks that his brother had delivered. He played ball, went to school, and hung out at a campus drugstore. There was a hamburger joint that was too pricey for him, so he was in the drugstore that day, a little while after Pearl Harbor, when the Thorn brothers came in talking about the Merchant Marines.

"Hell, I didn't know where Pearl Harbor was," he says. "But it occurred to me that something was about to happen. I had broken my wrist, had a couple of bad teeth, and I had my initials, so it looked like the only thing I could get was the Army, and I sure as hell didn't want the Army."

So he joined the merchant service, sailed around the world twice, and didn't come home until 1946. He finished his college at OCU, and he married Betty Jo in what he still regards as something of an upset. "I'd call and say, 'I'll be down Saturday and we'll go to a preview.' And they'd be an independent game in Union Valley, and I'd call her back and tell her." So Betty Jo got to watch her betrothed play ball, and then wash off afterwards in the horsetrough. "I's breaking her in to be a coach's wife," he explains.

He was making $75 a week working in a slaughterhouse, and coaching the OCU Chiefs part-time. After he graduated, he coached the freshmen there for five years, and when Noel Perry accepted the job at Oklahoma in 1955, Abe was named varsity coach. He stayed there for 18 years.

It was different then. An independent school that liked to travel could compete nationally. Abe loved to travel—his teams have played in 39 states, and he virtually opened Alaska to college basketball—so his teams travelled.

"We played everywhere," says Dr. Ron Bolen, an Austin dentist who played for Lemons in the late 1960's. "If there was a place he wanted to go, we found a team to play there."

His teams were intriguing collections of oddballs. Among Bolen's teammates were an Indian guard named Gary Gray and a big forward named Charles (Big Game) Hunter. Moreover, the world was beginning to discover the head coach who, when asked about the widespread practice of giving collegiate athletes easy courses, explained, "Well, they talk about basketweaving courses. We had a basketweaving course, but the Indians blew the curve so we had to drop it."

The Chiefs made the NCAA tournament seven times, the last time in 1973, when Lemons finally was lured away. A former OCU football coach named Ralph Schilling was the athletic director at Pan American University, hard by the Mexican border. He asked Lemons if he knew anybody that would like to coach basketball at Pan American for $25,000 a year or so. Lemons said that he certainly did, and he and Betty Jo moved to Edinburg.

His Pan American teams were 55–16, but it was while he was there that Lemons's reputation as an eccentric really took off. It probably helped a little that he had become friendly with Al McGuire, who undoubtedly saw in Lemons a soulmate and boon companion.

He might've stayed at Pan-American, even with players like Tree McCulloch, who once asked to go home to San Antonio because, "My aunt died again."

"I told him to wait a week, and we'd all go up and scrimmage Trinity, and stay overnight," Lemons says. "I asked him if he could delay the funeral a week. He said that'd be fine with him."

But Betty Jo didn't like Edinburg, which was a long way from anywhere, really. So, when Darrell Royal came to Abe in 1976 and asked him to take over at Texas, he grabbed at the job. "Nobody gave a damn about the basketball team for the very good reason that they'd never done anything," he says. "Darrell hired me by himself. After being at the other two places, Austin looked like the Treasure of Sierra Madre. You could see all the nuggets just laying around. I thought, How can you lose here? What can you do to lose here?"

Ingersoll coming up now.

There is a soft, golden-edged sunset, and then night falls on the Short Spring Cemetery, and on Jenkins B-B-Que, Beer, and Grocery. All the way up Route 74, there have been towns and stores, farmhouses and fields, oil pumpers and two-ton tanks of anhydrous ammonia. But there hasn't been a single human being, except for the lady in the mud-crusty green Buick back in Lamont. Nobody else. No witnesses. Ingersoll coming up now, and Abe is talking about UFOs.

"Around here, this is where they see all them UFOs. Always, it's only one guy sees them. He doesn't have anybody to substantiate it. He says, 'There's a UFO.' And they say, 'Who's with you when you saw it?' He says, 'Nobody. Who'd be with me way out here?'"

Ingersoll just went by.

To understand what happened to Abe at Texas, you first have to understand Influential People. Texas produces them the way it produces sand and hostile reptiles and, as Abe explains it, "I never worked at a place that had politics before." And then you have to understand Mike Wacker, and what happened to him, before you can understand Abe and what happened to him.

Wacker was a shooting fool out of San Marcos where his father, Jim, coached football at Southwest Texas State. He also was one of the most hyperactive basketball players who ever lived. Abe loved him. "The whole family was like that," he says. "All hyper. I'd go and see the kid, and he'd say, 'Will I play?' And I'd ask his Dad, 'What do you tell players when they ask that?' He'd say, 'I'm out of this.' So I'd say, 'Well, hell, I've seen you play four times and you lost every game. I don't know how good you are.'"

Wacker ended up at Texas, and in 1980, he was signing on with a successful program. The Longhorns had won 20 games in each of the previous three years, including a 26–5 NIT championship season in 1978. Everything Abe had learned in the boondocks, he put into practice at Texas. They played matchup zone, which hardly anybody ever did. Their offensive scheme was simple, but effective.

Moreover, Abe had become a fullblown celebrity, probably peaking as such in New York during the NIT, when he complained about the price of room service. "I ain't never seen the chicken that could lay a $6 egg," he said. Whereupon a helpful Texas farmer dispatched a crate of live chickens to Abe's office, where they ran riot during an ill-conceived photo opportunity.

"I started doing things that got me in trouble," Abe says.

"Part of it was that Abe was physically incapable of kissing butt," says Tom Douglass, who played for Abe at Texas and is now a graduate assistant to Tom Penders there. Bill Little, the Texas SID, agrees. "Abe was the most honest man I ever met," Little says. "Not everybody's ready for that."

He was not without allies among the Influential People, however. As athletic director, Royal backed him up, as did Frank Erwin, the legendarily powerful chairman of the school's Board of Regents. Between them, Erwin and Royal were able to insulate Lemons from those other Influential People whom he had disturbed. However, Erwin died and Royal retired, and by 1982, Lemons was perilously low on support.

Wacker was a sophomore when the 1982 season began, and he was still in overdrive, a fact that both endeared him to Abe, and also drove him crazy. On one occasion, Wacker was running around as wild as those chickens did in Abe's office. Abe blew the whistle. "Ahh-dammit, Wacker," Abe said. "Somewhere on this campus there's got to be a drug that will slow you down."

Somehow, that 1981–82 team jelled perfectly. The Longhorns began the year 14–0 and went into the Baylor game ranked fourth in the country. Abe would have to miss the Baylor game because his only surviving brother—another brother, Roy Willis Lemons, had been killed by a hit-and-run driver shortly after the war—was having heart surgery. That was fine with Abe. Abe hated Baylor.

"So, he's getting a bypass, and that was back 10 years ago now. Those guys were still practicing on those things," Abe recalls. "I decided to come up and wait with him in the veteran's hospital. That was the night Wacker got hurt."

Wacker's kneecap tore completely loose. The injury was so serious that Wacker didn't finish his college career until 1985, and then only while wearing a brace that made him appear to be standing with one foot in a golf bag. Texas lost to Baylor, and then they lost 11 of the next 13 games, finishing 16–11. After the season, Abe was fired. Some Influential People had gotten him.

"The first thing I thought was, This is gonna kill Betty Jo," he says.

Wacker's voice goes soft and cloudy when he talks about his injury, and the opening that it gave to the Influential People. "Hell, it didn't do Wacker much good, either," scoffs Abe, who, when pressed, will admit that Wacker is his favorite player, and that his last Texas team could have been the one for his lifetime.

"What happened to him wasn't fair at all," Wacker says. "He's a caring man. We'd go on a road trip, and we'd see what you then called street people, and he'd always go out of his way to be nice to them. He came to see me in the hospital, and he was just very kind.

"It puts me in a really peculiar situation. Realistically, if I hadn't gotten hurt, I don't think he would've gotten fired. I don't have a handle on that yet. I really don't."

Alva coming up now.

A small blanket of lights at the end of the road. Steakhouses. Farm equipment stores. Alva coming up now, and Abe is talking about the road.

"Just think. You could see this every night, if you lived in one of these old houses here. Just sit on your porch there, and watch the sunset, and sigh, and think to yourself, What in hell am I doing in Alva, Oklahoma? Besides, do you know how many people who know you and love you have absolutely no idea where you are right now?"

Alva coming up now. End of the line.

It is not Abe who goes to see the doctors about his Parkinson's Disease. It is Betty Jo. "I go and talk to them, then I come home and tell him what they say," she says.

"I think maybe I'm one of them Christian Scientists," Abe replies.

It visibly afflicts him only in his right foot and the ring finger of his right hand, but it certainly influenced his decision to retire at the end of this season. He claims it's just the result of seeing too many basketball games. "I'm like one of those old golfers," he says. "They gave me the yips.

"It's all real strange because I haven't been sick a day in my life. But, if something's going to happen, I don't want it to happen on a goddamn basketball court. It's the damn games that get to me. If I'm watching a game on TV, and it's two guys I know coaching the game, then I'll turn it off. Turn on something else. Clint Eastwood, maybe. At least I know that [SOB] is going to win."

He came back to OCU in 1983, after "redshirting for a year." He had some job offers, but, "the problem with most of them was you had to go live there." Instead, he came back to where he started. After unsuccessfully attempting to play Division I basketball in a new era, the Chiefs dropped back into the NAIA in 1985. "Hell, we couldn't beat anybody," Abe says. "The president came to me and said, 'What do you think about the NAIA?' I said, 'Have you already done it?' He said, 'Yeah.' I said, 'I think it's a great idea.'"

This year's Chiefs are big, but rather slow. They began strongly, but they've faded since the end of their monthlong Christmas break, which means Abe may fall a few victories short of 600.

Truth be told, he leaves most of the actual coaching to his assistant, a gung-ho Houstonian named Harry Masch. "I think Coach Lemons is coaching life more than he's coaching basketball," says Chiefs guard Rich Dozier, whose father also played for Abe at OCU. "I grew up with stories about the guy. He's an original."

Coaching still mystifies Abe, though, even after 35 years, even at the end of it. "Guys I like are them animal trainers," he says. "Gunther Williams there, how he gets them guys to do that. You could be a helluva coach if you did that. Get you some tigers. You could have a helluva fast break.

"You know what amazes me? How in hell does a guy get a damn whale to come up and jump through a goddamn hoop? You can't hit him. How're you gonna hit him if he's down in the water? Even if you hit him, how does he know that you want him to go through that hoop? Every day that I try to get a guy to make a good pass, I think about that guy with the whale. How does that initial contact get made? Those things amaze me."

He thinks about these things as he drives around to the places on the last schedule he will play. He drives through his past. He drives to Weatherford, where he went to college, and where his dorm is still there, and the drugstore is still there, but the pricey hamburger joint is long gone.

"You know," he says, "I promised myself once that I'd come back and eat every hamburger in the place. One day, I came back with a new car, and a pocketful of money, and I decided that I wasn't hungry anymore."

On the way out of Alva now.

The Chiefs have lost, blowing a five-point halftime lead to Northwestern Oklahoma State at least partly because the Chiefs have the worst fullcourt press on the planet. The towns come up faster in the dark—bright, sharp, and then gone, like winks from heaven. Alva's dropped behind us now, and Abe is talking about religion. Not in the grand cosmic sense, but at a basic level, acknowledging the absurdity of what happens when God, like all good coaches, comes up with a great plan, and finds that he has to hand it to human beings to execute.

"It's like the time when I first when to church with Betty Jo. She was one of them Church of Christs over to Temple there. I went with the whole family. So, afterwards, one of them says to me, 'How'd you like it?' I told him, 'Hell, I liked it fine, except I think y'all could use a piano.'

"He said, No, that it says in the Bible that you should raise your voices in song to the Lord. He said it doesn't say anything in the Bible about pianos.

"I told him, hell, it doesn't say anything in the Bible about chairs, either, but y'all got plenty of those."

Abe still lives near Oklahoma City with Betty Jo. His Parkinson's has gotten worse. He is still funnier than whistling fish.

The National **February 20, 1990**

Rich Man, Wolfman

It starts as a single dollar handed over in a little place very much like the N-N Express convenience store on Hall Street in Manchester, New Hampshire. All the single dollars from all the little places in all the towns in all this great country—a roiling stampede of single dollar bills chased across the landscape the way that the Indians used to chase the buffalo herds. All the single dollars come running together, and they all end up at a place in Boston, where they all wait together until someone calls for them.

Then, every December for the next twenty-five Decembers, 2,656,258 of the single dollar bills will move as one. (If you like, this can be reckoned as 303 of them every hour, 7,277 every day, 51,082 every week, and 221,355 every month.) They come running through the federal system and into the state treasury in a place very much like Concord, New Hampshire, where 28 percent of them are siphoned off.

The rest of them are herded into a bank account belonging to two people who, one day, in no particular hurry, walked into a place called the N-N Express in Manchester to find that the money stopped right there in front of them, close enough to grab by the scruff of the neck.

And now, every December until the year 2021, 1,912,506 of those single dollar bills will make their way from Boston into the bank account of Jason and Mary Sanderson. And despite that, nearly every weekend in a small Lions Club hall off a dirt road in the middle of the beaten New Hampshire woods, Jason Sanderson will pull on his tattered jeans. He will let down his hair. He will wave his hands and stomp his feet. He will roar his mighty roar. He will throw people on their heads for the vast amusement of the children and adults who pay ten dollars to watch him do it, who gaze upon Jason Sanderson as though they were looking at the awesome power of their own dreams come alive. He will keep doing it, even though he has sixty-six million good reasons not to do it. And because of all that, because if you follow the money you will find a story of the truest America, the best country yet devised in which to be lucky, there is only one way that this story can begin, and this is it:

Once upon a time.

Once upon a time, there was a Wolfman.

Wolfmen are not born but made.

So he was not born a Wolfman but became a Wolfman later in life. He is from the woods, though, sure enough, from a small town called West Burke in what is known as the Northeast Kingdom of Vermont—Baja Quebec, truth be told—where the Wolfman and the rest of the Sandersons had been pillars of their tiny community for nearly three hundred years. The Sandersons were constables and wardens. They were mayors and ballot clerks. The son of a carpenter and the woman who drove the local school bus, Jason Sanderson was born into what passes in the Northeast Kingdom for a political machine.

"There's one strain of the family that's Abenaki Indian, so I guess you can say we've been there since the earth cooled," Jason explains. "In fact, I'm about the only person in my family who's never held either an elective or appointive office since the family came over in 1640. I'm the one who finally figured it out and got the hell out of there."

West Burke has always been a rough and brawly place. A long time ago, the people of the Northeast Kingdom used to flock to wrestling matches staged by a particularly enthusiastic claque of Irish missionary priests. The matches drew their participants out of the fields and the sawmills. Yankee riverboat hands grappled with Quebecois lumberjacks. They were wild affairs, with clergy and laity alike sailing through the air and the gospel's injunction regarding the turning of cheeks seeming more than anything else an invitation to be bitten on one of them.

When Jason Sanderson was growing up, wrestling had just moved onto television, the stark Jurassic period of the glorified whizbang that professional wresting has become. Jason was fascinated by the shows beamed out of Montreal, the dimly lit exploits of the Vachon brothers, Butcher and Mad Dog. Jason would watch the matches endlessly. He would go out into the yard later, trying out on phantom opponents the moves that worked so well for *les frères* Vachon.

"It was," he says, "a living comic book."

He graduated from high school and left the Northeast Kingdom. He worked for a while on a dog ranch in Texas, herding chow chows and Great Pyrenees, mostly. He then moved back to Vermont. There was a period of about ten years during which Jason lost touch with wrestling. Then he moved back to Texas, living in Blanco, on the fringes of the Hill Country. He began following the legends of Texas wrestling—Jose Lothario in San Antonio, the Funk family from Amarillo, and the imperial Von Erichs, so many of whom came to such terrible ends. From time to time, Jason and the other ranch hands would clear out a warehouse or the back room of a bar, and they would engage in what Jason recalls as "scuffles," which were not all that different from the matches staged long ago by the grappling clerics of the Northeast Kingdom. Round and powerful, with a chest out of a waterfront saloon and hair and a beard out of the Book of Jeremiah, Jason threw himself into these scuffles with all the gusto—and science—he could muster.

"We'd just have a wrestling match," Sanderson says. "We'd try out what we saw on TV. If somebody saw a figure-four leg lock, he'd just try it. He wouldn't do it right, but he'd try it."

Eventually, in the mid-1980s, Sanderson moved back to New England. One weekend, a friend invited him to a mid-summer fair near Salem in New Hampshire. There, Jason met Mary, a small brunette whose passion for professional wrestling nearly equaled his own. Better yet, she had cable television, which allowed Jason to catch up with what had become a booming sport. Vince McMahon's WWF had managed to marry wrestling to entertainment with unprecedented results. (Later, of course, McMahon's empire would stagger beneath several garish scandals, and the power in professional wrestling largely would pass to Ted Turner's WCW operation in Atlanta.)

One night after they were married, the two of them went to a small WWF show near Salem. "She said, 'Why don't you try it?'" Jason recalls. "She told me that she'd rather I tried something and, even if it didn't work, it would be better than years from now me being a bitter old man about it."

Jason looked around for someone to train him; the most obvious choice was the wrestling school run by the legendary Walter "Killer" Kowalski in Massachusetts, but Jason couldn't afford the $1,700 fee. Then he found a former student of Kowalski's named Jeff Costa, who ran an independent wrestling outfit near the Sandersons. He walked into Costa's office, and Costa had Jason take off his shirt and let down his hair. "My chest, arms, and back look pretty much like my chin," Sanderson explains.

"I looked at him," Costa says, "and I knew I could do something with this guy." Costa asked him to snarl; Jason snarled.

All right, Costa said. You're the Wolfman.

Fine, Jason replied. I'm the Wolfman.

(Wolfmen are not born; they are made.)

Jason began working Costa's shows, most of which took place in the Lions Club Hall in Hudson. When he wasn't wrestling, he worked the door, or he sold popcorn, or he mixed the various effluvia used in the famous "toilet-bowl matches," in which the loser received what used to be called a swirly in all the better frat houses. Costa originally planned to use the Wolfman as a bad guy—a "heel," as the tradecraft of wrestling has it. At his first match as the Wolfman, he scared a nephew of one of his opponents so badly that the boy never came to another show. But Jason's heart was never in it, and, as the Wolfman quickly became one of the most popular of Costa's wrestlers, his career as a heel was a short one.

Last December, Jason and Mary were living in a two-bedroom apartment in Manchester with three dogs, two cats, and an odd number of birds. Most of the animals came through Mary's volunteer work at a local animal shelter. Money was as tight as space in the apartment. The payment on Jason's truck was overdue, and he'd recently changed jobs. One morning, Mary awoke from the strangest dream. She'd been dreaming of numbers—a random procession of them, no logic or pattern, just numbers. Three was one of them; so were 5, 13, 18, 45, and 20.

On December 17, there was a multistate Powerball lottery drawing. The purse was $66.4 million. Mary asked Jason if she should play the numbers that came to her in her dream.

Of course, Jason replied, and he rolled over and went back to sleep.

On the afternoon of December 17, while Jason was working on the road at his new metal-printing job, Mary went into the N-N Express store in Manchester. She handed a single dollar bill to Mohammad Nawaz, and she played the numbers that had come to her in her dream. A few hours later, she called Jason at the machine shop where he was working.

You have to come home, Mary told him. Right now.

It is Good Friday in Hudson, so the crowd in the Lions Hall is a thin one. An oldies station from Boston, piped through the public-address system, is warming up what patrons there are. Outside, the trees around the parking lot are stirring at their tops with the night's early breezes. Inside, the houselights go down. The hall is bounded by small yellow lights at its perimeter, and a great burst of shining white is at its center, where the ring is. The place smells of must and old popcorn. Children run freely through the folding chairs.

"And now," the announcer barks, "at 290 pounds, the world's richest wrestler—the *Wolf*man!"

He bounds through the arena door, hair flying to all points of the compass. He greets the folks in the ringside seats. He waves his arms. He stomps his feet. He roars his mighty roar. His opponent this night is a smallish fellow named Bart Hart, whom everyone calls

"Pinky," which he purports to hate. Which means that the crowd spends most of the match chanting it at him. Perhaps inflamed by this insult to his essential dignity—or at least as much of it as can be insulted in any man dressed in flaming-pink tights—Hart resorts to subterfuge, yanking the Wolfman's hair. It is a little like watching triple-A baseball or Ivy League football. The finely honed spectating synapses work a little faster than the action itself. A wrestler begins to tumble backward a split second *before* he is hit on the head. Still another grabs his back in obvious agony every time he is thrown— even if he is thrown onto his chest.

Finally, desperate to avoid being pinned, Hart lies facedown on the mat. "No playing possum on my watch," roars the Wolfman, who throws Pinky on his head, winning the match. The crowd is ecstatic. Jason stands in the ring, his arms above his head, deep in the long shadows of the arena.

He actually *is* the richest wrestler in the world. (The only person involved in the sport who is richer is probably Ted Turner, whom nobody gets to throw on his head.) When word got out that Jason and Mary had hit the Powerball with the numbers out of Mary's dream, Jeff Costa's promotional mind went into overdrive.

"The first thing that Jeff asked me was if I was still going to wrestle," Jason explains. "He said, 'I think we can get some publicity out of this.'"

Costa suggested to Jason that they work out a "run-in" with Captain USA and Lobster Man during the official lottery press conference. However, Mary failed to see the essential need for the presence of Lobster Man. If you do that, she told him, I am going to say that you're all gay and I'm just the housekeeper.

"His wife didn't go for it," says Costa sadly. "It would've been great, though."

However, Jason did mention an upcoming match at the press conference: Costa got the biggest crowd he'd ever put into the Lions Hall. Subsequently, Jason also consented to put the lottery money "at risk" in one of his matches. He won, of course. The purse was safe. The crowd was thrilled. "There were people there who actually thought they were wrestling for $66 million," Mary Sanderson says. "Amazing."

She immediately quit her job at the phone company ("You know those people who win the lottery and say that they're going to keep working?" Mary told her supervisor. "I'm not one of them"), and she devoted herself to her animals. Jason stayed on at his metal-printing job, and he kept working shows for Costa.

"For a while," he says, "I was wrestling every week." There was even some stirring from Atlanta, some talk that Ted Turner might want the Wolfman for his own shows to forge an alliance between the two richest men in wrestling. "Nothing ever came of it," Jason says. "The answer would've been no anyway. I like what I'm doing. I like the small halls—two hundred people or so. I like walking through the crowds, feeling like I'm back home, back in the small town where I grew up.

"You know, I've thought a lot about why I do it, why I still do it. The only thing I can say is that wrestling is like a love affair, but it's a love affair with a mistress that doesn't do anything good for you, and that's pretty demanding. Unforgiving, I'd say. I just love it. I love all of it—the stage aspect, the athletic aspect."

The first check came a few months ago, and it's almost gone. The Sandersons got a lawyer and an adviser to handle their money. Jason paid off his old truck on time, at last, and he bought a new one big enough to haul the ring around in. The mail was rough for a few months. "Congratulations on winning the Powerball," said one letter, "even though I need the money to survive."

But the Sandersons got one letter that Jason framed. It was from a woman who signed her name only as "Louise." She was not asking for money, she said. "You have to remember that everybody else's problems are not your problems," she wrote. "And your good fortune is not everybody else's good fortune."

"You know," Jason says, "I never gave money to anyone who asked for it, but there have been several times, when I knew somebody needed it, that I gave it to them without a second thought. It was just somebody who deserves a break. Knowing that I can do that and then doing it, if that's what a rich guy feels like, then I guess I feel like one."

Most of the first check went to buy a farm, a vast, rolling place at the top of a hill, an estate once owned by a toy tycoon and most recently the home of a dog-track millionaire. There is a fishpond and woodlots, and in one of the pastures there's a helipad that the Wolfman plans to rip up soon—with his bare hands, if necessary. The three dogs and the two cats have come along, and the Wolfman's going to buy some draft horses for the place, probably with the second of the checks that are going to come every December for the next twenty-four Decembers. All the furniture from the old two-bedroom apartment fits in one and a half of the seventeen rooms that are in the farmhouse where the Wolfman has come to live.

Plato—who had no Wolfman in his life, as far as the scholars can tell—once pointed out that, without public performance, the athlete becomes a mere brute. Every other Friday or so, the Wolfman loads up his new truck and drives it down the rolling hillside and over the back roads to Hudson, where, in a dark and noisy hall, he performs. He doesn't have to perform, but he does. And the people all cheer, and they are happy for a time, and then the Wolfman drives home again, over the back roads and up the little hillside to his place. And this is where the story ends, on a quiet hillside budding thick with the coming summer—a bright-green corner of the best country yet devised in which to be lucky, where all the single dollar bills finally came to rest once upon a time.

The Wolfman is still wrestling. The checks are still coming. The helipad is gone.

Esquire February 1998

The Son,
He Does Shine

The music suffuses the air like a warm cloud. It creeps around corners. It squeezes under doors. It wraps itself around the balustrade, and it drapes itself over the parrot's cage. Strong music, muscular melodies born in a harder place than this, a place where children starve in the long shadows of the old cemetery, where the guitar and the gun and the knife too often harmonize. All that blood and anger, but hope there, too, hope like the sun that comes up and makes the tombstones in the cemetery shine like the paving stones of the better world. The parrot squawks, and the music does not drown out the parrot's cry, but softens and subverts it, gives to it a kind of lyric grace. The old mother walks slowly through the house, sunlight blessing her face, and all around her is the music, her son's music. It is there, always, the soul of the big house. It hangs, lightly lilting, like moss, like memory, on all the sun-splashed walls.

"Every baby that's born," the old mother says upon hearing that her visitor's wife is expecting their third child, "your baby that's going to be born, is very, very special. Nobody in the world can be as special as your baby. Like you planting corn. That's what Jah blessing is like. Sometimes, you get beautiful, big ears of corn. Sometimes, you get little, tiny ears of corn. That is what the blessing is like. You can imagine all that corn go fertile. Now, from that one corn, you might be able to plant acres of corn. That's the way Jah blessing is.

Just keep on, keep on going. Some will fail along the way. The blessing is given. Some might not know how to handle it. Some might look more blessed than others."

She lost one son to cancer, and there were people on the other side of the world who mourned his passing. She lost another one to an unfathomable rage. "Don't stick to the anger," she says. "And there is anger, especially with what I been through. Not like I want to fight anymore, but it make me vexed. Why would anyone want to do me this? I did all the good I can. I take all the blessing Jah give me, and I share it with the world. Why turn against me like that?"

Rohan Marley grew up in this house in Miami, swathed in the music, his father's great music. Bob Marley brought his ineffable soul out of the Kingston slums, surging testimony to the indomitability of a single spirit. Rohan is one of Bob's eleven acknowledged children by four different women. As a child in Jamaica, his father suddenly dead, Rohan ran wild—the way his father had long before, when the Rude Boys were scaring the high-rolling tourists. So his mother sent Rohan to live in Miami with his grandmother, Cedella Booker, who had a son who shook the world and died too young and whose music rides the breezes through his old mother's house as though it is the very air of the place.

"We're Marleys," says Rohan. "Marleys can push through. To be a Marley is to push hard all the time, to feel like you're in control of the situation and not be afraid. Never feel like you're a puppy; you got to feel like you're a big dog. Don't want no one ever to step on you. We all know the struggle, and we see it every day in Jamaica."

A sophomore at the University of Miami, Rohan Marley plays linebacker like a deliberate bullet. At five feet eight and 200 pounds, cut sharp and fine in the weight room, Rohan hits as hard as a player half again as large. At first, the coaches tried to make him a cornerback. But the position carries Rohan too far from the delights of collision, which he continued to seek out, often to the detriment of the pass coverage. "What was the point?" Hurricanes head coach Dennis Erickson says. "He's just going to run to where the ball is anyway." And he is an exuberant, almost wild, competitor, even by the standards of Miami football, which are notoriously garish. He plays his position with a reckless, sunny glee.

"I love to make the hit," Rohan says. "It's just the sweetest thing there is. A nice hit, you feel it, oh, yeah. Best part about it, when you make a nice hit, you get a little headache. Sometimes, oh, yeah, I got to fix my face mask. That's when you know you did something." He made fifty-nine tackles last season, including nine in one game against West Virginia. He danced after every one of them. "That's my job, to keep my team motivated," he says. "I'm always lively, never down out there. The other team, they say 'You high?' I say 'Yeah, on life.'"

There is more to him, however, than simple football macho. He is a conscious keeper of tradition, living every moment with the knowledge that he is carrying forward something vital and alive. Being Bob Marley's son means more than having driven yourself to Palmetto High School in fancier transport than most of your classmates. It even means more than laughing when you are knocked out of bounds against San Diego State and, upon rising, hearing the Aztec bench singing "Buff-a-lo soll-jah!" at you. There is an obligation to testify from your blood and with your life, to seek out the Struggle and to fight it joyfully in the sunshine.

"My father, he told us once 'Don't cry. Don't ever cry,'" Rohan says. "It's part of the package, part of being a Marley. I play very hard because that's the way he was. He played very hard because he wanted to get his message across to everyone. That's why he played so hard, why he worked so hard at his music—to send that message out to everyone."

There is so much of the island still in Rohan, from the lilt in his speech to the utilitarian chaos of his pronouns. He professes the Rastafarian faith of his father, but circumstances prevent his using ganja, the marijuana that is the faith's primary sacrament. He eats no pork, however, and he will not even sit with someone who is. His grandmother looks at Rohan and she sees her firstborn son in her grandson's dancing eyes.

"He is so happy, like Bob was," she says. "When Bob was born, everybody want to see that baby, what a handsome baby he was. Most of his father is in Rohan. If he does anything wrong, and I scold him for it, he never frowns or anything. He always learns. Ro-

han, he's trying very hard and, because of his trying, I really appreciate him."

It is said of Bob Marley that he was never more at peace than when
he was with his children. They were scattered, living in different
homes, but they would gather with him when he came off the road.
He would talk with them, and they would all play soccer, which for
him was briefly an obsession equal to that of the music. "He was, in
many ways, an abandoned child," writes Stephen Davis, one of Marley's biographers. "Bob Marley was the most relaxed, the least shy
and withdrawn, the most *himself*, when his kids were around."

"Oh, yeah, he'd never leave his children," Rohan recalls. "Whenever he was in Jamaica, all of us would come together. We had different mothers, but we were all friends. They would argue sometimes,
but we were all friends."

The concept of family has grown so mutable, so protean, in its political utility. There are many types of families, united by blood and
by common agreement on what is precious enough to be carried forward. Sometimes the mother and the father are married to each
other. Sometimes they are not. Sometimes the mother and the father
have children with each other. Sometimes they have children with
other people. Sometimes all the children know one another. Sometimes all the children love one another. Sometimes, very rarely, there
is someone who makes sure all the children know who they are in
this world and why they are all sacred and loved. Sometimes there is
a complex web of blood ties and love, and sometimes only the people
within that web can understand how strong all the diverse strands of
it truly can be, how it can shelter them from danger and from sudden, capricious death. Sometimes, this is a family, too.

"Family tree?" laughs Rohan Marley, his eyes alight and wandering. "No, mon. Never seen one. No wall big enough for that."

The big war touched even the tiny villages deep in the green hills
above Kingston. In St. Ann, Cedella Malcolm worked in the sugar
fields beside her mother, and she listened to her mother sing the
songs that seemed as old as the island itself. In 1944, the British West
India Regiment was posted near Cedella's village, and she fell in love

with a captain of the Quartermaster Corps. Norval Marley was older than Cedella, and he was white. The romance was complicated. Her family didn't trust him, and his family thought the good captain's reason had melted away. A marriage was finally arranged, but Captain Marley was transferred before the ceremony. However, on February 6, 1945, Cedella gave birth to a son, whom she and Norval named Robert Nesta Marley.

Bob had little contact with his father. He lived with him in Kingston for a short time in 1951, but Captain Marley farmed the 6-year-old out to do chores for a local woman. Cedella found out, and she brought the boy back to St. Ann. Norval Marley died four years later. In 1952, Cedella and Bob moved to Kingston, settling in Trench Town, one of several self-explanatory slums, including Back O' Wall (which adjoined an ancient cemetery) and Dung Hill.

They were living in a flat at 19 Second Street. Also living there was a man named Mr. Toddy Livingston, whose son, Neville, became Bob's closest friend. Cedella and Mr. Toddy had a daughter together named Pearl. Within a year of Pearl's birth, Cedella met and married a man named Edward Booker. In 1963, Cedella and Booker moved to Wilmington, Delaware. Bob Marley stayed in Kingston. He was now living on the streets, where the Rude Boy phenomenon was vying with the Rastafarian faith.

Rastafarianism had blossomed in the 1930s, when a warlord named Ras Tafari Makonnen seized power in Ethiopia and took for himself the ancient honorific title Haile Selassie. His ascension was seized upon by those in Jamaica waiting for the fulfillment of Marcus Garvey's prophecy of a black liberator-king. They named their religion for the warlord Makonnen, who was revered as a god on earth. They preached abstemiousness—except from the omnipresent ganja—and in Trench Town, the Rastafarians served much the same purpose the Nation of Islam served in America's northern ghettos.

In 1966, Bob Marley became a Rastafarian. When Marley moved to Delaware that year, his faith became a source of great tension between him and Cedella, who was then a fundamentalist Christian, and Booker, a solid citizen of Wilmington's Jamaican immigrant community. With Booker, Cedella had two more children, Richard and Anthony. Bob Marley went home to Jamaica in October.

By then, the music was bursting in him. Reggae was the song of the Kingston streets, which had been his only real home. He formed the Wailers—Neville Livingston became Bunny Wailer—and throughout the 1970s he created some of the most compelling music ever made. It was more than simple rhythm. There was a power to it and a hunger of the spirit. He poured all of his childhood abandonment into it, and all of the anger of the streets of Trench Town. He became an international sensation and a Jamaican icon. He had married Rita Anderson in 1966 and had children with her, but he had children with other women as well. In 1972, he and a woman named Janet Hunt had a son they named Rohan.

As the decade ended, Bob Marley was exhausted. In 1976, he and several of his children were nearly killed in their house on Hope Road when gunmen opened fire on his recording studio. The violence that had never been far from the surface of his life and his music seemed to be overwhelming him; later, in testimony given during the baroque litigation regarding the Marley estate, one of the singer's associates would say that Marley had beaten him at gunpoint. In June 1977, Bob was diagnosed with a malignant melanoma. That year, Cedella moved from Delaware to Miami with her other two sons.

Bob fought the disease for four years, still giving concerts when he could. He died on May 11, 1981, at the age of 36. Ten days later, there was a memorial service in the big house in Miami. Bob was laid out in the main hall and Cedella sang his "Redemption Song." Rohan was nearly 9 and had come to Miami on a temporary visa. It was his first time in America.

He had been living with his mother in Jamaica, playing soccer and watching on television with odd fascination what the Americans call football. His father's death broke him, however. "I was running a little wild," he says. "When my dad passed, I started skipping school. I just turned around, oh, yeah. Finally, the principal tell me mother 'Why don't you just send him to live with his grandmother? He got two uncles up there; maybe they can discipline him.' They sure did that." In 1984, Rohan moved to Miami.

From the start, he was put in the charge of Richard and Anthony Booker, who were not that much older than he was. Richard had played high-school football, and he was the drill sergeant. He ran Rohan ragged, punishing him in the weight room. "He was my uncle, and a real big uncle, too," Rohan says, laughing. "He used to throw the football to me every day, as hard as he could. After a while, I loved it. I be outside, throwing it to myself. Like, when my friends come over, my uncle Richard would give us a little workout. One day, I wound up doing 500 pushups. He didn't put up with no mess because if I didn't do it, he'd punch me up, you know?"

Rohan took it all, and he came up smiling. By the time he enrolled at Palmetto High School, he had taken football as his primary passion. He approached it the way his father had approached music, searching for the Struggle in all its many guises.

"If you listen to his dad's songs," says Joe Mira, who coached Rohan at Palmetto, "it's all about odds, overcoming the odds and standing up for your rights. That's Rohan Marley. He lives his father's words."

He played at Palmetto for three years, blossoming finally as a senior. He is a graceful, gifted athlete with impeccable technique as a tackler. Erickson first saw him play in a high-school game (the coach's son played for Palmetto, too). It soon became clear that Rohan would be a Hurricane. At one point, however, there was some doubt as to whether he would achieve the 700 on his SATs required to be eligible to play. "I'll never forget it," says Mira. "Rohan just kept going, took his SATs and passed them. He came up to me and said 'Coach, I proved to all those people who said I'd never make it.' That's what he lives by today still—that the odds are always against him."

Meanwhile, he had become enormously popular. "I have never seen him without a smile on his face," says Mira. "I've never seen him down." As the knowledge of who his father was had spread through Palmetto, Rohan had never pretended to be more than what he was. "I never acted like I was anybody special," he says. "In Jamaica, you don't act like you're special. You just act like yourself. You don't act like you're special just because your father is a legend."

His closest companion was his uncle Anthony, who was only two years older than Rohan. Anthony was Richard's obverse. He was funny, and he was the musician of the two, the one through whom the family gifts ran most clearly. (However, one day at Palmetto, Anthony walked into the weight room and, just for fun, broke a school record in the bench press.) He and Rohan confided in each other. They sat talking in the big house for hours, Bob-music around them always like a blessing. Then, in February 1989, Anthony went back to Jamaica for a short visit.

The family believes that something happened to him there, that something was put in his food or drink. Anthony came back to Miami a different person. He sat in his room alone, Bob-music playing over and over. He shut himself off from everyone, including Rohan. "He was different," Rohan says. "One day, I spoke to him. I say 'A., I have a new girlfriend.' He didn't stop. He just kept going." Anthony went around the house, cleaning compulsively. One Saturday, he shot out a window in the big house. The next day, dressed all in white except for a bulletproof vest, Anthony came out of the house with a shotgun.

"I remember when he was leaving," Rohan says. "He asked me to get the Jeep keys. I said 'Huh?' He said 'Run and get me the Jeep keys.' I ran inside. I say 'Grandma, he wants me to get the keys.' I say 'Uncle Richard, he wants me to get the keys.' I couldn't do that much. I was scared. He had a shotgun. I can't argue with a guy who has a shotgun." Rohan got his uncle the keys. Anthony drove a short distance to the Cutler Ridge Shopping Mall. He stalked through the aisles, brandishing the shotgun and asking people if they felt like dying that day. He went outside and touched off a round at a uniformed policeman. Across the parking lot, an off-duty Miami detective lined up Anthony Booker and killed him with a single shot, just above the top of the bulletproof vest.

"It was a heavy thing," Cedella says now. "A heavy, heavy thing. I can question nothing. It's so hard, you know. Why did Anthony have to go the way he went? And he was strong, loving and caring. He just got away from me like that. What I think now is that Jah love them most and so he take them out of this wicked, cruel world."

Anthony's wake was in the big house, in the same front hall in which Bob Marley once had lain. Joe Mira came to the service. "It was the only time I ever saw a serious side to Rohan," Mira says. "He was saddened. I didn't know the customs, but it was almost like it was a peaceful mourning. Anthony was laid out in the house, right there in the living room. Incense was burning. Soft Marley music was playing. Rohan sat quietly and accepted his friends' condolences. He sat there and he went through what he had to go through and then—*snap!*—he was back. I don't think a day goes by when he doesn't think about his uncle and about his father."

Rohan Marley says that there are moments, wonderful, bright moments, when he will be walking down the street and a car will drive by with the windows open, and he will hear a snatch of one of his father's songs swirl by swifter than a breath. "Oh, yeah," he says, "I always hear Bob Marley tunes. I see my brother Ziggy on TV, or my dad, I stop and watch. I see that one video 300,000 times. I don't just listen to the music. I look deep inside. I know what my dad is singing. He's not really singing; he's preaching."

His grandmother feels the spirits of her two dead sons alive in the big house, where the Rastafarian rendition of *The Last Supper* is painted on the side of the kitchen counter and an old, battered guitar leans against the living-room wall. Glib jokes about the family religion aside—and, truth be told, between Waco and Bosnia, Christianity and Islam haven't been making a lot of sense recently, either—there is in this family a consistent set of values, born in Trench Town and carried forward through celebrity and money, through life and death.

Ultimately, Rohan plays as his father sang, with power and with feeling, with passion and with grace. "I'm ready to go any day," he says. "Practice? I'm always happy at practice. People say 'Where you get your energy?' I say 'I don't know.'" It is all around him, the way his father's music comes from the windows of the cars and the way it suffuses the big house where the old mother lives, still singing the way she did in the sugar fields of the high backcountry. Music around his life like the very air of it, lively as the new morning sun.

Rohan moved into the music business himself, as the companion/muse/ collaborator of Grammy-winning singer Lauryn Hill. In 1999, Ebony Magazine *named them one of America's 10 Hottest Couples. Together, they have two children.*

GQ September 1993

A Gathering of Lights

The summer people go home before the sky grows all muscular with the clouds that will bring the first snow down upon Chisago County in Minnesota. They are all gone by then—all the happy children, and the men in battered hats as thickly stuck with fishing lures as Moby Dick's hide was with harpoons. They come in the summer to fish the lakes for muskies—there is even a muskie painted on the water tower that greets you as you drive into Chisago City—and they take their leisure and the fish together, and they leave before the lake turns to deep, black ice. They leave and the farmers stay.

Dairy farmers, mostly, and the times have not been kind to them. Between 1984 and 1988, five percent of the farmers in the county lost their land. Debt ate them up, and they sold off their farms and left, and many of the ones that stayed now work second jobs. They are bank clerks and insurance men for eight hours a day, and they are farmers when they can afford to be. It is a stubborn culture. Tattered and ragged, it nevertheless coheres. The farmers in Chisago County rejoice together in the good times. In the bad, they gather themselves together and they help how they can. They bring food. They bring themselves. They provide community, a gathering of lights along the dark and narrow roads.

It is neither an easy life nor a safe one. It's no longer one man, one mule and a noble squint toward the far horizon. All modern farming relies on the operation of sophisticated, heavy equipment. The machines make the job of farming easier. They also make it as surely perilous as a job working the high steel. Almost every local farmer knows someone who has been killed or seriously injured by the machines that helped him earn his living. Just this fall, a young girl was riding a feed wagon driven by her father. The wagon bounced, and the child fell under the wheels and was crushed. Her father never knew it until it was too late. By nightfall, the other farmers had come. They brought food and they stayed a very long time.

Trouble does not creep into Chisago County unannounced. The land is flat, so you can hear the ambulance coming from a long way off. On Nov. 13, 1989, a cold morning with light snow blowing wild as confetti in the freshening wind, Don Johnson was finishing his morning chores. He was 67 years old, and he had been farming his land since he came home from the war. He had a healthy respect for the perils of his work. "Cattle are big," he says. "Handling cattle is dangerous." Johnson was walking back toward his house when he heard the siren go screaming down one of the rutty little back roads nearby.

The ambulance turned down Quinlan Road, and onto Bloom Lake Road, speeding toward the Bloom Lake Dairy Farm where Dick and Mary Beardsley live. Dick Beardsley was 33 years old and, some seven years earlier, he had been one of the finest marathon runners in the world. He had won the London Marathon in 1981, and, in the 1982 Boston Marathon, he had dueled Alberto Salazar for 26 miles, losing by a scant two seconds in what is reckoned by some to be the greatest marathon race in history. Salazar gave so much to beat Beardsley that his body temperature at the end of the race was 88 degrees. One doctor at the finish line compared Salazar's body to a potato chip. Shortly after the race, Salazar spotted Bill Squires, the remarkable coach who had trained both him and Beardsley. "My God," Salazar gasped to Squires, "You trained that kid to kill me."

Beardsley was a farmer at heart. He'd luxuriated in his grandparents' dairy farm and, as soon as he could afford it, he and Mary had bought a farm of their own in Rush City, on the other side of Chisago County. They'd sold that off (at a minimal profit) in 1986 so that

Dick could train fulltime to try and make the 1988 U.S. Olympic team. He had failed in that attempt. His running career was over. At least for the purposes of competitive distance racing, his legs were shot.

So Dick, Mary and their adopted son Andy came back to Chisago County, and they were living on the Bloom Lake farm, working toward eventually buying it from the owner. On the morning of Nov. 13, Dick Beardsley had been loading feed corn on an elevator that was attached to his tractor. His left bootlace snagged in the tractor's power-takeoff shaft. Beardsley's left leg was wrapped around the shaft, the way you can wrap a string around your finger. Every time the shaft took him around, it slammed him into the ground. Somehow, Beardsley managed to turn off the tractor, and to crawl up toward the farmhouse, and that's where Mary and the ambulance found him, lying in the new-fallen snow, his leg a tangled mess of torn ligament and muscle, five ribs broken and his left wrist shattered, breathing shallowly and fading into shock. The ambulance took him off to the hospital. You could hear the siren clearly from all the other farms.

They started coming by nightfall. Don Johnson came. So did so many others. They brought food and they stayed for a very long time. Over the next several months, they would help Mary work the farm while Dick recovered, because that is what you do when you farm in Chisago County and you hear the siren in the cold distance. "You help because you know that, the next time, that could be you, or somebody in your own family," says Don Johnson.

It did not stop at the county line, however. Help came from Boston, too, from two saloons and their patrons, from the people who stood along the streets in 1982 and cheered while Dick Beardsley did something rare and wonderful. Those people felt what the farmers felt. You do what you have to do. You bring food and you bring yourself. You provide community, a gathering of lights along the dark and narrow roads.

It all began because he'd thought the tractor was out of gas. He forgot about the trouble they'd been having with the fuel filter, which would plug up and then the tractor would stall as though it had run out of fuel. So he'd put some more gas into the tank, climbing up on the drawbar to do it. "I didn't check to see if the power-takeoff lever had been pulled," he says.

As he reached to turn the key, his pant leg rose up, exposing the long lace of his work boot. Beneath him was the tractor's drive shaft. In most newer tractors, there is a metal shroud over this shaft, but Beardsley's tractor was an old one. He turned the key and the world went mad on him.

There was no up and down. There was no left and right. He remembers it as being rather like a pilot caught in a hopeless spin. He just knew that, unless he stopped the machine, it was going to kill him. "As soon as I hit the key," Beardsley recalls, "all of a sudden, just like that, I'm just being sucked into the thing. I thought, 'My God, it's just going to wind my whole body around it and break my neck, or end up squeezing me to death or something.'"

He remembers getting one arm loose from his coveralls, all the while being spun around the power-takeoff shaft and slammed into the ground. "Finally, out of desperation, I threw out my arm and, it was like my fingers grew or something, and I was able to grab the lever and just hold on. My whole world was going in all directions. I knew that, if I lost consciousness that would be it. I was so afraid that I was never going to see Mary or Andy again.

"I was screaming, but Mary was in the milkhouse and Andy was off at school, so nobody could hear me. When it stopped, I was lying all wrapped up in this thing, and everything was going in every which direction. I somehow got myself untangled and I thought, 'Gosh, if I pass out where I am, Mary might not even see me and think I'm off in the fields chasing a cow or something.' So I tried to crawl across the road toward the house. I was getting weaker and weaker. Finally, Mary came out and saw me. By this time, I was shaking uncontrollably. They had to stabilize me before they got me into the ambulance."

They took him first to the Chisago County Health Services, a 40-bed facility just down Route 5 from the farm. He was there for $2^{1}/_{2}$ days, and he doesn't remember any of it. He was attached to an I.V. machine, and he could push a button every time he wanted a dose of painkiller. He pushed the button a lot over those two days. Then, he was transferred to the Fairview-Southdale Hospital in the Twin Cities, where an orthopedic surgeon named Richard Schmidt went about the task of putting Dick Beardsley's leg back together.

"Being in the city, we don't see too many farm accidents," Schmidt says. "But accidents with the power-takeoff shaft are pretty common. In Dick's case, he was lucky he got that machine shut off because it was getting ready to take his leg off at the knee."

Schmidt repaired all the ligament damage that had been done, essentially giving Beardsley a new left knee. An excruciating program of physical therapy began almost immediately. After the first operation, Beardsley awoke to find his leg strapped to a contraption that made it go around and around, almost like pumping a bicycle while lying flat on your back. He spent two weeks in the hospital, and then he went home.

By then, Don Johnson and the rest of the farmers had settled into a regular schedule of helping Mary run the farm. She assigned the chores. She told them what had to be done. "We did some. We did all we could," Johnson says, "But she was the A-1 person there."

"As hard as something like this is for you, it's 10 times worse for your family," Beardsley says. "It was so tough on Andy. I mean, Mary'd be in the barn showing people what to do, and he'd be in here with me, and I'd be in the bed. That was the worst part for me. I couldn't do anything." For two weeks, the pain kept him from sleeping.

He had to go back into the hospital twice, once for a virulent infection of a kind common to victims of farm accidents. "In a farm accident, there are all kinds of interesting little organisms that can get in there," explains Schmidt. The physical therapy continued. The medical bills ultimately topped out at $75,000.

For all the vaunted independence of a farmer, it is, in fact, a very precarious life. "They say that you are your own boss," says Don Johnson. "But, really, you've got a lot of bosses." Bankers. Loan officers. The occasionally erratic shifts in the local and national economy. All of them have power over the farmer that belies the independent image. One bad season can wipe out a life's work. One bad accident can do even worse damage.

The accident had caught the Beardsleys at the worst possible time. Their old medical policy had expired on Oct. 31, and their new one wasn't due to start until Dec. 1. There was not $75,000 in this little family. There was not even close to that. "We were just devastated by it," Beardsley says.

Some of the doctors chose to forgive the debts entirely. And a local bank started a trust fund for the family. That is when the checks started to come in. Not just local checks, but checks drawn on Massachusetts banks, checks from people who had seen Dick Beardsley run one great foot race and, touched by it, were paying him back.

He remembers the race in the same vivid detail with which he remembers the accident. They are the two central events in his life now. For good and ill, Boston and The Accident are the defining moments for him, intertwining with each other. "I'll never forget anything about either one of them," he says. He remembers the mob at the start, the crazed sprint by the leaders through the first mile. He remembers Salazar, cocky and hardbitten, waving at his friends as they coursed through his hometown of Wayland. To heck with this, Dick Beardsley thought. He waved, too. He remembers all of them falling away—Bill Rodgers first, and then a runner named Ed Mendoza virtually disappearing at the base of the hills in Newton. He remembers the last miles with Salazar, shoulder to shoulder in the 75-degree heat, too hot to be running this fast.

He remembers those last, frenzied miles. Some crazed fan trying to stuff a dollar bill down Salazar's shorts. The two of them nearly run down by the press bus, and the roads leading into the final stretch clotted thickly with people, and any pretense at crowd control long since abandoned. A long tunnel of noise and joy. He remembers the cramp he got in his right hamstring there in the last mile, and he remembers Salazar, smelling blood, taking off. Then he remembers stepping into a pothole directly in front of the Eliot Lounge, the hangout for runners and writers that has been the race's unofficial headquarters for almost two decades. Miraculously, the jolt of stepping into the pothole loosened the cramp, and Beardsley remembers taking off in a head-down sprint, and he remembers Salazar looking back at him in horror. And it was here, as they turned into the final straight, that Bill Squires almost fell off the building.

He and Beardsley had worked together for two years. Through his work with Rodgers, Squires had developed a reputation as a master at training runners to run on the roads, which was just then becoming a lucrative pursuit. At the same time, Squires also had developed a reputation as the marathon's premier eccentric genius. Conversations with him are constructed like beach houses, with wings and decks that go off in all directions. He has been known to write workout programs on napkins, envelopes, the pages of newspapers or anything else that was handy. In 1980, at the Falmouth Road Race, Beardsley got up to go to the bathroom late at night in a house that the New Balance shoe company had rented for the weekend. He found Squires asleep in the bathtub. "He gave up his bed for one of his runners," Beardsley marvels. "Now *that's* a coach."

Squires saw strength in Beardsley. "At first I thought, well, hey, this guy's pretty small," he says. "Then, I figured, hey, this guy works on a farm, so there's got to be some muscle there." Squires put Beardsley through a grueling regimen of long speed workouts on the roads, pointing him toward Boston in 1982. One of their last workouts before the race was a savage pounding up and down that stretch of the course that includes Heartbreak Hill. The workout was further complicated by the fact that a nor'easter had blown up, and Beardsley found himself running through a blizzard. "It was blowing 45 miles an hour, and the snow was coming sideways into my eyes," Beardsley recalls. "I must've been the only runner in Boston out that day. I got done with that and I knew I was going to run well. It just seemed so easy, like floating."

That was the place from which he summoned that final sprint. Salazar looked back and blanched. Above them, on the roof of the Hynes Auditorium, Squires was working as an analyst on WBZ-TV's live broadcast of the race. When he saw Beardsley closing on Salazar, Squires lost it completely. "Ayyyy, Dickie," he screamed, and WBZ anchor Liz Walker, a rawboned sort, grabbed Squires before he could become airborne.

Beardsley caught Salazar. Instead of simply sprinting past him, however, Beardsley fell into pace with him again, and Salazar threw out what he had left for a kick and won the race. The two men collapsed into each other's arms at the finish line, and the winner needed Dick Beardsley to hold him up.

Neither one was ever the same after that. Against Squires' advice, Beardsley overcompeted and, thus, overtrained. "I've always found it hard to say no to people," he says. "They'd say, 'Well, just come and you don't have to race hard.' But you get there, and they've paid your way and all, so you figure, 'Well, I'll race hard just this once.'" He tried to run that fall's New York City marathon. "I came off the Verrazano Narrows Bridge, and my left leg was like a rock," he recalls. "By five miles, my right leg was like a rock." Eventually, he would have surgery on his left achilles tendon, and his competitive career would end at the 1988 Olympic Trials. He would go home again. He would go home and he would be a farmer.

Word of his accident hit Boston around Christmastime last year. Two bartenders, Tommy Leonard of the Eliot and Eddie Doyle of the Bull and Finch Pub (the prototype for TV's *Cheers*, much to the dismay of Bull and Finch regulars who are tired of posing for snapshots with tourists from Iowa), began a drive for contributions to the fund set up by a Chisago County bank. The proceeds from the annual Jingle Bell Run were dispatched, as was one check that meant more than the rest. It was for $1,000 and it was from Bill Squires, who once had almost coached himself off a building during the greatest marathon anyone had ever seen. "I burst into tears when I saw that," Dick Beardsley said. "He's not a rich man, you know."

He still runs along the rutty farm roads around his house. "I do 15 or 20 miles a week at about a seven or seven-and-a-half minute pace," he says. "Now, I have before-the-accident PR's and after-the-accident PR's. Some day, I don't know where or when, I'm going to run a marathon again. My first goal is going to be to finish. My second goal will be to finish in under three hours. I still enjoy running. And I do cherish it so."

Someday, he may have to have an artificial knee, but he doesn't have to wear a brace, which would've meant the end of working his farm. He walks without the faintest trace of a limp. The contributions have offset most of the debt from the medical bills, and the Beardsleys are once again working toward owning the farm one day. For his part, Dick has taken an active role in various state programs regarding farm safety. The elevator he was working with when he was injured is still there, looming up above a snowcapped stack of feed corn. There is a new metal shroud over the drive-shaft of the tractor.

"I've always believed in people," he says. "I still remember that Monday, the night of the day that it happened, there must've been 20 farmers here. The next day, there were four or five corn-pickers in our field, getting the field work done. Food? We're still eating the food that people brought over here. I'm still overwhelmed by it all."

He takes a visitor around the farm. Two good farm dogs named Sam and Spike trot along behind. Sam has a game leg, but manages to be almost preternaturally cheerful anyway. On the other hand, Spike barks for effect and fools almost nobody. The cattle—200 head now—ignore the whole business, standing in the great clouds of their breath, content in the stolid job of being cows. There is a cold bit of winter in the air, the clouds in thick carousels along the horizon, the afternoon sunlight white and thin.

Alongside the barn, there is a row of small dens, each with a tiny corral in front of it. It is here where the newborn calves live, safe and warm in the straw against the bite of the winter wind. "In there, they feel fine, even if it gets down to 30 or 40 below, which it does pretty regularly," the farmer says. He goes into the barn and he comes out carrying the newest calf. He puts it in its pen, and it hunkers down within. A good hedge against winter's thin, gray prologue. A new calf for Christmas. The lights are coming on in the houses now, along the distant, darkening road.

In December of 1996, Dick Beardsley was convicted of forging prescriptions for various painkillers. He was sentenced to five years' probation. He has begun running again, and he now regularly lectures on the dangers of substance abuse.

The National December 21, 1990

Legends of the Fall

As I explained once to an editor friend, my column is like my house. I decide what gets hung on the walls. I decide what gets served for dinner. I decide what gets played on the stereo. If you don't like my paintings, my food or my music, don't come to my house. So, because this is my column, I am going to write right here about Peerless Price, a wide receiver for the University of Tennessee. I am going to do this because you don't often get to talk to someone named Peerless, unless you're Dick Tracy. It is one of the wonders of sportswriting that you occasionally get to meet people named Peerless, a pleasure denied to all those Beltway flatheads, who, I'm telling you, would act a lot less constipated on all those Sunday-morning television shows if they had a few more people named Peerless in their lives. This is my column, and this is my first Peerless, dammit. We will chat with him for a moment.

"Some people call me Peerless," he explains. "My friends usually just call me Peer." Of course they do.

One autumn afternoon, mark it, Peerless Price is going to make some poor Southeastern Conference cornerback leave his lingerie at about the forty-yard line, and a ridiculously gifted young quarterback named Peyton Manning is going to hang the ball on a deep line, and Tennessee is going to score a long and important touchdown. Peyton to Peerless. It rings.

Drop that note into the great chorus that still sings of a firehaired quarterback from Ole Miss who became the greatest legend Mississippi has produced since that July day at Gettysburg when Barksdale's boys failed to get up Little Round Top.

With the football, Archie Manning was juke-mad, a pocket-busting dervish in a time that celebrated the reckless and the improvised. He lit up the SEC to the point where people were writing songs about him; "The Ballad of Archie Who" was a respectable hit. Later he spent his professional career with horrid teams. He was battered, stomped silly all over the NFL, and he still came out of it smiling. He had three sons, and the middle boy is going to win the Heisman Trophy this season, unless he gets injured or General Grant comes back through Tennessee.

Last year Peyton Manning led his team to an 11–1 season. He threw for 2,954 yards and twenty-two touchdowns. He threw only four interceptions. His team's only loss came at Florida, in a game in which Tennessee led 30–21 at halftime before being hopelessly swamped in a driving rain after intermission. On New Year's Day, Manning and Tennessee caught Ohio State flat after the Buckeyes had punted away a national championship by losing to Michigan in the last game of the regular season. Manning caught Joey Kent with a forty-seven-yard touchdown pass that broke Ohio State and that, truth be told, marked the beginning of the 1996 season, in which Tennessee is nearly as solid a favorite for the national championship as Manning is to win John Heisman's trophy.

Peyton Manning's story is happily infused with his father's legend even as he has only begun to create his own. There is a lightness to the way the stories have begun to blend into each other. It is a burden neither to the father nor to his sons.

"I never had a child named after me," Archie muses when asked about the lore that is growing up around his son. "Best I ever did was some dogs and maybe a mule. But up here in Knoxville, they still print all the new babies' names, and there sure are a lot of little Peytons all of a sudden, boys and girls."

"I remember waiting for my dad after one of those bad games," says Peyton. "They'd have lost, and he'd be sore. He'd come out,

and he'd hug my mom, and then he'd sign his autographs. I'd be saying, 'Dad, let's go home.' I used to wonder about those people, Don't
they know he just lost a game? But he always told me to keep a smile
on my face. You know, a quarterback's got to be a patient person.

"What I remember most is that he never brought his sorrows
home."

Yes, sorrows. For this is a story about a family, a happy family, but
one that can trace its history back through one unspeakably sorrow-
ful evening in the Mississippi Delta. There are heroes in the story,
and that there may be a spot in the saga even for a minor character
named Peerless proves that Providence still wields a deft hand as literature. Peyton Manning is southern, a New Orleanian, but the
home of his legend is not there. Just as the wondrous old blues tells
us, its home is in the Delta.

Good Christ, this place is the kingdom of weird. It begins near Bel-
zoni, about twenty miles out along highway 49. You start seeing the
prisoners, lining the side of the road in their blue jackets reading
MDOC CONVICT, picking up the trash while the soft, loose cotton blows around the roadside. A little farther along, you start to see
the signs warning you not to pick up hitchhikers. The next set of
signs tells you that it is illegal to stop for longer than five minutes.
Then you see the prison, shadowy and vast in the morning mist. The
Mississippi State Penitentiary at Parchman.

Parchman Farm.

Its history is shot through with almost mythic terror. It was worse
to be there than to be sharecropping, worse to be there than back in
slavery, the old ones whispered. Young Riley B. King visited his uncle there once, and Parchman scared him so bad that the first chance
he got, he moved to Memphis, picked up a guitar and changed his
name to B. B. Most of the American popular culture that has been
worth a damn in the twentieth century owes something to this
haunted land, and Parchman Farm was the hidden charge behind
nearly all of it, good and bad, as though that ever mattered at all.
People bought the music and turned away from the bloody history
that produced it.

It was Archie Manning's country. He grew up in Drew, the nearest real town to the Farm, which casts its shadow over Drew as surely as it does over nearly everything else in the Delta. He would come to create his own legend in Mississippi, but he would come to do it from a place thick with long legends of its own.

"There were twenty guys on my football team," he recalls, "and six of them came from Parchman."

His father ran a farm-machinery shop in Drew. Buddy Manning was big and bluff and well loved around the town. Archie grew up as the best athlete in a very small place. Often he would go out to dances in the Delta to hear a band called the Gordian Knot, which was fronted by a singer named Jim Weatherly. Weatherly once started at quarterback at Ole Miss, and he ultimately went on to write not only "Midnight Train to Georgia" but also the vastly superior "Neither One of Us (Wants to Be the First to Say Goodbye)" for Gladys Knight and the Pips. The world was beginning to shake in Mississippi, and some of the boys Archie knew went to Ole Miss with the National Guard in order to escort James Meredith through the front gates.

"I'm not sure I really knew what it was all about back in those days," Archie recalls. "I probably should have."

This sounds more disingenuous than it actually is; after all, it beggars belief that he didn't really know what was going on in Mississippi. More likely, his is the cultivated ambivalence of a decent man on whom white Mississippi fastened at a time when it was groping for a white hero for anesthetic purposes. "Mississippi'd been getting beat up pretty good through the 1960s," he says. "The whole state pretty much clung to the team." One thinks of Parchman Farm and determines that Mississippi pretty much deserved what came to it. In a very real cultural sense, the Mississippi of the 1960s was the test track for the Montana of the 1990s, and Ole Miss still sticks in the craw of many talented black athletes because of all those things that went on while Archie Manning was coming up in Drew.

And one day in 1968, Kentucky brought two black players to Memorial Stadium in Jackson, and one of them, Wilbur Hackett, and Archie damned near knocked each other silly, and Archie patted the Kentucky player on the backside while everyone in the stadium went all hushed and still, even the highway patrolmen, not far removed from the days when their jobs entailed protecting the people who blew up little children in churches. Archie Manning's was the next-to-last Mississippi football class to play all four seasons without a black teammate, and it can be fairly said that Archie Manning became a hero to many people who didn't deserve the likes of him.

He had a glorious career, all torchlight and antebellum rituals. He met and romanced a homecoming queen from Williamsville named Olivia Williams. However, one season, he played such a miserable game at—of all places—Tennessee that he came back to school and briefly broke up with Olivia, severely distressing her father, a country shopkeeper named Cooper Williams. The following season, Archie helped Mississippi crush Tennessee in a piece of getback that cemented his legend for good, and he turned out to be smart enough to get Olivia back as well, old Cooper Williams being as thrilled as anyone.

Back home in the Delta, however, right before his junior season, in 1969, Archie came home from a wedding reception and found his father's body. Buddy Manning's health had gone and his business was failing, and so he took a gun to his chest. Archie called the doctor. He cleaned the room. This is the way things were done in the Delta, where they learn to deal with death as though it is nothing more than the dry wind that stirs the cotton.

"My father passed away," is the way Archie says it now.

Where he grew up, sorrow is of the land. He does not bring his sorrows home.

He never pushed his sons into football. He knew the game too well for that. Archie and Olivia married in 1971, a huge church wedding that people still talk about, and they had three boys, whom they raised in big houses in the Garden District of New Orleans. Cooper was the first one, a boisterous and hearty sort, a born operator and a gifted wide receiver. Peyton came next. He was more reserved, impeccably organized and something of a grind. "They never talked about the pros," Archie says. "All they ever wanted was to play college football." Both of the older boys (Eli, the youngest, is in high school now) were allowed to take up the game only when they were old enough for organized leagues in which there would be real coaches. They then went on to the Isidore Newman School, a private institution that is almost universally assumed to be a Catholic high school but which is actually quite secular and housed in what used to be a Jewish orphanage. Cooper went first, playing well enough to get a ride to Ole Miss, plunging enthusiastically into the heart of his father's legacy. Back in New Orleans, Peyton had begun to draw attention as a quarterback. With a Manning who was a quarterback, the stakes went up dramatically.

"He never pushed us into anything," Peyton says of his father. "If anything, we all took advantage of him. It was like, 'Hey, Dad. Whyn't you come work out with us? Show us how to do this and that.'" All along, Peyton had planned to go to Ole Miss, just as his father and his brother had. When the letters started to pour into the big house in the Garden District, especially the handwritten one from Bobby Bowden at Florida State, everything began to change.

The family determined that they would enjoy the recruiting process. Peyton took Cooper along on the visit to Notre Dame. When a congenital spinal defect ended Cooper's football career in 1992, the two brothers had become even closer than they'd always been. "It wasn't a hard call at all," says Archie, who knew the risks all too well to let his son continue to play. "I'll never forget the night I had to tell him. Tell you what, though. Cooper, he's a tough booger." Cooper told Peyton that he would just have to play football through him. So they both went to South Bend, where Peyton got the full treatment. "They had a ball," says Archie. "I'm not sure even I know all the stories." I am fairly sure he does not.

Every night during the recruitment phase, Peyton would lie across the foot of his parents' bed, and they would ask him if anything had clicked. He liked Florida. He liked Ole Miss. He even liked Michigan, although Archie secretly hoped that Peyton would stay in the South, where so much of his history was. It got ugly at the end, when Peyton picked Tennessee, nasty phone calls and all. "Ultimately," says Peyton, "I didn't want to be a celebrity quarterback the minute I walked on campus."

At Tennessee Peyton won a fierce competition for the job during his freshman season. Two veteran quarterbacks went down with injuries, and Peyton was given a chance at the job with another highly recruited freshman. Peyton ground the other guy out, spending endless hours studying film and winning the job so cleanly that his rival transferred to Texas A&M. During one of his first games, remembering what Archie had told him about how a quarterback has to be a leader, Peyton started yammering in the huddle. A veteran offensive lineman told him to shut up and "call the fucking play," which is something that has happened to every young quarterback on every football team in recorded time.

The easy comparison is to say that Archie was an instinctive player while Peyton is more calculating. What is more accurate is to say that Peyton has taken Archie's gifts and blended them with his own. He doesn't openly evince his father's reckless daring, but he is cool and precise, and that is a kind of daring, too. It takes courage to maintain enough distance to create your own legend and still not run away from the one into which you were born.

"I sensed pretty quickly that Peyton wasn't going to go to Ole Miss," Archie says. "I was never afraid of his not going there. What I was afraid of was that, in running away from Ole Miss, he might run away from the entire South."

They say he is a terrible spectator. They say he never learned. Archie Manning spent the first half of his football lifetime on the field, and he's spent the second half of it in the broadcast booth, so his sons say that the essential skills of being a fan simply elude him. He wanders, they say. He'll sit in two, three or four different seats in the course of each game, making new friends all the while. Last New Year's Day, as Peyton and Tennessee took apart listless Ohio State, Archie's wandering took him off through the murk and the gloom all the way to the wrong side of the Citrus Bowl. Olivia and the rest of the family considered sending Smokey the Tennessee hound off to find him.

He's disappeared again this bright spring day. They have brought the Volunteers out to sign autographs and to meet all the fans, great and small. The line for Peyton's autograph begins in front of him on the running track that encircles the football field. It extends halfway down the track, turns sharply to the left and then stretches the entire length of the fifty-yard line until it turns left again to run down the far sideline. From high above the field, Peyton's line looks like a spur from the Trans-Siberian Railroad. This line does not include the fans jamming the front row of the stands to take Peyton's picture. This line does not include the various cheaters who try to do things like toss a camera over Peyton's head to one of the security guards, or to Cooper, who is standing not far from his little brother. Archie is nowhere in sight.

"You seen Dad?" Peyton asks Cooper.

Cooper doesn't answer. He is remarkably lifelike this morning, considering that he'd fallen into evil company the night before. An old slyboots country lawyer—friend of Archie's, Matlock on steroids—had home-turfed Cooper somewhere way up in the hills until the sun began to rise. Cooper is not as quick as he might be, but he's showing definite signs of recovery.

"You seen Dad?" repeats Peyton.

"Yeah," Cooper replies. "He's over there, waiting in line for Will Newman." Will Newman is a sophomore and an offensive tackle, and he is famous primarily to the Newman family of New Market, Tennessee. As the brothers convulse, it becomes plain that it is a good thing that Peyton Manning will become a star professional quarterback, because, one day, Cooper Manning's going to own everything else.

"Peyton, he's pretty serious about things," their father muses. "He doesn't just ease into things. We know his commitments. We know what kind of kid he is. We've seen his grades. But we kind of remind him, you know? 'Hey, Peyton. Make sure you have some fun.'"

"I don't think I've ever had to say that to ol' Cooper."

Peyton Manning will contend for the Heisman Trophy, and Tennessee will contend for the national championship in a year in which the slightest early slip can dash both hopes. (Indeed, it can be fairly said that the Vols play a one-game season this year. Unless Tennessee beats Florida on September 21 in Knoxville, the team undoubtedly will be judged a disappointment.) He will try to enjoy himself, to catch a piece of the joy present in those moments when his father turned the corner out of the pocket and a cramped and sour world seemed to crack wide open for Archie Manning in all directions, playing for fun even though Archie was playing for mortal stakes.

For he was from a bloody and haunted place, its history clotted thick with the very worst of many things. It struck him young. He did his damnedest to redeem all of it, with his style and his flair, throwing footballs into the darkness of the place, trying to strike it, finally, at its heart. He drew people to him, and away, if only for a time, from all the hate and the anger. His son is a football star in the South now, and one of his teammates is a black kid from Dayton with a great name like Peerless Price. It is so very different from the way it was when Archie left Drew, out of the long shadows of his own past and the legendary prison. There is a sense that Archie Manning is owed this bright time, this peerless, shining day, these golden children, and that the legend is aging even more deeply and sweetly now, in the great oaken cask of the heart.

GQ **September 1996**

Ten Years Later,
He Can Laugh About It

And this is what the villain looks like, ten years on. A lone figure sliced by shadows—dim and then sharp, dim and then sharp—all splattery and soaked by a howling north-Atlantic gale that shakes the old bleachers of the ancient racetrack and makes the metalwork sing like rigging in a storm. He is in the lights, and then he is not, and then all there is in the light is a salt-stung torrent off the fiercest ocean in the world. Soaked and giddy children flock to the rails, leaning over to look at the villain, and the villain warms up, knees high, taking short dashes down the sloppy track, mud flying behind him with every step, and this is where the villain is now, ten years on.

It is a big night at the Charlottetown Driving Park on Prince Edward Island in what has become quaintly known as Atlantic Canada but what most people on both sides of the world's most amiable border still call the Maritimes. It is autumn now, running toward winter, as the prevailing winds grow sharper out of the northeast. The tourist season is long over. There are only a few Japanese walking the streets of Charlottetown, making the curious Anne of Green Gables pilgrimage that has come to mystify the locals even as it profits the island's economy.

It seems that the Japanese have come to adore the plucky heroine created by Prince Edward Island's own Lucy Maud Montgomery. (It is said that Japanese moms and dads return from North America business trips loaded down with copies of the Green Gables saga, since Japanese bookstores cannot keep the volumes in stock.) Consequently, every summer the streets of Charlottetown are filled with Asian women of all ages, all dressed in green jumpers and sprightly straw hats and all sporting long crimson braids. It is a town that handles the unusual with considerable aplomb.

There are close to seven thousand people gathered in the storm at the old driving park, which is meant to hold only a fifth as many. It is a historic track that has fallen into some disrepair. (The judges' stand, which looms over the infield like a lighthouse, was built in 1878, and the locals are trying to have it declared a national historical landmark. Until then, however, nobody is allowed inside the rickety old structure.) They have come to see something even more unusual than roving gaggles of giddy Japanese women in straw hats and pigtails. They have come to see a benefit race for the Children's Wish Foundation, the Canadian equivalent of the Make-a-Wish Foundation, which fulfills the requests of children with life-threatening diseases. They have come to see a man run against two horses and a car. They have come to see the villain.

He is smaller than you'd think he'd be, no longer the formidable presence he was in the mid-eighties, when he ran the dash the way a bull would, Jerome Bettis come to the sprints. His eyes are wide and clear, and there is still the sweet lilt of the Caribbean in his voice. He is guarded and bemused all at once. "I come here to help the kids," he says, each word edged and careful. "Remember, we all were kids once, you know?"

For the record, the trotter's name is Fast 'n Flashy, and it is driven by Wally Hennessey, a local hero in Charlottetown who went off to drive at Pompano in Florida. The other horse's name is Windsong, and it is ridden by Lloyd Duffy, a local hero in Charlottetown who went off to ride at Woodbine in Toronto. The car is the Auto Plus No. 25, and it is driven by Mike Ryan, who races it on the NASCAR stock circuit all over eastern Canada. The man's name is Ben Johnson, and he comes from Toronto, and he has raced all over the world, most notably in Seoul, South Korea, on one glorious fall afternoon when he seemed faster even than the sunlight that stabbed the stadium through. And then he became the villain, and this is where he is, ten years on, and this is what he's doing, ten years on. He is running a race against two horses and a car, through a soaking blast of headlong winter, on an old racetrack at the edge of the world.

Let me tell you about September 24, 1988, a day on which I saw a man run faster than a man had ever run before. It was a cool and brilliant day in Korea, with great shards of sunlight slanting low as the afternoon slipped toward evening. The participants in the men's 100-meter final bent into the blocks. It was a shivery, dead-level moment, as if time were running on a very thin and quavery wire. There was Carl Lewis, the defending Olympic champion, all springy and elegant, his eyes narrowed and clear, and there was Ben Johnson of Canada, thick and muscular, his eyes fierce and wide and yellow. Time stopped, the gun went off, and the race poured itself through the explosive sunlight.

I have never seen anyone run the way Ben Johnson ran that day. He was molten. He covered the distance in 9.79 seconds, and he had time at the end to look back at Lewis, whom he had beaten. After the race, Lewis intimated that Johnson had been using illegal drugs. Johnson denied it under persistent questioning. There were rumors like that all over the Olympics—of athletes drifting off to secret laboratories in the Caribbean or receiving their juice from their home-grown coaches.

That evening, I fell in with evil company in a place called Itaewon, which is a sort of Six Flags over the Seven Deadly Sins section of Seoul that caters to American servicemen stationed in the city. By my clock, I got fifteen minutes of sleep before the editor of my newspaper called to tell me that Ben Johnson had flunked a urinalysis—a steroid called stanozolol had been detected in his urine—and that Olympic officials were preparing to take his gold medal away. I felt rather terrible until I got to the main press center and saw a tableful of my Canadian colleagues, who collectively looked like a medieval depiction of the arrival of the Black Death.

The story from there is easily told. Having used steroids for some time, Johnson now used stanozolol to help him recover from a hamstring injury. Carl Lewis was awarded Johnson's medal. (Lewis later confided that his deceased father had come to his mother in a dream to tell her that God was going to make sure that everything was all right. The Almighty doth work in mysterious ways, but a urine sample doth seem one of the ickier ones.) A ruckus ensued in which the sports world eagerly joined the culture at large in losing its mind on the issue of drugs. Ben Johnson left Seoul a villain and, worse, a symbol. In the modern media culture, celebrity isn't necessarily just what we have that passes for a throne. In our vast and virtual modern town square, it's also what we have that passes for the stocks.

"I didn't kill myself," he says. "Why should I do that? God give me life, so I should appreciate that and live life. I cannot get my name back. Over the years, the media make me a monster, a villain. They make me a one-way figure on a two-way street."

Johnson disappeared, popping up again briefly in 1993, when he was banned for life because he was discovered to be toting around more testosterone than was thought appropriate. At that point, a Tory minister in Canada suggested that Johnson move back to Jamaica, where he'd been born. (This summoned up the joke that had flown through Seoul in the wake of Johnson's disqualification: The first day's headline was CANADIAN SPRINTER WINS GOLD! And the following day's was JAMAICAN SPRINTER FAILS DRUGS TEST!) It is estimated that the disqualification cost Johnson more than $10 million in endorsement money. He moved to a secluded home north of Toronto and went to work as a building contractor.

Still, he resurfaced from time to time, usually in his role as capital villain of his age. In 1997, his lifetime ban was upheld. In that same year, Johnson signed on as personal trainer to Diego Maradona, the Argentine soccer star who once was suspended from his sport because of a cocaine habit that would've embarrassed Led Zeppelin. He hooked up with Morris Chrobotek, a feisty little ball of enthusiasm and cologne who energetically promotes the dubious notion that Johnson can return, at age thirty-six, to the top level of competitive track—if only the international cabal of pooh-bahs and panjandrums that continues to conspire against Johnson will allow it.

"I think it's getting much better," Chrobotek explains. "He's still denied certain things, but his overall perception is positive. There are people who said to me, 'Isn't this demeaning? To run against horses?' They won't let him make a living. They won't give him a hearing. What's wrong with letting him run for charity? He's not making any money out of this. I mean, Fox TV—that Guinness program—has offered Ben a lot of money to run against a cheetah, and I said no. Nothing against Fox; they're good people. But Ben is not a circus."

Out on the track, Ben splashes up the backstretch, getting ready to race against two horses and a car. What I remember is a man who seemed to outrun the sunbeams. Pure or not, it's one of the damnedest things I ever saw.

The people have come out to see him—more than the driving park can hold, hanging off the gallery, flocking thick at the rail, salty wind whipping, stinging their eyes, driving the rain into their faces and down onto the track, where it splashes in the mud like tiny stars under the garish lights of the backstretch. And the villain is there in the light, and then he is not, and all there is in the light is the windswept rain, and there he is again, and everyone moves closer to the rail so they can see him—the villain or not, a strange man doing a strange thing in a strange place for a good cause. Behind him, the car grinds its engine, and the horses whinny and bridle, and then they're off! A man, two horses, and a car! Everybody cheers.

All right, so it was the eighties, and the country had lost its mind over drugs, demonizing vast numbers of citizens, truncating debate on an important issue, encouraging dangerously intemperate public rhetoric, poisoning politics, and taking good-sized chunks out of the Bill of Rights in the bargain. In retrospect, one thing seems obvious: Drugs indeed can make you crazy.

The frenzy began with the 1986 death of Len Bias, who overdosed on cocaine the night after he was drafted by the Boston Celtics in what was perhaps the decade's singular iconic tragedy. What happened to Ben Johnson in 1988 brought performance-enhancing drugs under the increasingly volatile rhetorical umbrella of the drug war. One respected sports journalist proposed dramatic, quasi-legal methods to combat what he called "bloodstream terrorists." Apparently, this fellow admired East German jurisprudence as deeply as he deplored East German sports medicine.

What was forgotten was that our performance sports would not exist as they do without artificial enhancement. Some enhancements are considered legitimate: Without the extensive use of some steroids—most notably, corticosteroids—the average professional-football career would be considerably shorter than it already is. Other forms of steroids are afforded all the tolerance usually reserved for crack cocaine. There are two arguments leveled against their use. The first is that banned substances should be banned because of their destructive effects on the athlete. The second is that the use of these substances is immoral on its face—contrary to the essential character of athletics and to the values of the society that the athletes undertake to entertain. Neither argument can stand without the other, and neither will stand forever.

In the first case, science marches on. By the next decade, anabolic steroids will be as obsolete as metal spikes. (Always ahead of the curve, the East Germans favored subtler potions by the time their country collapsed.) What will replace them likely will be more effective, easier to use, harder to detect, and—here's the real rub—safer to use.

We had a glimpse of the future this past summer, when Mark McGwire's pursuit of Roger Maris was briefly enlivened by a flap over McGwire's use of androstenedione, an over-the-counter dietary supplement that is allowed by Major League Baseball but banned by the NFL, the NCAA, and the International Olympic Committee. To his credit, McGwire said phooey to the whole business, broke the record, and made everybody happy. Sooner or later, there will come a pill that makes athletes better without destroying them. That will leave us with the purely moral argument, which at least is sturdily consistent. However, it is prone to the kind of gory illogic that fueled the heady early days of the drug war in the 1980s. (Baseball already is moving toward banning androstenedione for reasons that are purely cosmetic.) It also depends on an entire system of artificial enforcement that is incomprehensibly complex and whimsically applied. They test for the substance. Then they test for the substance that hides the substance. Next, they'll test for the substance that hides the substance that hides the substance. Soon, they'll wind up testing for substances as far removed from the actual drug as apple cider is from antifreeze. And out in the world, the tests don't even matter, because the presumption of guilt often depends on your country's medal count.

At the opening of the 1988 Olympics, there were just as many rumors concerning Florence Griffith Joyner as there were about Ben Johnson. The only difference at the end of the Olympics was that our beloved Flo-Jo didn't flunk any tests. To those uncomfortable with such ironclad guesswork, there is the case of Irish swimmer Michelle Smith, who in 1996 was presumed to be taking drugs largely because she had improved her times as radically as Griffith Joyner had improved hers, even though neither Smith nor Griffith Joyner ever failed an Olympic drug test. (Smith was banned last year over a contested sample, and she is appealing.) Ultimately, morality defined by jingoistic hooting over what may be contained in a person's urine is dubious morality indeed.

This past autumn was a strange one on the drug front. In October, the late Newt Gingrich got up at Auburn University and thumped the old familiar tubs, announcing that one of our new national priorities should be to get the NBA to start testing its players for marijuana. Since then, of course, the national concern over elongated bong-suckers has abated somewhat, since both the Speaker and the NBA have been largely disincorporated.

Elsewhere, the Australians moved loopily to criminalize all banned performance-enhancing drugs in anticipation of the 2000 Olympic Games in Sydney. Meanwhile, almost simultaneously, Juan Antonio Samaranch, Franco's old chum who runs the IOC, helpfully opined that it might be time to let athletes ingest anything they pleased. Then Florence Griffith Joyner died young, and the speculation that had spread underground in 1988 bloomed lushly in all the obituaries.

Finally, though, Samaranch's view likely will prevail, because the health argument will fall to technology, while the moral argument is fatally undermined by the ambiguous role of drugs in all our sports. If we demand to be entertained by sports at the level to which we are accustomed, then some drugs are undoubtedly necessary. Can anyone seriously argue that it is moral for some aging defensive tackle with arthritis grinding in every joint to shoot himself full of painkillers in order to play a game but immoral for the poor, staggering sod to smoke a joint afterward to help deaden the pain? Is it moral to take a drug that makes performance possible but immoral to take one to make performance better? It is a thin difference, fading into incoherence.

Ten years ago, after using steroids for most of his career, Ben Johnson took a steroid injection to overcome a hamstring injury. He ran the race of his life and became such a villain that he still cannot compete. Three weeks later, Kirk Gibson took an injection of steroids to overcome a hamstring injury. He hit a dramatic home run to win a World Series game for the Dodgers and became such a hero that Ken Burns blessed him with banjo music for all eternity.

He finishes third.

The standardbred horse gets spooked when the car engine starts, and it takes off, jumping the gun on Ben Johnson and the rest of the field. Johnson holds his own through the muck against the trotter, but he looks over just before the finish line, and the trotter goes by him. He beats the stock car, which slews all over the sloppy track. "I had a bad setup," says Mike Ryan, the driver, because this is what stockcar drivers say when they lose a race, even if they've driven out the gate and over a cliff.

"It was for me good exercise," Johnson says, toweling slop and grime off both his arms. "The horse was already in his movement, and I tried to hold on to my focus, because the fans and the people and the kids come out in this weather to see me, and it was a good cause, to be part of this night."

This is what it's like in the Gorky of the media age. The villain—or not—runs in the rain and raises $10,000, out of which some sick child will get a set of drums or some Maple Leafs tickets or a trip to

Disney World. Johnson insists he will win the appeal of his lifetime ban so that he can come back and compete again—which is not going to happen, because, even if the ban is lifted, Ben Johnson is thirty-six years old, and the game ran past him years ago. Now, the issues raised by the case of Ben Johnson, the ones that began on that glorious afternoon in Korea, still confound us and the people who still govern his sport and make us act contrary to both our greatest traditions and the best parts of our nature. And so he is here, in exile and in the rain, signing autographs along the rail, patting the children on the head, smiling his distant, distracted smile under the lights of an old racetrack at the edge of the world. The mud at his feet gleams like silver, like gold.

Ben Johnson subsequently failed another drug test, which he successfully contested. He continues to seek reinstatement. He is forty years old.

Esquire **February 1999**

The Next Superstar

A summer storm cell breaks, purplish and powerful, over the North Park Baptist Church on the north side of Orlando. Hard rain drums speedy and loud off the rusted tin portico of the recreation center, the bright little gym that Pastor Harry Bush calls "a little beam from God." It is the kind of place where basketball is born in the hearts of the people who play it. Shorn of numbers, salaries and reputations, they come to places like this to bring the game at one another, testing at the roots the fundamental authenticity of basketball's rewards.

The Orlando Magic have begun to filter into town, one or two at a time, as the season approaches. For a moment, several of them sit, and they listen to Pastor Bush, who talks to them of gifts and of God through the steady thrum of rain on the windows. They are veterans, most of them: big Stanley Roberts, soon to be the central player in a three-way trade that will send him to the Los Angeles Clippers; Dennis Scott, a gifted deep shooter trying to come back from a bad knee injury, and Scott Skiles, a 28-year-old guard with a sweet instinct for the game's geometry and a go-to-hell attitude that makes him, weight for age, perhaps the toughest player in the National Basketball Association. They politely pay attention to Pastor Bush, all of them looking like men in a rescue mission out of the 1930's, willing to accept a sermon as the price for a bowl of soup.

"Some of you have come here without families," Pastor Bush is saying. "Some of you have come down here without pastors."

The youngest of them is also the biggest. Even sitting down, he is perceptibly taller and wider than the older players. When he was a young boy, growing up in Newark first, then on Army posts around the world, Shaquille O'Neal was ashamed of his size. He shot up to 6 foot 8 as a sophomore in high school, but his coordination lagged behind. He slouched, making himself look even more ridiculous. "My parents told me to be proud," he recalls. "But I wasn't. I wanted to be normal."

He first wanted to be a dancer on the television show "Fame." He wanted to be lithe and smooth and lightly airborne, working on his break dancing until he could make himself appear to flow. He spun on his head, the way the sharpest breakers did. Until, one summer, he got too wide to flow and too big to spin on his head. He had out-grown his dreams. He was 14 years old.

He picked up a basketball because that is what the biggest children do. At age 16, he was the most sought-after high-school player in the country, enrolling at Louisiana State University. Last spring, he be-came the No. 1 pick in the NBA draft, signing in August with the Magic for an estimated $40 million over the next seven years. In ad-dition, he took the first steps toward being a multinational corpora-tion—wholly owned by himself. Reebok, the athletic-shoe company, has made him central to its drive to dominate that lucrative market. Soda companies have come calling. He also will have his own basket-ball and his own action figures.

The Magic is depending upon Shaquille O'Neal to reverse its sorry history as an expansion team, to make it a competitive basket-ball operation rather than simply another entertainment outlet fighting for tight discretionary dollars in the Kingdom of the Mouse. The NBA is counting on him to lead it into the next gener-ation and a continuation of the spectacular personality-driven growth of the last decade that has made the league the most aston-ishing success story in the history of professional sports. "He's a lit-tle mini-entertainment complex," says his agent, Leonard Armato, "before he ever steps on the floor." He is 7 foot 1 and 300 pounds. In March, he turned 20.

There are few doubts about his playing abilities. Of his most immediate contemporaries, he is bigger than Patrick Ewing of the Knicks, stronger than David Robinson of the San Antonio Spurs and a more instinctive defender than Hakeem Olajuwon of the Houston Rockets, for whom the game seems to have become a burden. Yet, in some ways, O'Neal is still amazingly raw. In his first exhibition game, against the Miami Heat, he committed nine turnovers, a ludicrous number for a center. There are moments when he seems to get hugely tangled in himself, and he has the devil's own time with free throws. What he has is enormous natural ability. All he lacks is acquired wisdom.

Says the Knick guard Glenn (Doc) Rivers, who played with O'Neal in a series of pickup games this summer: "He's going to stumble into 20 points and 10 rebounds a game just because he's so big. He's going to have to work on it, but he's just so . . . grown-up for his age."

In an October exhibition game in Asheville, N.C., the good and bad in him were on conspicuous display. Against the Charlotte Hornets, he put up 26 points and 11 rebounds, but he also lost the ball six times. He was duped into silly offensive fouls when smaller men moved in behind him as he powered toward the basket. Still, to watch him slap away a shot by Kendall Gill, a star of the Hornets, and then go 90 feet to drop a layup at the other end is to see almost limitless promise.

O'Neal took all of it with poise and equanimity. "I'm all right," he said afterward. "I'm at about 70 percent, or maybe 80."

Orlando coach Matt Guokas explains: "People tend to forget how young he is because of how big he is. He's still learning the pro game. He doesn't really even know the language yet." And if he sometimes looks like an Arthur Murray student confronting the footprints on the floor for the first time (once, against the Charlotte veteran J. R. Reid, O'Neal tied himself in an enormous knot, and Reid blocked his shot), he also clearly looks like the latest coming of basketball's most compelling mythic figure—the Big Man in the Middle.

Once, a center was called a "pivot man," with good and clear reason. Everything about the game, from its actual strategy to its psychic rhythms, revolved around him. Over the past 20 years, however, basketball has moved up and out, away from the big men in the middle. First, Gus Johnson and Elgin Baylor took it into the air, where Connie Hawkins, Julius Erving and Michael Jordan have followed. Then, Larry Bird and Magic Johnson, neither of whom could jump conspicuously well, redefined their respective positions, largely through their mutual love for and faith in the pass. Both were 6 foot 9, but both excelled at positions previously thought to belong to smaller men. Bird played essentially the small forward's slot, and Johnson was a point guard. Centers followed the trend as the game evolved. This led, at its best, to the multiplicity of skills demonstrated by David Robinson, and, at its worst, to the pathetic sight of Ralph Sampson, a 7-foot-4 man trying to play himself shorter.

In this, O'Neal may be the perfect synthesis of old myth and new reality. His is essentially a power game, but it is infused with the kind of speed and agility required by modern professional basketball. He will handle the ball on the perimeter if he must (the first play he ever made that caught national attention came in a televised all-star game after his senior year at Robert G. Cole Senior High School in San Antonio, when O'Neal grabbed the ball off one backboard and took it the length of the floor to dunk at the other), and he is working on a jump shot. But his greatest gifts remain in the classic pivot—close in, with his back to the basket. There, he is that thing most beloved by the savants—a "quick jumper," rising apparently from his ankles and calves without ever appearing to gather himself.

The Big Man in the Middle endures as an archetype, largely because he was so much of what first made basketball unique. Wilt Chamberlain once pointed out that "nobody loves Goliath," as an excuse for his enduring unpopularity. He was wrong, of course, even scripturally: the Philistines loved Goliath. If O'Neal comes up a little short of Goliath's six-cubits-and-a-span, his talents and, more important, his personality may make him the living refutation of the Chamberlain theorem. He has a quick smile that instantly takes five years off his age. This is what the Magic and the NBA are counting on—a Goliath everyone can love.

For to be merely a player—even a great player—is no longer all there is in the NBA. The league creates stars now, a culture of celebrity that could not have been anticipated in the late 1970's, when the NBA was in very real danger of collapsing altogether. There is an inexorable blurring of the line that separates entertainers and athletes. Most recently, Charles Barkley appeared in a cartoon brawl with Godzilla. This culture reached its apex at the Olympic Games in Barcelona, when the United States team, featuring Bird, Johnson, Jordan, Barkley and other NBA stars, careened across Europe like some strange, elongated outtakes from *A Hard Day's Night*.

That culture of celebrity has its benefits; for example, Jordan's carefully crafted public image largely insulated him from accusations of high-stakes gambling leveled against him last season. But it's also a fragile culture, largely black and formed during a decade of racial reaction. It needs constant renewal. Bird and Johnson are both retired, and Jordan insists that he will not play much longer. To survive, the celebrity culture that fueled the NBA's rise needs new, young, charismatic players while it continues to finesse the problems of race and class that bedevil every other institution today.

As soon as he left college last spring, Shaquille O'Neal became the de facto leader of that next generation. No less an authority than Magic Johnson sees that. "He's got it all," says Johnson, who worked out with O'Neal in Los Angeles last spring. "He's got the smile, and the talent, and the charisma. And he's sure got the money, too."

Indeed, Shaquille has a goofy kid's smile that runs up the left side of his face a little faster than the right. On his first day at a summer construction job at L.S.U., he jumped off the roof of the house on which he was working, terrifying the occupants. When a couple in Geismar, La., named their infant son Shaquille O'Neal Long—simply because they loved the name—Shaquille immediately drove out and had his picture taken with the baby.

And he does have something of a sweet tooth for cars. He drives a burgundy Blazer with the license plate "Shaq-Attaq," and his black

Mercedes sports a front plate that reads, "Shaqnificent." Both are parked at his new house in Isleworth, a luxury suburb outside Orlando. The first thing he did after signing his Orlando contract was to return home to San Antonio and treat two of his friends to a trip to an amusement park. This, from a newly minted millionaire who announced on his first trip to Orlando that he was looking forward to "chillin' with Mickey," and who explained on the opening day of the Magic's training camp, "I was a child star, just like Michael Jackson and Gary Coleman."

Dennis Tracy, who has signed on as his friend's unofficial media liaison, says: "I can't see him ever changing. He'll always be that kid who jumped off the roof because it was fun to do."

So far, O'Neal has done all the right things. He signed quickly and without rancorous negotiation. He defused a potentially messy situation over his college No. 33, surrendering it to his veteran teammate Terry Catledge. Over the summer, he impressed current NBA players with his love for hard work and, oddly enough, with his punctuality. "The most impressive thing is that he's such a mature person," says Doc Rivers. "When we were playing at U.C.L.A., we started at 9 o'clock in the morning, and he was there right on the dot every day. You don't see many college kids like that."

O'Neal listens attentively as Pastor Bush winds up his talk, and then he takes the floor. He is playing with Skiles, who is already in game shape and driving his teammates hard. Roberts, a former L.S.U. teammate of O'Neal's, tries to shoot a jump shot over him, and O'Neal slams the ball off the floor in a 10-foot carom. Skiles is not impressed. "Shaq," he says, "block it back to someone on your team." Shortly thereafter, Stanley Roberts has had enough, and he walks off the floor, claiming an injured leg.

Thunder peals outside, and there is a flash that shows the wire threaded through the thick window glass above the bleachers. On the first day that Shaquille O'Neal came to Baton Rouge, the skies darkened and roared, and a small tornado blew through town. Scared to death, he rode around on Dennis Tracy's bicycle with the storm blowing up all around him.

There is portent to the way he plays. His team wins. The lightning cracks.

"O.K.," says Scott Skiles, looking up at his newest teammate. "You guys bring it back."

It is a comfortable world that Shaquille O'Neal joins. Between 1981 and 1991, the NBA's gross nonretail revenue grew from $110 million to $700 million—an increase of 636 percent. Its gross retail revenues, which include the vastly profitable licensing of team jackets and caps, exploded even more vigorously, now totaling more than $1 billion per year.

As recently as a decade ago, there was serious talk of folding at least three and possibly as many as six franchises. Now, the average franchise is worth approximately $70 million, and there is talk about selling the Boston Celtics alone for $110 million. "There is no one place that it changed," says the NBA commissioner, David J. Stern. "A number of things that the owners and players did provided a better stage for all our players." Indeed, on the two most volatile issues of the past 20 years in professional sports—money and drugs—the NBA and its players have developed workable solutions, while largely avoiding the acrimony that has become customary in both baseball and football.

The league's greatest triumph has been to inculcate in everyone a fundamental loyalty to the idea of the league. Hence, Stern talks about "the NBA family." "It may not be a traditional family," he says, "but it is an extended family." This has provided NBA players with a stable foundation from which to kick off their own lucrative careers. Each generation builds on the previous one. Erving's abilities as a player and as a public person made it easier for Bird and Johnson, who made it easier for Michael Jordan, who took the whole business to another dimension. Without Erving, who proved once and for all that black athletes were neither brooders nor cartoons, Jordan's entree into the corporate class would've been that much more difficult. In turn, Jordan's success eases the burden on O'Neal.

He joined the family at the end of last year's college season, leaving L.S.U. with one year of eligibility left. He was tired of being triple-teamed and physically roughed up. "I played my heart out," he says. "But there was one game, I was catching alley-oops all day. So, in the second half, I was doing my spin move, and guys were putting their butts into my leg, coming under me. It was not a money thing. I was taught at a young age that if you're not having fun at something, then it's time to go."

The lesson came from his father. In the early 70's, with Newark just beginning to turn from the riots of 1967 into something even more lost and hopeless, Philip A. Harrison decided to get out. He joined the Army and, before he could marry Lucille O'Neal, he was shipped overseas. She had their baby without him. Looking through a book of Islamic names, she called him Shaquille Rashaun O'Neal, which, she says, means "Little Warrior." "I wanted my children to have unique names," Lucille says. "To me, just by having a name that means something makes you special."

The couple married soon thereafter. The family held together in the gypsy jet stream that is military life. "The best part for me was just getting out of the city," Shaquille recalls. "In the city, where I come from, there are a lot of temptations—drugs, gangs. Like, when I used to live in the projects, guys'd ride by in their Benzes. Kids want to have the fancy clothes and the Benzes. They say: 'Look at Mustafa. He's done this and done that. I want to do that.' When I was little, I was a kind of juvenile delinquent, but my father stayed on me. Being a drill sergeant, he had to discipline his troops. Then, he'd come home and discipline me.

"The worst part was, like, traveling, you know? Meeting people, getting tight with them, and then having to leave. Sometimes, you come into a new place, and they'll test you. I always got teased. Teased about my name. Teased about my size. Teased about being flunked. You know, 'You so big, you must've flunked.' I'd have to beat them up. It took a while to gain friends because people thought I was mean. I had a bad temper. Guys used to play the 'dozens' game with me where they used to talk about your mother, and I'd get mad and hit them. One day, I just woke up and walked away."

They moved to Germany twice, the last time just before Shaquille entered junior high. It was a tight, regimented existence. In Fulda, where Sergeant Harrison was stationed, there was some anti-American agitation; in one bizarre protest, the townspeople painted American military vehicles a bright blue. It is significant, then, that, for all his travels, Shaquille still calls Newark his home, and that "the projects" loom so large in his personal iconography despite the fact that he spent very little of his life there. "He didn't want to leave," his father explains. "He wanted to stay there with his grandma."

But that was not the way that the sergeant's family functioned, and all four of his children knew it. "Society is always dictating to the parent who's the boss," says Harrison, who will retire as a staff sergeant in September 1993 and move his family one last time—to Orlando. "You know who the boss is today in the family? The children. My dad disciplined me. Your dad disciplined you. What was said about it? Now, everybody's in the middle. Back then, the people in the middle were your friends, so you didn't disrespect them. Now, somebody runs to the court."

One day near Fulda, Shaquille went to a basketball clinic run by Dale Brown, the energetically eccentric basketball coach at L.S.U. Brown presumed that the big young man was a soldier. Discovering that Shaquille was, in fact, barely a teenager, Brown's coaching antennae vibrated into the red zone, and he asked to meet the sergeant. Five years later, after Harrison was posted to Fort Sam Houston in San Antonio and after Shaquille became a high-school all-American at Cole, L.S.U. recruited and won him. It was presumed that Harrison made the choice for his son. "That was him alone," Harrison says. "We pushed the boat away the day he decided to go there. We told him, 'Go out there and take what we taught you and what you learned in life and apply it and do what you have to do.'"

In college, O'Neal became a superstar, despite breaking his leg during his sophomore seaon. By the end of last season, he was averaging 24.1 points per game. But the Pier 6 strategy of rival coaches was wearing his patience thin. In addition, Brown seemed unable to keep O'Neal as the focal point of the L.S.U. offense, something that drove NBA types mad when they looked at tapes of the Tigers, and something that they blame for the rough edges that still exist on his game.

"I saw one game last year when this kid touched the ball about twice in the entire second half," says one NBA scout. "I said, 'Is this guy kidding or what?'" O'Neal managed to restrain himself until the

Southeastern Conference tournament, when he became one of the instigators of an ugly brawl in which even Brown was seen throwing haymakers at the opposition. Shaquille was suspended for the Southeastern Conference championship game the following day. After L.S.U. was eliminated early in the subsequent N.C.A.A. tournament, he made his decision to turn professional. He closed his bank account and went home to San Antonio.

His father always had insisted that O'Neal would stay the full four years at L.S.U. His parents had tried to impress upon their son the value of a college degree. In addition, Philip Harrison had emphasized the vast differences between the college game and the one that is played in the NBA. But the scene at the Tennessee game gave even the sergeant second thoughts. "I told him I wanted to leave," Shaquille says. "It was not that hard. He just thought about it and finally, he said, 'If I was you, I'd want to leave, too.' Not because of the money, but because I wasn't having any fun. Everybody thinks he's a dictator. He's not."

His father laughs now. "Everybody's got this myth that, when the sergeant speaks, everybody listens." He points at his wife: "When *she* speaks, everybody listens."

Shaquille announced his availability for the draft on April 3, and he was taken into Stern's NBA family almost immediately. Through Dale Brown, the family had met a Los Angeles-based agent named Leonard Armato, who also represents Hakeem Olajuwon, and who also had helped straighten out the tangled public image of Kareem Abdul-Jabbar. Armato agreed to represent Shaquille. In June, he went to the NBA finals in Portland, where he was interviewed by Ahmad Rashad. Endorsement offers bloomed everywhere. It was a dizzying time, and Shaquille handled an array of new situations with conspicuous aplomb.

Counselors who work with them say that military children adapt quickly, that they develop social skills faster than other children their age. Shaquille was formed within a dynamic that was at once very stable, and at the same time in predictable flux. Every three years, as the sergeant was rotated between duty stations, there were new places to see and new friends to make. Even though he seems to cling to Newark as some sort of cultural touchstone, Shaquille learned very early in his life to function in different contexts with ease and confidence. He has been an urban homeboy and an American abroad, a Texas schoolboy legend and a college star. He is going to be a professional star, a commercial spokesman and a national celebrity.

"Ego is acting like you're all-that," he says. "Like they say on the block, 'all-that.' Can't nobody touch you," he says. "Confidence is knowing who you are."

At various times during his career, the Orlando general manager, Pat Williams, has treated NBA crowds to halftime entertainments involving singing dogs and wrestling bears. He has become known as the league's premier showman, occasionally at the expense of his reputation as a basketball man. Williams needed to sign O'Neal quickly. For the first few seasons, the Magic were content to sell the entertainment side of the NBA experience. But, in an area where there were so many other entertainment options, it became incumbent upon the team to move toward competitive basketball, lest it drop down past Sea World on the food chain of local attractions.

"As great as Disney and Sea World are," explains Jack Swope, the Magic's assistant general manager, "they're not considered something that local people can identify with. It's hard to root for Disney World." It's just as hard, however, to root for a basketball team that wins 20 games a year. O'Neal would be the link between the entertainment function of the Magic and the athletic one.

Immediately after the draft, a nervous Williams couldn't even find his new star. There was nothing coming from the O'Neal camp, he says, like "yippee, we're glad Orlando won the lottery. There were no warm-fuzzies coming out of that end for about a month," he says. In addition, Williams was having trouble with the NBA salary cap. It stabilized the league's fiscal situation, but it also requires general managers to contort themselves regularly through baffling mathematical gymnastics just to get their rosters filled.

Orlando's situation was complicated further when the Dallas Mavericks signed Stanley Roberts, a restricted free agent, to an offer sheet that totaled $15 million over five years. The Magic had to match that offer within 15 days or lose Roberts without compensation. Moreover, because of salary-cap restrictions, the Magic had to sign O'Neal before matching the offer to Roberts.

Williams was going in several directions at once. To make room for O'Neal under the salary cap, he traded guard Sam Vincent to Milwaukee and restructured five other existing contracts. On Aug. 4, O'Neal signed for a reported $40 million over seven years. Orlando also matched the Dallas offer to Roberts, whom the Magic then traded to the Clippers in September in a deal that brought two first-round draft picks, which will be used to put the required supporting cast around O'Neal.

It was a remarkably civil negotiation. "To their credit, Shaquille and his people were bright enough to understand," Williams says. "They worked with us in those 15 days. Most people thought we couldn't do it. But we did it."

That left Armato free to develop the rest of what he calls Shaquille's "entertainment complex." While the Magic own the rights to everything with their name on it, O'Neal is free to make whatever outside deals he can. (For example, he can do television commercials, but he can't wear his uniform in them without the prior approval of either the team or the league.) Soon, a lucrative deal was signed with Spalding for the Shaquille O'Neal basketball, and one is in the works with Kenner for a line of Shaquille action figures. Since Armato made his reputation primarily as a shrewd money manager—as opposed to as a hardball negotiator like David Falk, the Washington attorney who represents Patrick Ewing—O'Neal feels confident that his long-term interests are secure.

"We've got good investments going," he says. "We've got stocks, T-bills. We're all right."

Armato plans a unified marketing strategy and a logo currently being designed by a team of graphic artists in Los Angeles. "We're thinking of a single image for Shaquille through all of the products in a way that benefits all of them," Armato says. "Let's say it's a soft drink: The 'Shaq-Pack.' On the package as a prize, maybe there's a

Shaquille basketball, or a pair of shoes. The NBA is putting Shaquille in 100 different countries by itself."

The most obvious modern endorsement is a shoe contract. It's almost unfathomable today to realize that Kareem Abdul-Jabbar once made only $100,000 a year to wear Adidas basketball shoes. In 1983, Nike had passed Adidas as the leader in worldwide sales. The following year, however, Reebok, a smaller, Boston-based company, took over the market from floundering Nike, largely by catching the aerobics boom that Nike missed. Later in 1984, though, after Nike signed Michael Jordan to an innovative promotional deal, Nike won back the market again—by September 1985, the company had sold more than 2.3 million pairs of Air Jordans alone—and Reebok now plans to counter Jordan with Shaquille O'Neal, whose size 20 feet will be shod in Reeboks in exchange for a reported $10 million over the next five years. Nike and Jordan made this deal possible, and Reebok and O'Neal plan to repay the favor by bringing them down out of the air.

"He is going to be the focal point of basketball for us," says Mark D. Holtzman, Reebok's director of sports marketing. "We want to portray him as the strongest man in the NBA, and we want to do it worldwide. We're going to put him in 50 countries." Reebok is hanging new technologies on the "Shaq Attaq" shoes as well, which will retail for more than $100. O'Neal spent part of September shooting the first commercials for them.

Every step he takes now has consequences. Every move he makes sets off tremors, and his first NBA season is barely a week old. When he and Catledge were wrangling over No. 33 in Florida, the NBA licensing people grew edgy in New York, since they didn't know what number to put on their official Shaquille gear.

O'Neal is aware that the commercials he so enjoyed making will contribute to a deadly consumer culture that grips the projects where he has anchored his past, to that look he saw in the eyes of the kids who wanted the Benzes long ago. He is going into a culture of celebrity that has been accused of abandoning its most impoverished adherents.

"I'm worried about that," he says. "I'm not going to make myself a superhero that people can't touch. The commercials are going to show both sides of me, what I like to do off the court, like listen to my rap music.

"The question was asked of me, should athletes be role models? The answer is, yes, to a certain extent. Like, when I was a kid, I could look up to Doctor J, but if I needed some advice about the birds and the bees, I couldn't ask Doctor J. I couldn't call one of these superstars. I had to call Mommy or Daddy. I mean, we should carry ourselves well on TV. We should not do things like beat our girlfriends up, do drugs or alcohol. Now, if all those kids lived with me, then I could be their role model."

The Forum Club is hopping. Once the NBA was armories in places like Davenport, Iowa, and Rochester. Today it is the Great Western—formerly Fabulous—Forum in Los Angeles. Once it was steelworkers and mill hunks. Today it is agents and movie stars and singers. In the Forum Club, there is taffeta and lace, leather and gold. There is loud talk of agents and properties and the hot places to go later that night. Ice rings like delicate chimes. It is a basketball evening in Los Angeles, and the sky outside is a perfect parfait.

Every August, Magic Johnson hosts a benefit game for the United Negro College Fund. O'Neal has come to play this year. His coach is Arsenio Hall. Coaching the other team is Spike Lee. The singer Al B. Sure sits in one section with the female singing group En Vogue. At midcourt, Jack Nicholson sits with his infant daughter, whose parents will later mutually determine that they no longer want to live together in separate houses. It's a long way from North Park Baptist Church, a great distance from Pastor Bush and his little beam from God's eye.

O'Neal plays with consummate ease and confidence. He blocks shots by catching them. He whips down the lane for a dunk off an in-bounds play, and he winks at Leonard Armato's 4-year-old son while he does it. He tosses the veteran Pistons center Olden Polynice this way and that, once bouncing the ball off the backboard, retrieving it with a lightning first step, and then slamming it through as the women from En Vogue rock and Arsenio grabs his head. He ends up with 36 points and 19 rebounds. "Shaquille, the best part about him is that he's mean," Magic Johnson says later. "He's going to be one of those guys that, after you play him, you sleep real good. He's gonna put guys to sleep."

He does not look mean. He does not look like a product here. He looks like a 20-year-old discovering himself all over again. There is a purity that extends from north Orlando to this gathering of gaudy dilettantes. He will be comfortable in both places. He will be a kid and a corporation. He will be for sale and he will be free. He will be a Goliath for everyone to love.

New York Times Magazine **November 15, 1992**

The Trials of Jobe

Once upon a time, before spectator sports became an airless bubble of corporate enterprise, college basketball was coached by fractious rogues like Al McGuire and Abe Lemons. As a young man, McGuire worked in the family saloon, leaping feet-first over the bar to stop—and, on rare occasions, to *start*—the weekly Saturday night hooley. For his part, Lemons was a child of dust-bowl Oklahoma; to this day, he carries around an old newspaper photograph of what appears to be most of southern Kansas in a dust cloud, looming black and biblical over the main street of his hometown. Once you've seen that, it's logical for you later to peruse a breakfast menu upon your arrival in New York City and announce "I ain't never seen a chicken could lay an $8 egg."

In their own way, both of them carry with them the Depression, the great historical event of their time. It is not there in the younger coaches. They float free, from one job to the next. They are shallow, hollow people, dangerously out of touch with the players they coach and with the culture that produces those players. They are unstuck in history, unmarked by either the civil-rights movement or the Vietnam War, both of which cleaved their generation as surely as the Depression colored the generation that produced McGuire and Lemons.

There are exceptions, of course. Danny Nee at Nebraska fought in Vietnam, and when most college programs mindlessly went along with the jingoistic yahooism attending the Gulf war, Nee announced that they would have to "pull me off of my son before I'd let him go through what I did." Certainly, there is no making sense of Georgetown's John Thompson unless you realize that he went off to Providence College angry and confused in the days after the March on Washington in 1963. Touched by great events, by the simple fact that history has its bloody side, neither man is as monomaniacal in his outlook as are many of their contemporaries.

And, down at Southern University, in Baton Rouge, Louisiana, there is Ben Jobe, the head coach of men's basketball, a man of older and deeper traditions trying to get by in a job that measures history with a shot clock.

His basketball credentials are impeccable. Jobe learned the game from the venerable John McLendon, who himself learned it from Dr. James Naismith—learned it so well that McLendon's teams at Tennessee A&I became a dynasty among the country's black colleges. "I like to say that I am the third generation removed from Dr. Naismith," Jobe says. "Coach McLendon told me once—we were riding along in a car—that Dr. Naismith once told him that the one thing that bothered him most was seeing kids playing at just one basket. Dr. Naismith said the game should be played for ninety-four feet."

Jobe's Jaguars would delight the game's inventor. They run and they press, and they put the ball in the air with astonishingly promiscuous glee. In their first two games this season, Southern launched 195 shots, albeit launching them over a pair of obscure outposts called Patten College and Paul Quinn College. By the midpoint of the season, they were averaging nearly eighty shots a game.

Last season, the Jaguars burst into national attention by upsetting fourth-seeded Georgia Tech in the first round of the NCAA tournament's West Regional. Jobe was ambivalent about the big win. In the first place, it came at the expense of Georgia Tech coach Bobby Cremins, one of Jobe's oldest friends. In the second place, it thrust Jobe onto a national stage, attention he instinctively distrusts. And, finally, it put him in the spotlight as a basketball coach, which to Jobe seems in many ways a refutation of what history—his personal history and our common history—has made of him.

He is a product of America's black colleges, those stubborn remnants of the curdled promises of Reconstruction. After the Civil War, the freedmen were promised forty acres, and a mule with which to plow them. They were promised that they would be educated. But when the price became too politically dear, the country lost its nerve: The land always belonged to someone else; the mule always died. The colleges, however, stayed. They are proud places: Howard University, in Washington, D.C.; Morehouse College, in Atlanta; Fisk University, in Nashville, where Ben Jobe was educated; and Southern, still an endangered stepchild of the educational system in Louisiana. At these schools, college is not merely a pleasantly beery way station on the path to inexorable entitlement. Here, an education has always been a struggle against the inertia of history, and a degree, earned with dignity and grace, an unlikely triumph.

Jobe has spent most of his career in places like these, long enough to develop a mistrust for the larger educational Establishment that (among its other perversities) controls major college sports. So, when his team beat Georgia Tech and Jobe found himself praised as a coach, he felt his entire past tugging at a suddenly spotlit present. What in God's name did Ben Jobe (Fisk, '56) have to do with all of this country-club hoohah run out of the preposterously white-bread precincts of Overland Park, Kansas?

"It is a decadent profession," Jobe says. "You have to remember that I go back to the days when we were educators, at the same level of the English teachers or the math teachers. Now, we are entertainers, and we are choreographers, and we are Ringling Brothers directors."

"I don't think Ben thinks of himself as a basketball coach," says Donnie Walsh, an executive with the Indiana Pacers who worked with Jobe (and with Cremins) on Frank McGuire's staff at the University of South Carolina. "I don't think it would occur to him."

He has walked away from coaching three times. He has left to sell real estate, to sell insurance and to sell athletic shoes. He has walked away from the country once. But he has come back to the game and to the country, drawn by the conflicting impulses that are so much a part of the history he has lived. Du Bois and Washington. Malcolm and Martin. Black Power and the Rainbow Coalition. Anger and conciliation, and so very much more than simply basketball, a game in which so many people find a narcotic escape from their own time and place, and where they can ignore all the history that grows, full and spreading, like the great willows that sway over a long bend in a ceaseless river.

Ben Jobe left America in 1960. One day, in his hometown of Nashville, Jobe had taken part in a sit-in to protest the city's racial segregation. Nashville was alive with Movement fervor in those days; a theology student named James Lawson had been conducting regular workshops in nonviolent resistance. This loose network of activists included students at Fisk University, from which Jobe had graduated three years earlier.

After the Civil War, the Jobe family had moved from northern Mississippi to central Tennessee, where they lived on the land promised to them by the federal government. Arthur Jobe was born on that land. So was Arthur's son, Ben. Arthur drilled into his children that they would one day take advantage of the education they had been promised. He insisted that his children collect that which was their due, even after he was cheated out of the farm ("He couldn't read," says his son. "He signed the wrong papers") and the family moved to Nashville. They would go to one of the black colleges. Fisk, maybe. Or Southern, down there in Louisiana, big and growing, under the direction of Dr. Josiah Clark.

In 1881, Southern University was established in what used to be the old Hebrew Girls School, on Calliope Street in New Orleans. In 1914, the university moved to what had been the Walker plantation, a tract of land along the Mississippi River in Scotlandville, just outside Baton Rouge. According to Charles Vincent's centennial history of the college, one white citizen fumed to a local newspaper, "A Negro with an education is useless for all practical purposes."

The abiding figures in Southern's history are Clark and his son, Dr. F. G. Clark. They presided, in succession, over SU from 1914 until 1968. The elder Clark impressed upon his students the delicate line that the educated black citizen had to walk in a segregated society. Later, his son explained: "I seek to do the paradoxical job of try-ing to administer with integrity . . . a legally segregated college in a democratically pronounced commonwealth." It was a stance doomed to fail due to its obvious internal contradictions. The schools were producing mechanics and farmers, as was their mandate from the white educational Establishment, but they were producing lawyers and doctors and dreamers, as well. The good intentions of the Clarks eventually were overrun by events. In 1969, after a week of student unrest, Louisiana law-enforcement officials fired into a crowd that had gathered on the Southern campus. Two sophomores, Denver Smith and Leonard Brown, were killed. No one has ever been prose-cuted in the shootings.

Ben Jobe wrestled with Dr. F. G. Clark's paradox at Fisk more than a decade before Smith and Brown were killed, taking courses from, among others, W.E.B. Du Bois, who was a visiting professor. Segre-gation's idiocy becomes even more apparent when you educate its victims.

"I was a sophomore in college in psychology class," Jobe recalls. "The professor walked in and he said 'Well, the Supreme Court just handed down a decision and now there's going to be integration.' I had never heard the word before. Later on, he injected the word 'de-segregation.' I liked that word better. It meant I had a choice to go wherever I wanted.

"You know what the worst was about segregation? For me, any-way, it wasn't lynchings. The worst thing was the signs, the signs say-ing 'WHITES ONLY,' the signs that programmed you."

So, that day in 1960, he went downtown with some of James Lawson's people, and he sat in at a lunch counter. Next to him was a woman from the North who had come to Nashville to offer her support. They were soon surrounded by a roiling mob. "I remem-ber smelling something burning," Jobe says. "Someone had set fire to her hair." He walked out, angry and bitter, and soon accepted a Ford Foundation fellowship to teach in Sierra Leone. He needed to get away. He had no talent for joining and even less for non-violence. "I tried," he says today. "But deep down in me, there's a violence."

Upon his arrival, he took a boat to the capital, Freetown. On the banks of the harbor there stood a cottonwood tree thickly festooned with ancient, rusting chains. Time was when British corsairs would intercept slave ships bound for the Americas. They would disembark the freed slaves at the nearest African port. In Freetown, the slaves would nail their shackles to the tree. When Ben Jobe arrived there, the shackles hung in the branches and swayed, clanking like old ghosts. "It was very emotional for me," he explains. "I thought, I am going where I will be governed by my people." He stared at that cottonwood tree until the boat made it all the way to shore.

After three years, during which he taught commonwealth history to the sons of the country's elite and coached them in cricket, Jobe returned to the United States and enrolled in graduate school at the newly integrated University of Tennessee. It was an edgy time, the old order peeling away until only raw nerves were left. He was in a class the day John Kennedy was murdered. He saw frat boys speeding through the campus in their convertibles, blowing their horns and waving Confederate flags in celebration. In their joy, Jobe heard the chains rattling on the cottonwood tree, and he vowed to get out of the University of Tennessee in one quick hurry. That day, he and three other black graduate students were escorted to their dormitories by campus security, and they were kept there throughout the long weekend.

He took a job as the director of student teaching at Rust College, a small black school in Mississippi. They made him coach basketball, too. From Rust, he moved on to Talladega College, in Alabama, and then to South Carolina State, both black schools. He would stay here, in the places where education was a triumph, where the horns did not blow in celebration of a murdered president. He was through with integration. "Then," he says, "I met the Irishman, and I changed my mind again."

Frank McGuire hired Jobe to be one of his assistant coaches at South Carolina, in 1973. McGuire already was a legend, having built a monumental program at North Carolina, where he had revolutionized recruiting by spiriting away players from New York City's

Catholic high schools. Jobe joined Walsh and Cremins on McGuire's staff, and he became very close to the latter. Cremins invited Jobe home to meet his father, who had come to New York from Ireland. Jobe and the elder Cremins immediately hit it off. "He was a dude," Jobe recalls. "He'd wear a hat like the black guys in Harlem would wear a hat, all broke down." Unfortunatley, the elder Cremins insisted on giving Jobe whiskey. A lifelong teetotaler, Jobe would accept the drink, and then discreetly pour it into a nearby plant. "I figured it could handle it better than I could," he says. "I often wonder about that plant."

The three assistant coaches educated one another. Walsh and Cremins took some of the edge off Jobe's anger, and Jobe made them hear the clank of shackles in the cottonwood tree. "I learned so much from Ben that had nothing to do with basketball," Walsh says. "I was able to get some perspective on what it was like growing up black in the South—things I never knew and there was no way I could know."

Jobe left South Carolina in 1978, worked briefly for the NBA's Denver Nuggets and, after two years out of coaching, became head coach at Alabama A&M. In 1986, he took the job at Southern, where his record after last season was a gaudy 146–67. He is drawn to those places that embody the promise that was made to his family long ago, before the land passed from them and before the mule died. He brought to Southern a piece of its own history, a lien on its soul. And Southern itself testifies that black colleges produced not only mechanics and farmers but also gypsy dreamers such as Ben Jobe, who have gone out and called Thomas Jefferson's great bluff.

One morning, Ben Jobe got a call from Dale Brown, who coaches basketball across town, at Louisiana State. It is a unique experience to get a phone call from Dale Brown. (Once, a few years back, Brown called me at home to talk about something critical I had written about a Soviet player to whom Brown had become close. Brown told me that he hoped what I'd written would not imperil the incipient thaw in the Cold War. I told Brown that it probably wouldn't and that, anyway, it was unlikely that Gorbachev's copy of *Basketball*

Times had yet reached the Kremlin.) On this particular day, Brown was puzzled, and he was asking Jobe for help.

"Tell me," Brown said to Jobe. "What's the problem with black people, anyway?"

"I told him 'Dale, how in hell do I know? I'm just one of them,'" Jobe says. "Then he says 'How come none of my players know about [civil-rights leader] Vernon Johns?' I told him 'Dale, it's because Vernon Johns never played for the New York Knicks.'"

It is not unreasonable to state that college athletics as it is presently constituted is doomed to a bloody collapse, probably within the next decade. History indicates that no sport can sustain itself as an amateur enterprise once it attains mass popularity. Golf and tennis opened themselves up to professionalism simply because they couldn't carry the weight of their own public hypocrisies. That is the crisis that is building in college basketball, a billion-dollar enterprise supported by an unpaid, largely black labor force.

Over the past year, black coaches have moved into open revolt. In fact, in January, the Black Coaches Association threatened to boycott the games played over the weekend of Martin Luther King, Jr.'s birthday. The ostensible flash-point issue was the NCAA's decision not to add one scholarship to the thirteen allowed each school for its basketball team, but the BCA has also bristled at the continual tightening of academic standards, particularly the NCAA's pigheaded reliance on standardized testing. The BCA called off the boycott when the Justice Department agreed to mediate the dispute. But there seems to be little doubt that if the BCA ever does go through with a boycott, a substantial number of white coaches and all of the players involved would honor it. This would bring the entire artificial edifice of the sport crashing down, at least for one weekend.

Now, it is true that the BCA has its own agenda, much of which is oriented merely toward winning basketball games. Nevertheless, the ongoing controversy has exposed the great fault line running through all of major college sports: namely, that they are operated for the pleasure and profit of administrators who have little understanding of the people who are doing the work. Consequently, the NCAA cannot understand that the members of the BCA look at the misguided efforts at "reform" and see poll taxes, literacy taxes and a whole train of sour historical baggage.

The BCA has something of a point. Using the SATs as a marker for anything is preposterous; even Harvard keeps its admissions policy flexible, so that it is free to admit the idiot grandnephews of the Roosevelt Cabinet. And there doesn't seem to be any compelling reason for Southern to have the same admission standards for athletes as, say, Duke, when the standards for their respective student bodies are so radically different.

Jobe is of two minds about all of this. He believes that black students can meet whatever challenges are required of them; that is the faith that built places like Fisk and Southern in the first place. However, he also clearly perceives that the new standards are an attempt by a group of powerful people to set rules for powerless people about whom they know nothing. That is what places like Fisk and Southern have taught their students to know as reflex, as instinct.

"These presidents, the people who are talking about raising standards," Jobe says, "in another time, they didn't care. They turned it over to the NCAA, which ran with it. Then all of a sudden, they said 'All these black kids, they're taking over athletics.' Also, they said 'I didn't know you could make money in athletics. Whoa, we got to control this.'"

"The problem with this whole thing is that if every school in Louisiana had the mission the black schools had, there'd be no need for black schools," Jobe says. "If every school in the United States had as its mission to serve all of its people, then there would be no need for Southern University."

He doesn't care what people think anymore. He has lost a father and nine siblings to cancer. He is 61 now, so he is pushing Gregor Mendel's odds in this regard to the very wall. He will coach one or two more years, and then he will leave again, this time for good. He has seen so much history that, even though things seem to be coming unglued around him, he has something to hold on to. A sense of place, a feeling of debt and honor.

"I mean, we need to operate within an integrated society," he says. "No doubt about that. But we must never forget who we are."

It is all around him as he comes to work, the determined ghosts of his family, his school and a way of life that is rapidly losing ground. His office is in an athletic center named after Dr. F. G. Clark. If you walk west from it, you will pass the Smith-Brown Student Union, named for the two students murdered in 1969. Sooner or later, you will reach the graves of Dr. F. G. Clark and of his father, who together spent fifty years here redeeming the curdled promises of American history. It is a quiet spot where students come to spoon or to study in the deep shade of a willow tree that has been there forever, waving gently over a long bend in the ceaseless river.

In August of 1996, Ben left Southern and took the job as basketball coach at Tuskegee University in Alabama, another place at which history is as thick around him as it is within him.

GQ March 1994

Iverson, Allen

These are Allen Iverson's blues.

It is six years since he went to jail and four years since the conviction was thrown out. It is two years since they stopped him with the Glock and the blunt in his car. He will make nearly $71 million over the life of his contract with the Philadelphia 76ers. He was—arguably—the most valuable player in the NBA last season and—inarguably—the most entertaining to watch. These are his blues, one stanza at a time.

"I say all the time, when I go, all I want you to say is that this guy, he was a good man. I want my momma to say he was a good son. I want my friends to say he was a good friend—no, check that. He was the best friend."

And: "I am going to take care of my responsibilities and have fun, because you never know when it can be over. You're not promised anything. Go in there, take a nap, and it can be a long nap. For real."

And, finally: "Misunderstood. Forever. I'm gonna put that on my tombstone."

These are Allen Iverson's blues. They are true, real, and earned, and, in their own way, sadly magnificent—songs of tombstones at the top of the world.

The truth. Self-evident. This is the only nation on earth that could've produced an Allen Iverson.

He rides in the limo with two friends on this fine Manhattan day. Andre is big and wide, and he wears a headband designed to look like a chain of $100 bills. Robert is smaller and more animated. In the middle, Allen Iverson shuts his eyes for long stretches of the drive. He is in their conversation, but he is drifting out of it, too. He is resting, but he is among his friends, which means that the stage he carries with him, always, is comfortably crowded.

This is not a king and his court. It is deeper than that, more democratic. It is a complicated business, these friendships, and they support something in him that otherwise would seem almost exhausted. "What people fail to realize," explains John Thompson, Iverson's coach at Georgetown, "is that these are not just people he grew up with. These are people who kept him alive."

He's twenty-four now and was last season's star, regardless of how efficiently Tim Duncan managed to push the San Antonio Spurs to the title. Duncan is seven feet tall, enormously gifted, and a model citizen. In a year in which the NBA sacrificed half the season in order to establish control over its players and its public image, the league couldn't have asked for a better ending. But whereas Duncan glowed, Iverson burned. He's the embodiment of what the NBA gussies up and sells, which are young black males, to audiences that usually arrange to have them followed in shopping malls. It sells hip-hop to the gated-community crowd, but the reality doesn't sell— eight friends dead back in Virginia before Iverson was sixteen.

And isn't that the most American thing about it? The old preachers sold the devil as hard as Mario Puzo sold his gangsters, as hard as the penny press sold the James brothers, as hard as the singers sold the badman, Stagger Lee. They sold him so well that the preachers often found themselves wrestling with their own best work. And here, now, is the best player in the NBA, riding in the limo with his two friends at the heart, and the NBA would like you to buy the style of this friendship but not its substance, because its substance is what so unnerves the NBA's primary audience.

"What human being don't have nobody?" says Iverson. "They looked out for me and I looked out for them. I got good friends, and I am a good friend."

The old poet heard the truth in the outlaw music of his country. He heard it in that towering adjective—*self-evident*—that hangs within the seminal colonial heresy like a bell in a tower. What follows—all men created equal, and those things with which they've been endowed by Whomever and all that—is not merely the truth, it is a pig in the parlor. The word cracks history wide open. Freedom is itself set free.

The old poet saw what happened next. Freed itself, freedom produces as it will. Mainstream and underground, Sousa march and Delta blues. Two countries, for sure, but really one, their unacknowledged coexistence the foundry in which the country's peculiar genius is forged. Puritan Boston and pagan Vegas and everything in between, which is to say New York. Abe Lincoln and Frank Sinatra and everything in between, which is to say Jack Kennedy. Malcolm and Martin and everything in between, which is to say "What's Going On?" Beats and Baptists, whiskey and soda pop, Oppenheimer and Elvis. "I Like Ike" and "A-wop-bop-a-loop-bop-a-wop-bam-boom" ... at the same friggin' time on the same friggin' radio—can you dig that? Lenny Bruce. Allen Iverson.

The Answer, with all the questions.

"The pure products of America," the old poet wrote, "all go crazy."

The game is the easiest part about him. Watch him now, since Larry Brown brilliantly moved him off the ball in the middle of last season. Watch him in last year's playoffs, cutting heads on Orlando's Anfernee Hardaway—ruining him to the point that Hardaway complained that he could either shoot or guard Iverson but he couldn't do both, which momentarily distracted folks from noticing that he couldn't do either one.

Watch him against Indiana, against Larry Bird, the toughest basketball audience there is, and listen to Bird talk about him as an equal, almost, seeing much of his own struggle in Iverson's game and realizing as so very few do that joy can be tough, fierce, and unsmiling.

"They don't want him?" Bird once said, unsmiling. "Hey, send him along. I can find a use for him."

"Bird was a great player," Iverson says, "but he didn't have all the natural ability—I mean the *athletic* ability—that Mike had. So what made me concentrate on his game was that, hey, I've got the athletic ability, but I was like, 'Damn, how Bird do what he do there?' He just knew the game."

It was Brown who nudged Iverson away from the position he had played all his life, freeing him to create from shooting guard. Now, with Iverson on the cusp of greatness, Brown talks about that position as a delicate, ambivalent place. "He's still so young," Brown says. "I mean, this should be his rookie year. He's come so far, and he's always felt that people don't want to see him succeed, and that comes from where he's from."

Let us sum up how the transcendent game developed within the person: a troubled childhood, an absent father, a burning desire to succeed in a world seemingly set in opposition, trouble with the law, staying loyal to old friends, and, at last, success, wealth—joy, fierce and unsmiling.

So here you have it. A new story for the NBA to market and sell.

Allen Iverson—the New Larry Bird. Ain't that a bitch?

The game is the simple part.

There are not many worse things to have in this twenty-four-hour-news, all-sports-radio world than a life of reiteration, and yet that is the life that Allen Iverson lives, now that he has become a certified star in a league that thrives on them. Everything that he does brings along his time in jail, the gun and the blunt, the hair, the tattoos, and the friends. It all stands for the glibly categorized sum of other people's fears. Pack up all of the NBA's problems as we enter the third millennium of the Christian Era, and here's what it comes down to: scary Negroes.

Which is not to say this is not a useful concept. It helped the NBA concoct a winning public strategy in the battle for the next century's revenue streams—a battle that cost it half a season to the roaring applause of the league's ticketholding suckers.

"My only worry about Allen is whether people will let him grow out of this marketing thing that they've got him in," muses John Thompson. "Michael learned as he grew up that he couldn't wear those sweats to meetings anymore. I hope Allen gets the room to grow, because this is a smart kid."

"Like I always say," Iverson argues, "you can have a twenty-five-year-old man, and he has the cornrows and the baggy jeans and the gold, and he can be standing next to a ten-year-old kid with a suit on, and they walk past the guy and grab their pocketbooks, but that little boy, he might be a gangbanger or a murderer. And you know that's true. You *know* it."

The cristal arrives in the suite in golden buckets of ringing ice. It is set upon by Andre and Robert and Goldie, who hooked up with them after the photo shoot was done. Iverson is looking at a present he's been given—an old Robert Johnson CD, older blues than his. It's not music to give to just anyone.

"Who's this?" he says, flipping over the case, devouring the brief biography on the other side.

He's you, Iverson is told, sixty years ago.

"He's me, huh?" Allen says. "That's cool." And maybe later, when he records his album, there will be a touch of the old outlaw music, the self-evident truth, freedom itself set free.

To grow up alone is to grow up in opposition. Allen Iverson was alone as a child. Nobody was around to define him, so he defined himself. A life in opposition. He brought his friends into it, but they respected his rules, so they stayed his friends. They let him be alone among them.

"I am going to wear my hair the way I want to," he says. "I am going to dress the way I want to. I am going to hang around the way I want to, my way. So when it's all over, I can look in the mirror and say, 'You did it your way. Nobody made you be nobody.'"

It is very much an immigrant creed, because that's what he is—not an outcast in his own country but an immigrant within it, passing over borders that are as real as any border on any map, living through the tension between identity and assimilation, the way all immigrants do.

He brought his village with him, the way all immigrants do. But internal migrations are different, all perceived danger and threat, no promise and opportunity—as when millions of blacks moved north into the cities, the greatest unacknowledged story of the immigrant century.

They were already here. They knew the truth was self-evident. They brought their music, the outlaw music, all dread and menace and joy besides—the self-evident truth, denied but rising, still rising, rising still.

Esquire **November 1992**

Two Tough Mothers

The yachts rock softly at anchor under the pale, watery sunlight of late fall. Big, seagoing things, they bob there along the waterfront known as the Crystal Coast, and the old men come down to the boardwalk and point to them, then out to sea, south toward the Caribbean. In the late 1970s, when the federal government authorized a multimillion-dollar renovation of the docks in Beaufort, N.C., the town became a prized anchorage for trust-fund sailors running the inland route on their way to the Bahamas. The yachts tie up for a while and then they go, the town's real money hoisting anchor and heading south.

Inland from the anchorage, the houses get smaller and farther apart as you come into that part of town they call North River. Up past East Carteret High, past the Thomas Seafood Company and the little brick church of uncertain denomination, there is a dirt road. A long driveway, really, it is gullied by the rain. Cars and trucks rust along the side of it, and battered boats jut like ruined teeth out of the tall weeds. At the end of the road is a trailer home. There's a house rising up now behind the trailer. Because of one woman, this is where some of the big money came to Beaufort and stayed.

"I didn't really look on it as a contest," says Bettie Taylor. "I was a mother doing what was right for her child. I don't know anybody around here who wouldn't have done that. I don't know one woman who wouldn't go to bat for her child."

She is not a big woman; her son Brien towers over her. She is still young, 39, but she's stooped a little bit from working. Her voice is light and lilting. Wherever the steel is, and it is there as sure as sun and rain, you've got to look close to find it.

Last spring, the New York Yankees made Brien Taylor the first pick in the annual baseball draft. The team offered him $300,000, which is more money than anyone in North River had ever seen. Bettie Taylor looked at the offer, studied baseball precedent and turned the money down. She saw what the Oakland A's had given Todd Van Poppel the year before, and she saw that it was a lot more the $300,000, and she told the Yankees that, no, this wouldn't do at all and that Brien would go to college instead. The pressure mounted. Bettie was flogged in the baseball press. Some of her neighbors wondered if she had lost her mind. However, in August the Yankees came down to Beaufort, up the driveway through the weeds, and they gave Brien Taylor a $1.55 million deal. Some of the money has gone into the house that's going up behind the trailer, which to the Yankees these days must look a great deal like Appomattox Court House looked to Robert E. Lee.

"Like any business, you've got buying and selling," Bettie Taylor says. "Look at it that way, and Brien's a commodity. It's not a very pretty picture. I can appreciate where [the Yankees are] coming from. They're trying to do what's right for them. But I was trying to do what I know was right and fair for my child, and that's all I cared about."

This is a new phenomenon in sports, and sports is not entirely prepared to deal with it. Because young athletes are increasingly coming out of single-parent homes and an overwhelming number of those homes are headed by women, mothers are becoming more and more involved in the career plans of their gifted children. College coaches involved in recruiting saw this first. At Kentucky, Rick Pitino hired Bernadette Locke-Mattox as an assistant basketball coach in 1990, at least in part to have a woman who could approach the mothers of prospective Wildcats. "You're seeing [involved mothers] more than you did 10 years ago," says Maryland basketball coach Gary Williams. "I think a mother is more likely to be concerned with the human being who is her kid, while the father might see the athlete more."

As these athletes move toward professional careers in their sports, their mothers inevitably collide with the huge corporate enterprises that are professional teams. And the people who run these enterprises are not used to dealing with assertive women or with the fact that a mother's perspective on her child's welfare might be different from their own, largely male, perspective.

"A mother will probably have more of a tendency to think about the real interests of her child," says Carl Lindros, whose wife, Bonnie, has become a controversial figure in Canada because of her conspicuous involvement in the career of their son, hockey wunderkind Eric Lindros. "I think the mother might have a broader sense of things, particularly if the father was involved in the sport himself. He might be actualizing his own dreams through the kid, whereas the mother won't focus on anything except the well-being of the child." The fact that both Bonnie Lindros and Bettie Taylor have husbands makes them no less determined to secure the best future for their children.

Because the sexism laced through American culture is closer to the surface in sports than it is elsewhere, there's considerable resistance to the involvement of women in their children's careers. The sports world seems to classify women as either disposable or a nuisance, a continuum fairly well defined at one end by Margo Adams and at the other by Lisa Olson. In both of their celebrated cases, sports had an opportunity to confront its fundamental attitude toward women. In both cases, sports botched the job and went blithely onward. Indeed, every one of the male athletes interviewed by *SI* in the immediate wake of Magic Johnson's announcement that he had contracted the AIDS virus described a world in which women were either prey or predators and professional athletes were naïfs struggling with temptation.

At one time or another, people have tried to pigeonhole Bettie Taylor and Bonnie Lindros as either disposable or a nuisance. No one accused Carl Lindros of brainwashing his son. Willie Ray Taylor, Brien's father, has spent his entire adult life fashioning stone and laying brick. He went to all of his son's games. He, too, thought the Yankees had brought far too little to the table. But nobody claimed that he wasn't smart enough to guide his son's affairs. Bettie Taylor was seen as a woman who just didn't understand. "Most of the time," her husband says, "she means what she says. I don't think they knew that. I did."

They do not lose, these two women. Bettie beat the Yankees, and it's better than even money that Bonnie is going to stare down the NHL. After all, both of these mothers hold an unassailable bit of high ground—it is their children that the nervous executives need. And it's awkward for any sports team to promote itself as entertainment for the whole family while it attempts to pillory a woman for acting upon one of the most basic family values of all: Don't Sell the Kids.

"I never hear Daddy jokes, *never*," says Eric Lindros. "What I hear are Mommy jokes."

Eric went to Dallas last summer to be photographed for a series of trading cards. All the No. 1 draft picks were there. The Charlotte Hornets' Larry Johnson, whose mother, Dortha, raised him alone, was there. So was Brien Taylor. Eric is baseball silly, so he fell into conversation with Brien, and they talked about their mothers. Good mothers both, but more than that. Strong women, bred in their own ways to compete and to win. Fearsome opponents for the whiskey hours of the poker game.

Bonnie Lindros, 42, is talking about her days as a high school track star. "I was," she says, "a great standing broad."

There is a two-beat, and then there is this huge, 200-watt laugh. Brassy, it would have been called some years ago. Flo Ziegfeld would have cast Bonnie Lindros on sight, and she would have made Fanny Brice look like a Carmelite. Bonnie's laugh is good to have if you're going to be a Hockey Mom. You can laugh at all the cold, cracked-gray dawns and all the crowded, sweaty rides and all the coffee poured hot and thin out of battered machines and all the tin-pot rinks from Trois-Rivières to Norman Wells and back again.

Hockey Moms are cheery sorts, fiercely uncompromising in their belief that the next great player is munching potato chips there in the back seat. They are dedicated to working through the system. The stolid conformity endemic to the sport is first instilled by the Hockey Mom, who is an establishment figure first and always. One morning not long ago, it flashed upon Bonnie Lindros that the next great player was indeed asleep in the next room. And hockey's panjandrums, equally convinced that Eric Lindros was the best young player in the game, anticipated dealing with just another Hockey Mom. They were, ah, incorrect.

"I don't chew gum, and I don't have a [team] jacket," says Bonnie, and then there's that laugh again.

She grew up outside Chatham, the town in Ontario where Ferguson Jenkins was born. Bonnie Roszell's father, Blake, was a justice of the peace, and he was amused when big Carl Lindros would ride his bicycle out from town to the Roszell place, a guitar bouncing off the handlebars. Blake Roszell's teenage daughter was being classically wooed, albeit in the key of D Minus. "It was sweet," she says, "but his singing was brutal."

They were a striking couple, tall and athletic. Eventually, Carl would be drafted by Edmonton of the Canadian Football League and played hockey in the Chicago Blackhawks' system. Though her sister, Marcia, went on to set a Commonwealth Games record in the shotput, Bonnie's career in track and field came to an abrupt end one afternoon in 1965. Anchoring a relay team, she came all the way from last place to second, whereupon she looked over to one side and lost the race. Instead of applauding her effort, the coach tore into her for peeking. Bonnie quit on the spot.

"I have a very strong sense of fairness and a strong sense of what's right," she says. "I learned it in a one-room country schoolhouse, and all of us had to play together. If something happened to you, your siblings came to make sure it was fair."

Bonnie and Carl were married in 1969, and Eric was born four years later. He was the neighborhood ball of fire, and out of sheer desperation his parents enrolled him in a small local hockey league.

He so took to the sport that he refused to remove his equipment, pedaling his bicycle down the street in full pads like a strange little tank. His talent became plain early on, and Bonnie became very visible at Eric's games. Once, when the tabloid *Toronto Sun* ran several pictures of her in the stands, other Hockey Moms openly wondered whether she had paid off the photographer. "If I was going to pay to be in the paper," she told them, "it'd be on page 3," referring to the *Sun*'s daily pinup picture.

"See?" she says. "That's why I get in trouble."

Eric rose swiftly through the regimented system of Canadian youth hockey until, in 1989, he was ready to ascend into the Ontario Hockey League, his last scheduled stop before the NHL. It was here that Bonnie Lindros first went national. It was here that she first became a target.

Both Bonnie and Carl agreed that Eric should play close to home so as not to disrupt his schooling. Unfortunately, the first pick in the OHL draft was held by the Greyhounds of Sault Ste. Marie, a town far from the Lindros home in suburban Toronto. Bonnie and Carl said flatly that Eric would not play there; he would play on an amateur team in the U.S. instead. Figuring this for a bluff, the Soo drafted Eric anyway. On the way out of the draft, a local reporter cornered Eric. Since her 16-year-old son had just had his whole life turned upside down, Bonnie told the reporter to get lost. Her reputation has never recovered.

"That day at the OHL draft was when it started," Eric recalls. "She just told me, 'Eric, shut up and get in the car.' That's when I started to hear about my mother ruining my life and stuff." Bonnie's eyes still tear up at the memory of those days.

"It was a sad time," she says. "He takes his finals, and then he's off to a new country, new school, new home. Simple, right? But I knew that it just wasn't right to stick a microphone in the face of a 16-year-old at that controversial time. To me, that's a violation of a child." Later, of course, the OHL decided that it was absurd to have the league's biggest drawing card playing amateur hockey in Detroit, so it magically adjusted the rules to allow the Soo to trade Eric to the

Oshawa Generals, who play near his home. The Lindros family had not been bluffing, and the OHL threw in its hand.

Resentment lingered everywhere Eric played. He was named an OHL All-Star after playing only one league game. To protest Eric's selection, the players at the Soo wore black armbands for their next game. Worse than that, however, was the general feeling among Hockey Moms that Eric was the worst kind of whippersnapper, and that Bonnie—not Carl; never Carl—was pushing around all of junior hockey. After all, the other Hockey Moms had played by the rules. They had put their kids in an archaic system in which children as young as six might be forced to practically sign away the next 12 years of their lives. That was the way the game worked.

"When Eric was drafted by the Soo," Bonnie says, "we didn't criticize. We just said, 'That doesn't work for us.' Isn't that fair? Can't we say that about our own child? That's what I can never understand."

Today the Lindros family finds itself in an eerily familiar predicament. Eric's NHL rights are owned by the Quebec Nordiques. No one in the family wants Eric to play in Quebec City. He would again be playing far from home. Indeed, given Quebec's desire to separate itself from English-speaking Canada, Eric would be playing in what is virtually another country. Not only would his endorsement opportunities be limited in a francophone culture, but he might also find himself in an intolerable bind if relations between Quebec and the rest of the nation worsen—and the tabloids are already full of wild talk in two languages concerning the possibility that Quebec will one day play the role of Croatia in some Great White Götterdämmerung. In such an event, it wouldn't be easy being the most famous English-speaking person in town. Thus, one young hockey player—and his mother—find themselves in the middle of Canada's struggle for its soul.

"One time, I heard [a man say] on the radio that Eric should go to Quebec because that's the rules," Bonnie says. "I wanted to ask that guy, 'Where do you work? What if I told you you had to go to Winnipeg and work? Would you like that?' Why don't people understand that? It seems so simple to me."

Still, the Nordiques have no intention of trading the rights. Hence, Eric Lindros is playing today for the Canadian Olympic team. The Nordiques are the latest folks to call the Lindros family's bluff, and, again, Bonnie has been made the fall person. "Bonnie has looked them right in the eye," says Carl. "They're not used to that." After all, it's easier for the Nordique faithful to vilify Eric's mother than it is for them to vilify Eric, whom they still hope to applaud one day. And it's easier to vilify Bonnie than it is to vilify Carl, who is, after all, a man and who therefore, of course, understands the game. It's more insulting, in the eyes of Eric's detractors, to imply that he's doing what Mommy says.

There is a certain precedent for this. For years Gordie Howe's wife, Colleen, was the object of carping around the NHL for her great success in managing her husband's career. The carping, of course, was largely surreptitious, because nobody who played against Howe was crazy enough to bad-mouth his wife in public and thereby risk an impromptu splenectomy. Colleen Howe also helped along the NHL careers of her sons Mark and Marty. Once, after negotiating a contract with Gordie Howe, an NHL executive was heard to sneer, "I hope that makes Colleen happy."

So there are leaks and whispers about how or how often Bonnie has done this, that and the other thing. There are more rumors about Bonnie Lindros than there ever were about Margaret Trudeau. For her part, Bonnie is quick to cite a newspaper report that certain people in Quebec treated some visiting Indian hockey players in an inexcusably racist fashion—neatly implying that all Quebecois are racist, which is a form of prejudice in itself. While Bonnie's role remains strictly advisory, it's clear that her advice will be heeded and that Eric Lindros is unlikely ever to be a Quebec Nordique.

"Sometimes," Eric muses, "I get scared, you know? Things between me and my mom get a little strained. It's like, 'Mom, don't say that.' But that's when I'm not thinking clearly. When I was at the Canada Cup this summer, my roommate was Brent Sutter, and he said, 'Don't worry about it. Your mom's just doing the best she can for her kid.'" Sutter is an expert on Hockey Moms, his own having sent six sons to the NHL.

Nordique general manager Pierre Pagé, not surprisingly, takes the high road. "Part of what makes Eric a great player is what comes from his parents, that drive to be the best," says Pagé, who took over as Quebec's coach last month. Bonnie's critics, meanwhile, continue in their attempts to make her into a cartoon character—*hockey maman de l'enfer*. However, there's a bright edge to her that cuts through the caricature.

"I know who Eric is," Bonnie says. "He may be 6'5" and 225 pounds, but he's an 18-year-old kid. He's my 18-year-old kid. He might be precocious in a lot of ways, but I know he's vulnerable.

"There are ways in which I deserve to be a target. You know, I looked up *outspoken* in the dictionary. I think in the States, that's cool. But I don't think they like outspoken up here."

People once thought Bettie Murrell was trying to go above her station. After all, East Carteret High School was white. Bettie was trying to go there, and she would just start trouble, and who did this child think she was, anyway?

"My mother didn't want me to do it," says Bettie. "She thought I would be so alone. But I couldn't back down. It was my right to go there." She learned that from her people, who were righteous in their church, quick with the Bible and quicker with the switch. She especially learned it from her granddaddy Columbus Murrell, who preached his lessons as deacon of the Mount Tabor Baptist Church. Everybody in Beaufort knew Deacon Murrell, who preached so hard one morning that he collapsed, just died right there in the pulpit and went straight to Jesus. Her real father was long gone, but 10-year-old Bettie Murrell didn't feel the loss until the Deacon died. "It was that day that I first realized I didn't have a father no more," she says.

She learned the Deacon's lessons well, and they helped her when she became one of two black children to integrate East Carteret in 1965. The lessons helped her in the tobacco fields, too, where she worked alongside a gentle boy named Willie Ray Taylor. They courted, and they had a child, Brien, in 1971. Two years later, they were married. They bought the trailer at the end of the dirt road. Bettie worked at the Thomas Seafood Company, taking the meat out of crabs for eight hours a day. Willie Ray worked as a bricklayer and stonemason. They had three more children, and they raised them the way Bettie had been raised, quick with the Bible and quicker with the switch.

"As a child," Brien says, "I was real bad in the house. I knew how to behave outside and all, but I'd do wrong at home. This is when I was six, seven, eight years old. I got beat so early that by the time I was 13, I didn't get a kick out of being bad anymore."

Brien grew up long and lean, and the neighbors were amazed by how he could throw a stone and knock a bat out of midair. Soon, he was pitching for East Carteret, the school his mother had helped integrate, and his fastball was being clocked at 97 miles per hour. Scouts began to come to North River. By his senior year, Brien Taylor was 9–2 with an ERA of 0.92, and the feeling was that he would be picked first in the major league draft by the Yankees. The Taylors were all Yankee fans, as were many others in Beaufort, a fluke of fan demography caused first by an atmospheric glitch that allowed the old-timers to hear radio broadcasts of ball games from New York and second by the fact that Babe Ruth used to come down to Beaufort to hunt birds. His picture hangs in a number of the old hunting shacks that are still occupied deep in the scrub woods up behind the town. It was a very big thing to have Brien Taylor drafted by the Yankees last June.

The Taylors knew that Brien was going to need advice in dealing with his new employers, so they enlisted the aid of a Los Angeles–based attorney named Scott Boras. It was Boras who had wrung the Van Poppel contract out of Oakland, largely by threatening to have the pitcher go to college, which would have cost the A's their rights to him. Boras instructed Bettie about the intricacies of the sports business, and he found a bright and apt student. "By the time the Yankees came down here," Boras says, "she was ready with all the questions."

New York first offered Brien $300,000, then $650,000. The family thought it over, consulted with Boras and turned the deals down flat. Baseball, which was once again trying to rein in salaries, was agog. Bettie was adamant. She knew what Van Poppel had gotten, and she knew what was fair. If the Yankees didn't want to give Brien what was fair, then he would go pitch at Louisburg College, near Raleigh. The Yankees fumed. *Newsday*'s Tom Verducci, expressing an attitude widely held in baseball, ridiculed the notion of Brien as a student. This got Bettie even angrier. People seemed to assume that the threat of college was less credible coming from a poor black kid like Brien than from a suburban white kid like Van Poppel. She called on those same reserves that had gotten her through the doors at East Carteret on that first day of school.

"When somebody tells me I can't do something," she says, "it makes me want to do it all the more. Push me against the wall, and you've got a battle on your hands. O.K., so I looked like the bad guy, but I wasn't going to do what they wanted just so I wouldn't look like the bad guy."

People were talking in Beaufort, too. Bettie would hear them behind her in the store. They thought she was crazy to turn down that money, that she was being too damn high and mighty about it, just the way she had been when she had to go to that high school. There were others, too, more vicious than the rest, telling people they hoped that the nigger wouldn't get a nickel. This attitude was so prevalent that it chilled even Bruce Paul, a sportswriter at the *Carteret County News-Times*, and Paul's previous job had been as a Marine aviator taking surveillance photos of Iran during the hostage crisis. Paul wrote a column decrying the racism that was fueling some of the reaction to Bettie Taylor.

In any event, Brien says, "it was really my decision. I didn't have no doubts at all. She raised me up, and I was not going to sign until it was right to sign."

The situation reached its nadir in late July when Bettie publicly wondered whether the Yankees were trying "to take advantage of a poor black family." In August a man named Don Koonce, who represented the Major League Scouting Bureau, showed up at the trailer and tried to pressure Brien into accepting the original Yankee offer. Bettie, who by then was fed up with rich people trying to knuckle her, threw Koonce out. Inevitably, George Steinbrenner got into the act, saying that Yankee general manager Gene Michael "ought to be shot" if he failed to sign Brien.

Oddly enough, once Michael and Bettie met, later in August, they shook out the deal very quickly. "He talked about how [it was for him] coming up, how hard he had it, and I believed him," Bettie says. "I thought, 'This is a nice man.'"

On the day that the agreement was struck, Brien was at Louisburg, waiting to hear if he should go to his first class. The Yankees met the Taylors' $1.55 million demand, while the Taylors agreed not to insist on a major league contract. This gave the Yankees not only flexibility—they wouldn't have to protect Brien in an expansion draft before he arrived in the major leagues—but also a minor victory they could proclaim. "Once we got them off the major league contract," Michael insists, "it was easy to get it done."

Afterward, however, Steinbrenner, his feet firmly planted on both sides of the fence, said that Michael should be ashamed of himself for having agreed to the deal. Houston Astro owner John McMullen fumed that Michael had been "snookered by a 19-year-old kid from North Carolina." Indeed, last month baseball's owners moved to close the loophole through which Brien had threatened to escape by proposing that teams be allowed to keep the rights to their draft choices for as long as five years, a provision so blatantly restrictive that the NHL might have thought it up. Regardless, Brien went off to the Instructional League, where he pitched superbly. Shortly thereafter, with $15,000 contributed by the town's newest millionaire, work began again on the house behind the trailer, which had been going up slowly as time and money allowed.

Not much else has changed. Willie Ray works at what work he can find, and Bettie's job at the seafood company has dropped down to three days a week now that crabbing season is over. Fewer people come down the road through the tall weeds, although Morley Safer brought the *60 Minutes* crew to the trailer in November. Every Sunday, Bettie Taylor goes back to Mount Tabor, where her granddaddy went straight from the pulpit to glory one day when she was very small.

"If Brien had gone to college," she says, "our standard of living would've been just what it is now. I've adjusted to it. We haven't fared that badly. We never missed a meal here. We never didn't have clothes on our backs. Our bills get paid—not on time always, but they get paid. It would've been easy for me to go on." Her business has always been the business of living—the business of raising the children and feeding them and keeping them safe and making for them a life of value and substance. Nobody owns your children. They are yours until they are their own.

Other businesses will bend to this business of living, or no business at all will be done in North River. There is something unreal about sports, after all—something very much like the little shops down along Beaufort's waterfront, where the gold-leaf letters catch the dying sun and where you pay an extra 10 cents on the ashtrays for the *e* that they hang on *Old*. Something artificial that works so very hard at being genuine.

It almost succeeds. But then it rubs up against something real and fine, and it bends out of deference, the way that the old men ignore all the little shops and look out beyond the big yachts, out to where there is just the sea. Sometimes not all the money that comes to Beaufort rocks at anchor for a while and then heads south through the channel. Sometimes, if you hold on tight to the best of what you are, good things come here and stay.

As of this writing, the mothers are fine, but the sons have had their problems. In 1993, Brien Taylor dislocated his left shoulder in a brawl outside a saloon near his home. He was acquitted of all criminal charges, but the injury effectively ended his pitching career. Eric Lindros eventually played for the Philadelphia Flyers, being named the National Hockey League's Most Valuable Player in 1997. At the end of the 2000 season, Lindros suffered his seventh concussion in two years. His playing future was in doubt.

Sports Illustrated

Transition Game

We have raised a generation with the gun. A wicked connivance between social cowardice and political expedience has now brought us whole lives lived in the cross hairs. In the cities, far too many children have seen far too much blood. After a summer in which a respected spokesman of a major political party proposed a religious war as an anesthetic for the national conscience, we find we are already a nation of tiny Belfasts.

On the Fourth of July of 1991, a 16-year-old kid named Shannon Bowman left Dorchester to go play basketball at a playground in Roxbury's Orchard Park. His family was not pleased. Orchard Park is not a neighborhood where anyone travels lightly, not even a six-foot-four, 220-pound rising basketball star. But the best players go where the best games are, and on that bright holiday afternoon the best game was in Orchard Park, so Shannon Bowman went off to play there.

Bowman's life was going very well. Raised by his grandmother, an indomitable woman named Teresa Chatman, he had come through some bad times with his parents, with whom he now had only a nodding acquaintance. That fall he would be entering Beaver County Country Day School, an oak-shrouded prep school in Chestnut Hill, a place where 300 boys and girls pay $14,000 a year for a privileged education, the kind of place where the head basketball coach is also the head of the English Department. Bowman's uncle, a veteran Boston cop named Al Rue, is an assistant basketball coach there.

Rue wanted his nephew out of Dorchester High School, but he was concerned about the distance between Dorchester and Chestnut Hill, and he was not thinking about mileage. "I knew what an adjustment it would be," Rue says. "Not just academically, but socially as well." Still, the opportunity was a golden one, and Rue was not about to let it pass by his nephew.

On the day that Bowman went to play on the courts at Orchard Park, there was a beef in the neighborhood, the kind of thing that Rue once settled with his mouth and/or fists when he was king of the courts coming up in Jamaica Plain. Today, though, somebody had mf'd somebody else, and the somebody else came back strapped. The somebody was gone, and the somebody else was ready to open up in frustration at anybody who was handy. On the Fourth of July 1991, playing basketball on a court in the city of Boston, Shannon Bowman was shot because there was nobody else around to shoot.

He took the bullet in the left side. It went straight through and came out the back, and it missed everything that was vital. "I got scared," Bowman says today. "Did I walk to the hospital? No, I ran to the hospital." He got to Boston City, and he counted himself one of the lucky ones. He had two scars and a pretty good story to tell. But he also carried away something else, a reflexive sense of his own mortality. One night that winter, after he had enrolled and prospered at Beaver Country Day, after all the coaches had begun to call, he was riding home to Dorchester with his uncle. Somewhere along Route 9, the car backfired. Bowman flinched.

They know him now in Bob the Chef's, which is a good place to get yourself known, especially if you want to eat very, very well. One of the guys at the counter shakes his hand. Charlie Titus, the AD at UMass-Boston, stops by at the table. "How're you doing?" asks Titus. "And I'm not talking about the basketball now." Late last summer, Bowman's AAU team played in a tournament in Philadelphia, but he couldn't make the trip. He had to stay home and finish *The Handmaid's Tale* before school started, in September, because that's the way things are at Beaver Country Day School, even for the best basketball player the school has ever had.

"It was pretty scary the first time that I went there," he admits. "It was a different kind of scared. It wasn't the academics so much. I felt like I could handle studying. It was more the whole place, you know? Do I belong? You come home from there to Dorchester, back to my neighborhood, and it's a different world, a whole different world."

There can be a terrible pulling and hauling in such an adjustment, and it is the social cost of all that clamoring for "parental choice" in education. Leaving aside the fact that most choice plans will simply take the best students from the city and leave the rest to a public school system that will be abandoned to wither further, "parental choice" without a firm commitment from society to equal opportunity in every other area of life simply means that some African-American students will be educated in neighborhoods in which they might otherwise be stopped and frisked.

It is hard enough for a young person to find his place in one world, let alone two. Opportunity is not without obligations, and the sub-rosa argument the prep school makes is that Shannon Bowman's home and his friends and his whole previous life are things to be overcome, like a speech impediment or polio. There are dangers in this terrible pressure. Robert Sam Anson's book *Best Intentions: The Education and Killing of Edmund Perry*, about the young New Yorker who had just graduated from Exeter when he was shot while apparently attempting to mug an undercover cop, is suffused with a drifter's melancholy. It is the story of a child without a home, orphaned by opportunity itself.

Al Rue knew that his nephew would encounter such pressures at Beaver: "It was going to be a shocker. So I prepared him for what he was going to be facing here. The way I presented it to him was that the high school he was going to didn't offer a challenge to him. Here, I told him, he could get a chance to go to college, and, since I knew he didn't have the money to go to college, I told him he could use his abilities [in basketball] to get there."

Now in his senior year at Beaver, he has become a genuine prospect. There is a subtlety to Bowman's game that is far beyond his

18 years. Too strong for most high school forwards to handle, he also has soft hands and a gift for passing that is passing rare in any young player. His game does not lend itself to basketball's summer camps, where the emphasis is on individual skills that show up in drills. But put him on a team, and let that team play, and Bowman becomes central to every part of the game. This past June, almost a year to the day after he was shot, Bowman and the Boston Amateur Basketball Club (BABC) won the national AAU junior men's championship. Bowman won the tournament's Most Valuable Player award, a prize taken home previously by both Magic Johnson and Michael Jordan. That was when the coaches began to call.

"He went from someone who people thought would be a good Division 2 player to someone whom the mid-major Division 1 teams really like and the really big Division 1 schools are willing to look at," says Tom Manning, the English teacher who coaches Bowman at Beaver.

Manning was sensitive from the start to charges that he had brought Bowman in simply to improve his basketball team. "It was something that I was aware of, even though I didn't get charged with it," Manning muses. "If anybody said it, they didn't say it to me, but I heard that it was around." Fortunately for everyone, Bowman quickly adapted, discovering that he had a gift for languages and playing so well that Manning had to upgrade the team's opponents so that his star player could continue to progress on the court as quickly as he has done in the classroom.

Off the court, he has fit in seamlessly, which is not to say without a lot of effort. "Last year," Bowman says, "I was up at 6:30 so that the school van could pick me up. I wouldn't get home until 6:30 or 7 at night. When basketball started, I wouldn't get home until 8:30, after dark. Sometimes, at home, it's not too good after dark, you know?"

It is summer evening with a hint of fall in the air. Tank tops have given way to Starter jackets, and the old men in the folding chairs have blankets on their laps. There is a good crowd here at Evans Field, in North Providence. The BABC is beating a team called Buddies from Fall River, and Jamal Jackson of East Boston High School is having the most conspicuously good game, but the real savants in the crowd are talking about Shannon Bowman, how he upfaked a guy into the lights and tucked a pass around him to Jackson, who dunked. The dunk is for the kids in the Starter jackets; the pass is for the connoisseurs.

He will make it, comes the thought. He was shot and he survived. He has delicately walked between the most explosive issues of race and class, and he has taken the best lessons he can find from the journey. Between two worlds, where there could be fear and hate and hopeless division, he has found a home and safety and a life for himself.

The ball goes up again. A bad jumper from the top that rebounds with a great *whang!* off the iron rim. Shannon Bowman goes up and gets it, and that's the lasting image of him: one arm reaching, reaching high, against the perfect parfait of the late-coming twilight sky.

Shannon Bowman graduated from Fairfield University in 1997. In his final game, he helped the Stags nearly defeat the University of North Carolina.

Boston Magazine November 1992